Breaking Down Barriers

George W. McLaurin. Courtesy Western History Collections, University of Oklahoma Libraries (OUPS 30218).

Breaking Down Barriers

George McLaurin and the Struggle
to End Segregated Education

David W. Levy

University of Oklahoma Press : Norman

This book is published with the generous assistance of the Wallace C. Thompson Endowment Fund, University of Oklahoma Foundation.

Library of Congress Cataloging-in-Publication Data

Names: Levy, David W., 1937– author.
Title: Breaking down barriers : George Mclaurin and the struggle to end segregated education / David W. Levy.
Description: Norman : University of Oklahoma Press, 2020. | Includes bibliographical references and index. | Summary: "Explores George W. McLaurin's two-year battle to gain admission as the first African American student at the University of Oklahoma, the help he received from the NAACP and attorney Thurgood Marshall, the legal maneuvering in state and federal courts to secure his rights, and the segregated conditions to which he was subjected once he was on campus"—Provided by publisher.
Identifiers: LCCN 2020008300 | ISBN 978-0-8061-6722-0 (paperback)
Subjects: LCSH: McLaurin, G. W.,—Trials, litigation, etc. | Oklahoma State Regents for Higher Education,—Trials, litigation, etc. | University of Oklahoma—Admission—History—20th century. | Segregation in higher education—Law and legislation—Oklahoma—History—20th century. | Colleges and universities—Admission—Law and legislation—Oklahoma—History—20th century.
Classification: LCC KF228. M3925 L48 2020 | DDC 344.73/0798—dc23
LC record available at https://lccn.loc.gov/2020008300

The paper in this book meets the guidelines for permanence and durability of the Committee on Production Guidelines for Book Longevity of the Council on Library Resources, Inc. ∞

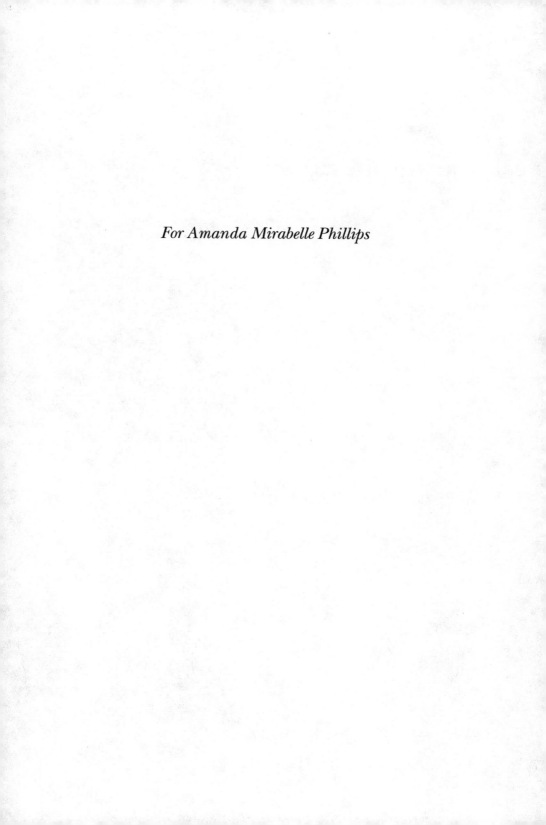

For Amanda Mirabelle Phillips

The classroom for that course was very large and built on a step-up incline, with one row of seats on each of about six levels. In back of the last row of seats was a single large wooden chair behind a wooden rail. Attached to a pole on the back of the chair was a large printed sign that said COLORED. The room was about half-filled when I walked in. I did not look about, just walked straight ahead and up the levels to the chair. . . .

Did the fact of our separation violate the Fourteenth Amendment? On June 5, 1950, a unanimous United States Supreme Court answered yes. . . . The next day, I moved down to the front row. I have not sat in the back ever since. *McLaurin* made that possible.

—Ada Lois Sipuel Fisher, *A Matter of Black and White* (1996)

Contents

Abbreviations

BWC	George Lynn Cross, *Blacks in White Colleges: Oklahoma's Landmark Cases.* Norman: University of Oklahoma Press, 1975.
ChO	*Chronicles of Oklahoma*
CMF	Carl Mason Franklin
DO	*Daily Oklahoman*
EOHC	*Encyclopedia of Oklahoma History and Culture.* Edited by Dianna Everett. 2 vols. Oklahoma City: Oklahoma Historical Society, 2009. Also available online at http://www.okhistory.org/publications /encyclopediaonline.
GLC	George Lynn Cross
Levy 2	David W. Levy, *The University of Oklahoma: A History, Volume Two, 1917–1950.* Norman: University of Oklahoma Press, 2015.
MBW	Ada Lois Sipuel Fisher, *A Matter of Black and White: The Autobiography of Ada Lois Sipuel Fisher.* Norman: University of Oklahoma Press, 1996.
MQW	Mac Q. Williamson
NAACPPM	National Association for the Advancement of Colored People (NAACP) Papers. Part 3: The Campaign for Educational Equality, Legal Department and Central Office Records, 1913–1950. Series B: 1940–1950. Microfilm.
NT	*Norman Transcript*
OD	*Oklahoma Daily*
RD	Roscoe Dunjee

RM   Minutes of the University of Oklahoma Board
             of Regents. Evans Hall, University of Oklahoma,
             Norman.
SM   *Sooner Magazine*
TM   Thurgood Marshall
WHC   Western History Collections, University of Okla-
             homa Libraries, Norman

Prologue

On the morning of Wednesday, October 13, 1948, an elderly African American man named George Washington McLaurin and his wife, Penninah, climbed into their car and drove the twenty miles from their home in the black section of Oklahoma City south to Norman, the site of the state's leading and all-white university. Accompanying the couple were two other passengers: Amos T. Hall, a prominent black attorney from Tulsa,[1] and Roscoe Dunjee, longtime crusading editor of the *Black Dispatch,* the state's most widely read black newspaper, and for many years the mainstay of the Oklahoma State Conference of the National Association for the Advancement of Colored People.[2] At a little after 10:30, the four of them arrived at the campus, found a place to park, and walked up the manicured North Oval to Evans Hall, the university's stately administration building. As they neared the arched Gothic doorway, a young lady approached McLaurin. "I'm so happy for you I do not know what to say," she exclaimed. "I have been pulling for you all the time and it is good to know that Oklahoma has finally done the right thing."[3] The University of Oklahoma had been teaching

---

1. On Hall, see Hannah D. Atkins, "Hall, Amos T. (1896–1971)," *EOHC* 1:639.

2. On Dunjee, see John H. L. Thompson, "The Little Caesar of Civil Rights: Roscoe Dunjee in Oklahoma City, 1915–1955" (PhD diss., Purdue University, 1990); Bob Burke and Angela Monson, *Roscoe Dunjee, Champion of Civil Rights* (Edmond, Okla.: UCO Press, 1998); and Worth J. Hadley, "Roscoe Dunjee on Education: The Improvement of Black Education in Oklahoma, 1930–1955" (EdD diss., University of Oklahoma, 1981).

3. The following account of McLaurin's registration, including the quotation, is drawn from "56-Year-Old Segregation Rule Broken at Okla. University," *Black Dispatch,* October 16, 1948, 1–2, 5; and from Q. M. Spradling to Roscoe Cate, October 15, 1948, GLCPP, Box 50, Folder: "Negro Question (#2)."

students since 1892, and now, after fifty-six years, George McLaurin was about to become its very first African American student.

The little group entered the building, climbed the stairs to the second floor, and found their way to Room 210, the office of J. E. Fellows, dean of Admissions. They were met by Norma Geddes, the dean's assistant, and then introduced to Dean Fellows, who smiled, greeted them cordially, and said, "We are going to try to make your stay here on the campus both pleasant and profitable." From there they were escorted down to the first-floor office of the university's president, George Lynn Cross, passing through "a battery of photographers and reporters" waiting in the president's outer office. Cross himself was absent that day, as he was traveling home from New York City, where he had attended Dwight Eisenhower's inauguration as president of Columbia University. The four instead met briefly with acting president Roscoe Cate, Cross's finance officer and trusted adviser and friend. After chatting with Cate, they returned to Dean Fellows, who handed McLaurin the required forms to fill out for enrollment in the College of Education. From there they were directed to the office of the Graduate College, where they were joined by Associate Dean Joseph Pray and Professor John Bender, who was to serve as McLaurin's academic adviser. For the better part of an hour, they planned the new graduate student's schedule and enrolled him in twelve hours of study. In addition to three hours of independent reading, McLaurin signed up for courses in Educational Psychology, Problems of Teaching in the Secondary Schools, and Principles and Practices in Guidance. Then the party was sent down to Room 107 for the payment of fees. "The enrollee presented himself without funds and was handled as a deferment [sic] with the promise of payment of the fees by Monday, October 18."[4] Finally, McLaurin and the others were taken for a talk with H. E. Wrinkle, dean of the College of Education.

Around 2:00 P.M., after the paperwork and visiting were completed, university officials hosted the group for lunch. Since no restaurant in Norman would serve them, they were taken to the

4. Spradling to Cate, October 15, 1948.

cafeteria of a nearby dormitory called Wilson Center. McLaurin was effusive. "We were entertained royally," he told one reporter. "Everything seemed to be natural."[5] To another he acknowledged that "university officials have been very co-operative. . . . This is a happy day in my life. If things continue the way they have gone today, I think everything is going to be all right."[6] Dunjee's *Black Dispatch* quoted McLaurin as saying that he had never "had a more pleasant half day in my life, and I really feel my studies here are going to give me much comfort, happiness, and satisfaction."[7] On the other hand, he was careful to make it perfectly clear that he would be commuting to his classes from Oklahoma City and not attempting to stay overnight in lily-white Norman, where he would have been decidedly unwelcome and probably subjected to threats of violence. The interurban buses between the two locations ran hourly, and according to university records, 1,996 white students were making the same commute.[8]

On Thursday, October 14, the day after enrolling, McLaurin took the bus down to Norman and made his way to his first class, Educational Psychology, in Room 104 of the old Carnegie Library, now home to the College of Education. He was provided with a chair and a small desk, not in the actual classroom itself, where the white students would be sitting, but in a small, adjoining "anteroom" or "alcove"—his attorney would later describe it (erroneously) as a "broom closet." He would be able to see the blackboard and the professor at a 45-degree angle, but technically he would be "separated" from the other students in accordance with Oklahoma's segregation laws.[9]

5. "Negro to Have Own Anteroom for OU Work," *DO*, October 14, 1948, 1–2.
6. "Negro Admitted to O.U.," *SM* 21 (October 1948): 9, 22.
7. "56-Year-Old Segregation Rule Broken," 1–2.
8. Ibid.
9. There has been a minor scholarly discussion about whether that alcove was especially constructed by the university in order to provide a separated space for McLaurin, or whether the Carnegie Building already had such a convenient available place. A definitive answer to the question comes from a recent article by Eric Lomazoff and Bailie Gregory. They have compared floor plans of the building from 1920, 1928, and 1934, to prove conclusively that the alcove or anteroom off

McLaurin arrived ten minutes before the class was to begin at 2:00 P.M. He found the classroom empty, but the hallway outside the room was crowded with some of the same reporters and photographers who had covered his registration the day before. Curious students and faculty members peeked into the room for a glimpse of a sight that they knew to be unprecedented and historic. A young man and a young woman walked up to him. The man said: "We want to welcome you here, sir, and let you know that we hope you will find a warm welcome." "I'd like to welcome you too," said the woman. "We are glad to see you." McLaurin smiled and said "thank you." The boy said, "I'm George Bassett, and this is Edith Long." "How do you do," the old man said. "I guess you know that my name is McLaurin."[10] It was a safe enough guess. By the time he walked onto the campus, tens of thousands of Oklahomans, blacks and whites alike, already knew his name.

Meanwhile, thirty-one white students were sitting one floor above, and their professor, Frank Balyeat, was having a quiet talk with them. He told them that their class had been moved down a floor to Room 104 and that they would be gaining another classmate, a black student. "I know all of you will agree with me that we are going to make the necessary adjustments as smoothly as possible."[11] Any of the whites who might have objected to being taught in a mixed-race setting could have simply left the building as Balyeat led his students down the stairs, but, he later recalled, "All filed into the room with no apparent resentment."[12] The reporter from the *Daily*

Room 104 had been there for years and that no special construction was required. Lomazoff and Gregory, "Thurgood Marshall's 'Broom Closet': The Structure of Segregation in *McLaurin v. Oklahoma State Regents*," *ChO* 97 (Spring 2019): 26–43. The authors cite half a dozen scholars who erroneously claim that the alcove was constructed to house McLaurin. I am grateful to the authors for allowing me to read their article before publication.

10. "Class Moves to New Room So Negro Can Sit to One Side," *DO*, October 15, 1948, 1.

11. Ibid.

12. Quoted in John T. Hubbell, "The Desegregation of the University of Oklahoma, 1946–1950" (master's thesis, University of Oklahoma, 1961), 48. Hubbell interviewed Professor Balyeat.

Oklahoman noticed the tension in the air: "As the class led by Balyeat came into the downstairs room where McLaurin waited, students either looked at their Negro classmate full in the face or walked self-consciously past his desk. None of the students—both graduates and underclassmen—spoke to him before the session."[13]

The photographers went into action, taking from various angles their shots of McLaurin seated at his desk. Those pictures! Those incredible pictures! They were breathtaking, horrifying, devastating, heartbreaking, easily worth the proverbial thousand words. The elderly black man sitting alone, serious and dignified and dressed in suit and tie. The white students looking indifferent or as if they were somehow superior and knew it—as if the old black man was not quite worthy of their notice. As if they were in danger of being somehow tainted by too close contact with a man who had been teaching school since before they were born, a man trying to attend a university that was younger than he was. (The pictures failed to show that before many days had passed many of McLaurin's fellow students would prove to be friendly and sympathetic.) Within a week, the damning photos were appearing in hundreds of places all over the United States and Europe. It would be hard to overestimate their impact, the resulting national outrage at Oklahoma's callous and humiliating treatment of one of its own citizens.

The university's *Sooner Magazine* tried to put the best possible face on it. "Looking through opened double doors," McLaurin had full view of Professor Balyeat. "But for the glare of an occasional flashbulb fired by a photographer . . . the class was not out of the ordinary." When it ended, Balyeat "stopped by McLaurin's desk to inquire if he were able to hear and see well. McLaurin assured him that he could."[14] Then McLaurin left the classroom, caught the bus, and returned home to Oklahoma City.

George McLaurin's battle to break down segregation at the University of Oklahoma was a long and complicated one, undertaken in the face of bitter official and popular hostility to the mixing of

13. "Class Moves to New Room," 1.
14. "Negro Admitted to O.U.," 21.

George McLaurin and his "alcove" off Room 104 of the Carnegie Building. *Left:* Courtesy Western History Collections, University of Oklahoma Libraries (Ada Lois Sipuel Fisher 4). *Below:* Courtesy Library of Congress, Prints and Photographs Division, NYWT&S Collection (LC-USZ62-126449).

the races. And it would not end with his admission or attending his first class. In fact, it had just begun. But before it was all over, he and his attorneys and his many supporters would have been instrumental in bringing the beginnings of change to the university and the state, to the racial practices of southern higher education in general, to the legal strategies of the leaders of the civil rights movement, to the racial experiences and perceptions of countless white college students, and to the lives and opportunities of thousands of southern African American men and women who were to follow his lead. McLaurin's struggle—both before that day in October 1948, when he became the first black person to enter the all-white school, and afterwards—is the subject of this book.

CHAPTER 1

A Tradition of Segregation

By 1948, when George McLaurin took his seat in that alcove off Room 104, segregation of the races was as solidly established among Oklahoma's white citizenry as Christianity or the Democratic Party. One might find, of course, a handful of white opponents of segregation, just as one might occasionally stumble upon an atheist or run across, here and there, a smattering of lonely Republicans. But with the exception of a few obstreperous and vocal dissenters, these outcasts tended to keep their heresies to themselves at neighborhood barbeques or get-togethers at the Rotary Club or meetings of the city council. The idea that black people and white people must be kept rigorously separated was a deeply ingrained article of faith among the great majority of white Oklahomans, an unquestioned principle endorsed by long tradition and sustained by certain readings of Holy Scripture and by certain beliefs about the importance of "racial purity." Not surprisingly, segregation was also frequently accompanied by fervent declarations of white supremacy and acts of discrimination. Segregation tended to be so universally upheld by whites that support of it might very often go unspoken. But whenever the black community challenged—or even *appeared* to challenge—some aspect of the practice, as the black community frequently did,[1] the white response was likely to be swift, vehement, and very often violent.

1. For one dramatic early example of black resistance to segregation, see Sara Doolittle, "Contingencies of Place and Time: The Significance of *Wilson v. Marion* and Oklahoma Territory in the History of School Segregation," *History of Education Quarterly* 58 (August 2018): 393–419.

Any person who set about to oppose the racial status quo had to be aware of this.

The tradition stretched far back into Oklahoma's pre-statehood history. The first blacks to set foot in what was to become the state of Oklahoma accompanied those intrepid Spanish and French explorers, gold-seekers, traders, and travelers who passed across the landscape in the sixteenth, seventeenth, and eighteenth centuries. Their presence was brief and neither they nor their white associates made a noticeable impact on the land.[2] It was not until the first half of the nineteenth century, when large numbers of African Americans arrived, against their will, that one could speak of a real black presence in Oklahoma's cultural and political life.

The large migration of African Americans to Oklahoma was closely tied to the infamous Trail of Tears. As is well known, it was the clamor among whites for Indian lands in the southeastern United States that led to President Andrew Jackson's decision to forcibly "remove" the Five Civilized Tribes in the 1830s.[3] These tribes—the Chickasaw, Cherokee, Choctaw, Creek, and Seminole— were regarded as "civilized" because they had adopted such aspects of white culture as constitutional government, agriculture, literacy, and Christianity. Among other practices they copied from their white neighbors was human slavery, and they had employed it for many years before making the arduous westward journey to what is now eastern Oklahoma. Enduring that forced migration with their Indian masters were several thousand African American slaves.[4] Because the territory assigned to the Indians and their slaves was

2. Arthur L. Tolson, *The Black Oklahomans: A History, 1541–1972* (New Orleans: Edwards Printing, 1974), chaps. 1–2.

3. Grant Foreman, *Indian Removal: The Emigration of the Five Civilized Tribes of Indians* (Norman: University of Oklahoma Press, 1932, 1972).

4. A small number of slaves arrived in Indian Territory before the removal policy of the 1830s; they came with an advanced group of Cherokees between 1807 and 1819. Annie Heloise Abel, *The American Indian as a Slaveholder and Secessionist* (Cleveland: Arthur H. Clark, 1915), 49–50. See also Michael F. Doran, "Negro Slaves of the Five Civilized Tribes," *Annals of the Association of American Geographers* 68 (September 1978): 335–50; Wyatt F. Jeltz, "Relations of Negroes and Choctaw

located south of the Missouri Compromise line of 36° 30', the legality of slavery was effectively guaranteed. The number of slaves brought to Indian Territory is not precisely known. One estimate puts their numbers in 1839 at between 4,500 and 5,000,[5] but by the outbreak of the Civil War in 1861, there were probably more than 8,000 of them, and, not counting a few free blacks and a small number of whites, they comprised around 14 percent of the Indian population.[6] At the war's beginning, there were three times as many slaves living among the Five Nations as there were whites.[7]

Their treatment in Indian Territory varied from tribe to tribe, but in general the laws governing slavery were copied from those of the southern whites, who had been their neighbors before removal. By general agreement among historians, the least harsh treatment came at the hands of the Seminole and Creek Nations. In the cases of the Cherokee, Choctaw, and Chickasaw, the usage of slaves was similar to that of southern whites. Blacks in those three nations (and after an especially harsh slave law of the mid-1850s, among the Creeks as well) were denied the right to vote in tribal affairs, were not permitted to intermarry with Indians, and were not allowed to enroll their children in tribal schools.[8]

---

and Chickasaw Indians," *Journal of Negro History* 33 (January 1948): 24–37; and J. B. Davis, "Slavery in the Cherokee Nation," *ChO* 11 (1933): 1056–72.

5. Joseph B. Thoburn and Muriel H. Wright, *Oklahoma: A History of the State and Its People* (New York: Lewis Historical Publishing, 1929), 1:297. Doran, "Negro Slaves of the Five Civilized Tribes," 345, notes that "before 1860, the federal government was specifically barred from carrying out enumerations of the tribes, due to their official status as 'domestic dependent nations.'"

6. See Doran, "Negro Slaves of the Five Civilized Tribes," 347; and Doolittle, "Contingencies of Place and Time," 399. A thorough discussion of the enumeration of slaves in Indian Territory is Michael F. Doran, "Population Statistics of Nineteenth Century Indian Territory," *ChO* 53 (1975–76): 492–513. According to the U.S. Census for 1860, the Choctaws held 2,349 slaves (14% of the Nation's population); the Cherokees held 2,511 (15%); the Creeks held 1,532 (10%); the Chickasaws held 974 (18%); and the Seminoles, who resisted enumeration, held around 1,000 (29%). *Eighth United States Census* (Washington, D.C.: Government Printing Office, 1864), xv.

7. Doran, "Negro Slaves of the Five Civilized Tribes," 349.

8. For a summary of the pre–Civil War treatment of blacks by the Five Civilized Tribes, see Ollie Everett Hatcher, "The Development of Legal Controls in Racial Segregation in the Public Schools of Oklahoma, 1865–1952" (PhD diss., University of Oklahoma, 1954), 30–40.

Even though southern whites had been the ones, thirty years earlier, to expel the Indians from their ancestral lands in the Southeast, and even though there were bitter divisions of opinion about secession in each of the Five Nations, the tribes had powerful reasons for casting their lot with the Confederacy.[9] Many Indians felt as much resentment and animosity toward the policies of the national government in Washington, D.C., as they felt toward land-hungry southerners. The agricultural commodities produced in Indian Territory, especially cotton and grains, were floated down the Arkansas and Red Rivers to New Orleans, and that commercial intercourse soon involved cultural and social connections. The wealthiest and most influential figures among the Five Nations, often of mixed race, were connected to the Old South by family ties and by educational institutions to which they sent their children. Above all, Indian leaders—who themselves were heavily invested in and dependent on slave labor—feared for the future of the institution should the North prevail.[10] Of the four states surrounding Indian Territory, moreover, three were similarly committed to slavery—and the fourth, Kansas, succeeded in alienating Indian Territory leaders with ardent and vocal abolitionism and the undisguised desire of many of its citizens to invade Indian lands and use them for their own purposes. Added to all that was the Confederacy's greater interest in an alliance with the tribes in contrast to the Union's relative indifference—the federal forts in Indian Territory were quickly abandoned by the Union Army and taken over by Confederate forces in June and July of 1861.

The Union's ultimate victory in the Civil War brought disastrous consequences to the Indians. By punitive treaties signed in 1866, the Five Nations were required to cede the western half of

9. Lary C. Rampp and Donald L. Rampp, *The Civil War in the Indian Territory* (Austin, Tex.: Presidial Press, 1975); James L. Huston, "Civil War Era," *EOHC* 1:290–93. For tensions between blacks and Indians regarding secession and the immediate postwar, see Donald A. Grinde, Jr., and Quintard Taylor, "Red vs. Black: Conflict and Accommodation in the Post Civil War Indian Territory," *American Indian Quarterly* 8 (Summer 1984): 211–29.

10. It was the mixed-race leaders of the tribes who owned the great majority of the slaves. In no Nation did slave owners amount to more than 3 percent of the tribal population. Doran, "Negro Slaves of the Five Civilized Tribes," 348.

their lands to the federal government. In addition, the Indians were forced to permit railroad construction through the Territory, thus hastening the arrival of eager whites. And, finally, the tribes were compelled to emancipate their slaves and accord them both property rights and citizenship. Suddenly new questions about the relations between Native Americans and the newly freed blacks had to be confronted.

The status of the freedmen varied within each of the Five Nations, with the Chickasaws and Choctaws being the least welcoming of their former slaves and the Seminoles the most.[11] One of the principal areas of concern was the education of the children of the two races, and Indian children and black children were rigidly segregated in the school systems of four of the Five Nations. The Cherokees, for example, established two schools exclusively for their freedmen in 1867,[12] and by 1871, the Creeks were maintaining twenty-five schools for Indian pupils and six for the children of their freedmen. Only the Seminoles permitted the children of both races to attend school together, but this did not mean much as the Seminoles "were practically without schools from 1866 to 1893, and were the least educated of all the Five Tribes."[13]

The huge western part of Indian Territory that was forcibly ceded to the federal government in 1866 soon became the home for other tribes, some of them removed southward from Kansas and Nebraska, others eastward from the American Southwest. From 1866 to 1889, the white presence in this vast territory was limited largely to military personnel stationed there to monitor Indian activities, a few traders, and the cattlemen leasing grazing lands. Several proposals

11. Grinde and Taylor, "Red vs. Black," 215; Kevin Mulroy, *The Seminole Freedmen: A History* (Norman: University of Oklahoma Press, 2016); Kenneth W. Porter, *The Black Seminoles: A History of a Freedom-Seeking People* (Gainesville: University of Florida Press, 2013).

12. By 1872, the Cherokees were operating fifty-seven schools, three of them for freedmen. A high school for freedmen was established in 1890. Grinde and Taylor, "Red vs. Black," 216.

13. Hatcher, "Development of Legal Controls," 61. For a review of each tribe's post–Civil War policies regarding separate schools, see ibid., 54–61.

were floated during the last three decades of the nineteenth century to allow blacks to "colonize" the "Unassigned Lands" (lands not designated to one of the tribes), even leading, in some schemes, to the creation of an entirely black state within the Union. Meanwhile, the numbers of black settlers continued to increase. In addition to the freedmen of the Five Civilized Nations, were freedmen from the southern states and a large number of blacks who had moved to Kansas in the "Exoduster Movement" of 1879, but who by 1890 were finding Kansas less congenial than they had hoped.[14] Between 1865 and 1910, almost two dozen all-black towns were established in the two territories and later in the state of Oklahoma as pioneering blacks sought to escape prejudice and create community.[15]

It was, however, the ever-growing and ever-more-insistent demand by white "boomers" that carried the most weight in Washington, D.C. The pressure on Congress and the president to open to white settlement the "Oklahoma District," as it was now being called, proved to be irresistible. Starting with the legendary "land run" of April 22, 1889, and followed by a series of other runs and sealed-bid auctions, whites flooded into the area in overwhelming numbers.[16] In May 1890, Congress created "Oklahoma Territory," and the march to combining the "twin territories" into a new state proceeded with a certain inevitability.

In the years between 1890 and 1907, both of the territories experienced tremendous growth. According to the 1890 census, Oklahoma Territory had a population of 78,475; by 1907, that

14. Nell Irvin Painter, *The Exodusters: Black Migration to Kansas after Reconstruction* (New York: Alfred A. Knopf, 1977). Danney Goble, in *Progressive Oklahoma: The Making of a New Kind of State* (Norman: University of Oklahoma Press, 1980), 191, writes that the majority of the first black settlers of Oklahoma Territory probably came directly from Kansas.

15. Norman L. Crockett, *The Black Towns* (Lawrence: Regents Press of Kansas, 1979); Hannibal B. Johnson, *Acres of Aspiration: The All-Black Towns in Oklahoma* (Austin, Tex.: Eakin Press, 2002).

16. A number of African Americans also participated in the scramble for lands in both territories, but they comprised only a small minority of the total of new settlers. Grant Foreman, *A History of Oklahoma* (Norman: University of Oklahoma Press, 1942), 256.

number had increased tenfold, to 783,062; Indian Territory, during the same period, grew from 180,182 to 685,115. Regarding the racial composition of the two territories, the greatest change occurred between Indians and whites. In 1890, Indians comprised roughly a quarter of the population of the territories; by 1907, they accounted for only around 5 percent of the total. The black percentage of the population in the two territories remained roughly the same between 1890 (when blacks comprised 8.4 percent of the total) and 1907 (when they were 7.9 percent). But between 1900 and 1907, the number of blacks surpassed the number of Indians in both territories, and in 1907, there were 112,160 African Americans in the new state and 75,012 Indians.[17] Whites had always been more numerous, but in the years from 1890 (when their share of the population was 66.7 percent) to 1907 (when they comprised 86.8 percent of the new state) they gained an unassailable majority.[18]

Both Indians and whites were determined to maintain their policies of segregation and black subordination. Many whites who entered Oklahoma Territory through Kansas were Republicans and, in general, more sympathetic to the former slaves, but by the turn of the century not even they could be counted on to champion black rights and aspirations. As they soon learned, placing black candidates on the ballot sometimes meant losing the entire ticket, and a faction of "lily-whites" emerged within the GOP. Republican leaders, however, still wanted to retain the loyalty of black voters. By the late 1890s, the principal means for keeping blacks voting Republican was to quietly appoint black leaders to minor patronage positions.[19] Those whites who entered through Texas, Arkansas, or Missouri often had direct ties to the Old South (many were veterans of the Confederate Army or their sons and daughters) and were fully committed to racial separation and white supremacy. For them, electing or appointing an African American to any office was outrageous, and all that talk about forming a "black state," and all those glowing promotions of black towns that urged southern

17. Bureau of the Census, *Population of Oklahoma and Indian Territory 1907*, 7–8.
18. Ibid.
19. Goble, *Progressive Oklahoma*, 92–94.

blacks to pack their things and come to Oklahoma, were even worse. Probably the nastiest manifestation of brutal racism in both territories was the series of expulsions of blacks from white towns. Before statehood, white mobs forcibly drove their black neighbors from the towns of Lexington, Norman, Sapulpa, Waurika, Lawton, Perry, Marshall, and Shawnee.[20]

The question of what to do about the schools was debated with intensity in December 1890, the first legislative session of the newly formed Oklahoma Territory.[21] The presence of Republicans in the legislature, together with a Republican governor appointed from Washington, prevented the Democrats from imposing strict segregation in public education.[22] The legislature instead adopted a "county option" alternative, giving the voters of each county the power to decide whether there should be one or two school systems. There were some places in Oklahoma Territory, during the next half dozen years, where black children and white children went to the same schools, but these grew fewer rather than more numerous as time passed.[23] That first Territorial Legislature also created three institutions of higher education and, theoretically, threw open the doors of these schools to any citizen of the Territory irrespective of race. As far as can be determined, however, no African American applied for admission to the Normal school in Edmond, the Agricultural and Mechanical College in Stillwater, or the University of Oklahoma in Norman.

The situation for the Territory's black citizens worsened decisively in 1896–97, and it worsened on two separate fronts. First, the entire white South, by the mid-1890s, was indulging itself in an orgy of segregationist measures, and Oklahoma Territory was not

20. Tolson, *Black Oklahomans*, 61–68.

21. Doolittle, "Contingencies of Place and Time," 408–11; R. Darcy, "Constructing Segregation: Race Politics in the Territorial Legislature, 1890–1907," *ChO* 86 (Fall 2008): 260–89.

22. For the make-up of the Oklahoma territorial legislatures, see R. Darcy, "The Oklahoma Territorial Legislature, 1890–1905," *ChO* 83 (Summer 2005): 144–77.

23. F. A. Balyeat, "Segregation in Public Schools of Oklahoma Territory," *ChO* 39 (Summer 1961): 191–97.

immune from the trend.[24] The creeping lily-white attitudes among the Territory's Republicans, combined with the consistent racist proclivities of both Democrats and Populists, now extinguished any hopes for equality that black settlers might have entertained. The new legislature speedily repealed the county school option. In its place, the lawmakers decreed that in the Territory's educational system, from the lowest grades through college, "it shall hereafter be unlawful for any white child to attend a colored school or any colored child to attend a white school."[25] Historian Danney Goble argues that the word "shall" in the 1897 law was "more normative than imperative" and that mixed-race instruction persisted in some Territory schools until a statute of 1901 "ordered" the end of interracial schooling. The 1901 law also made it illegal for whites to teach in black schools and for blacks to teach in white ones.[26]

Second, in 1896 the United States Supreme Court, in the landmark case of *Plessy v. Ferguson*,[27] spoke authoritatively about the legality of segregation. In a contest that involved a Louisiana law providing for the separation of the races on the state's railroads, the High Court ruled that keeping the races apart was constitutional (i.e., that such separation did not violate the "equal protection of the laws" clause of the Fourteenth Amendment) as long as the facilities for both races were substantially equal. Justice Henry Brown, writing for seven of the eight participating judges, argued that the aim of the Fourteenth Amendment "was undoubtedly to enforce the absolute equality of the two races before the law, but in the nature of things," he explained, "it could not have been intended to abolish distinctions based upon color, or to enforce social, as distinguished from political equality, or a commingling of the two races upon terms unsatisfactory to either." Indeed, "laws permitting and even requiring their separation" have been recog-

24. C. Vann Woodward, *The Strange Career of Jim Crow* (New York: Oxford University Press, 1955).

25. Oklahoma Territory, *Session Laws* (1897), article 1, sections 1–11.

26. Goble, *Progressive Oklahoma*, 135–37.

27. 163 U.S. 537 (1896). See Steve Luxenberg, *Separate: The Story of* Plessy v. Ferguson, *and America's Journey from Slavery to Segregation* (New York: W. W. Norton, 2019).

nized as a proper exercise of power by state legislatures.[28] And although the case before the Court had nothing to do with separate schools, Justice Brown noted that the most common examples of laws requiring separation of the races were "connected with the establishment of separate schools for white and colored children, which has been held to be a valid exercise of the legislative power." The majority in the *Plessy* verdict flatly rejected the central contention of Homer Plessy's attorneys. In Justice Brown's words, "We consider the underlying fallacy of the plaintiff's argument to consist in the assumption that the enforced separation of the two races stamps the colored race with a badge of inferiority. If this be so, it is not by reason of anything found in the act, but solely because the colored race chooses to put that construction upon it."[29]

In Oklahoma, the first response to *Plessy* occurred in the field of higher education. Blacks already had been excluded from white colleges and universities, but there were no colleges or universities for blacks. This obvious violation of "separate but equal" caused the Territorial Legislature to create, ten months after the Supreme Court had spoken, a higher education opportunity for the black citizens of Oklahoma Territory. It was called the Oklahoma Colored Agricultural and Normal University, and it was located in the rural all-black town of Langston, a dozen miles northeast of Guthrie, the territorial capital.[30]

For the next six decades, the doctrine of "separate but equal" became the standard way to argue the validity of measures separating the races, and, at the same time, the allegation that in actual practice the separated facilities were *not* equal became the standard way to argue against particular segregated arrangements.

In June 1906, the United States Congress passed and President Theodore Roosevelt signed the Oklahoma Enabling Act.[31] It ended

28. 163 U.S. at 544.

29. Ibid., at 551.

30. Oklahoma Territory, *Session Laws* (1897), sections 37–41. See Zella J. Black Patterson, *Langston University: A History* (Norman: University of Oklahoma Press, 1982), chap. 2.

31. 34 *U.S. Statutes at Large*, 267 (June 16, 1906).

the debate between those who favored the formation of two separate states and those who favored combining the twin territories into a single state, by deciding in favor of the latter. The act decreed that on November 6 the citizens of the two territories would go to the polls to choose delegates to a constitutional convention to be held in Guthrie on November 20. Each of the territories was to choose fifty-five delegates (and two more were added to represent the Osage Nation, not yet incorporated into Indian Territory). Once the delegates had drafted a constitution, it would be sent to President Roosevelt for his approval and then to a ratification vote by the people of the state. If the voters endorsed the constitution, Oklahoma would be proclaimed America's forty-sixth state.

There were some good reasons to expect that the Democrats would elect a majority of the delegates to the constitutional convention. First, except for the four years of Grover Cleveland's second administration (1893–97), Republicans had occupied the White House every year from 1889 to 1907. These Republican presidents sent their political allies, all of them fellow Republicans, to serve as the governors, judges, and marshals of Oklahoma Territory. The Republican governors had additional patronage powers including the ability to choose party loyalists for every office from public notaries to the regents for the Territory's institutions of higher education. The result was a flood of "carpetbagger" Republicans, many of whom arrived from outside the Territory and went back home when their terms expired with the election of a new president. By 1906 these professional bureaucrats were the targets of enormous public resentment, and allegations of cronyism and corruption fueled the demand for choosing good Democrats, whose homes and loyalties were here and nowhere else, to govern the Territory. Second, the Democrats were able to identify their Republican opponents with the big business, banking, and railroad interests, and to argue that these aristocrats were interested only in their obscene profits and were hostile to the interests of everyday workers and farmers. To many the allegation was confirmed when the Republicans named Henry Asp, the chief lawyer for the Santa Fe railroad, as one of their candidates for a seat at the convention. And third,

the Democrats could assure the voters that they were fully committed to keeping black people in their proper place, fully committed to preserving white supremacy. In a campaign characterized by
extreme race-baiting, it was not subtly implied that Republicans,
those practitioners of dangerous collaboration with blacks, were in
favor of every outrage from mixed schools to mixed marriages. The
Democrats even put into play the terrifying (and preposterous)
fear of "black domination." Of course, that rhetoric on the part
of the Democrats ignored the growing conviction among Republicans that their traditional alliance with black voters was becoming a liability. Under the influence of the growing lily-white faction
in their party, Republicans were also lining up behind segregation
and black subordination.[32]

If there was every reason to presume that the Democrats would
control the constitutional convention, nearly everyone was shocked
by the overwhelming domination they enjoyed. Of the 112 delegates in Guthrie, no fewer than 99 were Democrats; there were only
12 Republicans (one of whom was Henry Asp) and one independent. The Democrats brought with them a set of progressive ideas
aimed at regulating the big corporations and railroads and assur-
ing the power and the prerogatives of "the common man." The
proposed provisions for establishing the mechanisms of the initiative and the referendum in the constitution, for example, passed
the convention by a vote of 81–5, and the stringent regulation of
banking, by 88–1.[33] There was, in short, valid reason for considering the constitution produced in Oklahoma the most progressive
of any state constitution in the United States.

But the Democrats also brought to the convention in Guthrie
their notions about race, and no one voiced disdain for black people
more vehemently or viciously than one of the delegates from the
Chickasaw Nation. He was a thirty-seven-year-old white lawyer named

32. Goble, *Progressive Oklahoma*, 142–44; Jimmie Lewis Franklin, *Journey toward
Hope: A History of Blacks in Oklahoma* (Norman: University of Oklahoma Press,
1982), 37–38.

33. Goble, *Progressive Oklahoma*, 213. Goble gives other examples of the progressive temper of the Guthrie convention.

William H. Murray, already known as "Alfalfa Bill." Born in Toad-
suck, Texas, in 1869, Murray migrated to Indian Territory in 1898,
married the niece of the Chickasaw governor, and soon ingratiated
himself with the Nation's leaders. Murray played a prominent part in
the unsuccessful effort to create a separate Indian state, to be called
Sequoyah, and in the process learned a great deal about writing constitutions. He was elected president of the Oklahoma constitutional
convention, and many of his ideas found their way into the document drafted in Guthrie. In his opening speech to his fellow delegates, Murray addressed the matter of race relations in the new state.
He claimed to "appreciate the old-time ex-slave, the old darky—and
they are the salt of their race—who comes to me talking softly in
that humble spirit which should characterize their action and deal-
ings with white men, and when they thus come they can expect any
favor from me." After all, hadn't Murray appointed blacks to be the
janitors at the constitutional convention? In general, Murray told
the men who had come to create Oklahoma's fundamental law, the
black man "must be taught in the line of his own sphere, as porters,
bootblacks and barbers and many lines of agriculture, horticulture
and mechanics in which he is an adept." It was, however, "an entirely
false notion, that the negro can rise to the equal of a white man in
the professions or become an equal citizen to grapple with public
questions. The more they are taught in the line of industry the less
will be the number of dope fiends, crap shooters and irresponsible
hordes of worthless negroes around our cities and towns."[34] One of
Murray's first acts at the Guthrie convention was to set off a section
of the visitors' gallery and have it marked "Negroes Only."[35]

There is little doubt that the majority of delegates to the Oklahoma constitutional convention wanted to produce a document
that would thoroughly segregate all aspects of social life in the new
state. They were stopped only by the threat of President Roosevelt's
refusal to approve it. His rejection of the document would forestall

34. *Proceedings of the Oklahoma Constitutional Convention* (Guthrie: Leader Printing, 1907), 33. For the colorful career of William H. Murray, see Robert Dorman,
Alfalfa Bill: A Life in Politics (Norman: University of Oklahoma Press, 2018).
35. Franklin, *Journey toward Hope*, 40.

a ratification vote and postpone the actual award of statehood.[36]
The segregation of schools, however, was a different matter. Even
the Enabling Act of 1906 had held out the possibility of school
segregation,[37] and other southern states had enshrined the policy
in their constitutions. That might get by Roosevelt. As for segregating everything else, that would just have to wait until Oklahoma
became a sovereign state and could pass laws without fear that some
Republican in the White House might say no. Thus segregation of
the schools was embedded into Oklahoma's constitution and faith
was placed in the post-statehood legislature for the rest.

The constitution also stumbled toward a definition of the term
"colored." According to Article 23, Section 11, "Whenever in this
Constitution and laws of this State, the word or words 'colored'
or 'colored race,' 'negro' or 'negro race,' are used, the same shall
be construed to mean or apply to all persons of African descent.
The term 'white race' shall include all other persons."[38] No quantity
of African inheritance was stipulated—would a child who had one
black great-grandparent be prohibited from attending school with
white children? On the other hand, by a miracle of phraseology,
American Indians and Asians suddenly became "white."

Thereafter things went smoothly enough. The president approved the draft, and on September 17, 1907, the people of the
twin territories went to the polls. It was the subtly phrased boast of
the Democrats that the new constitution would appeal to everyone
living in the new state except, of course, "Carpetbaggers, Corporations, and Coons."[39] More than 70 percent of the citizenry who
voted were convinced. By a vote of 180,333 to 73,059 (Republicans

36. Goble, *Progressive Oklahoma,* 219.

37. Section 510 of the Oklahoma Enabling Act required the provision of "a system of public schools" that would be "open to all the children" of the future state.
But it added that "this shall not be construed to prevent the establishment and
maintenance of separate schools for white and colored children."

38. This section of the Oklahoma constitution was repealed in November 1978
by a referendum.

39. Danney Goble, "The Southern Influence on Oklahoma," in Davis D. Joyce,
ed., *"An Oklahoma I Had Never Seen Before": Alternative Views of Oklahoma History*
(Norman: University of Oklahoma Press, 1994), 287.

and African Americans stayed home in large numbers) the constitution was ratified. It was approved in every county, and only in the northern substantially Republican counties was the vote even close. A little before noon on November 16, after a long, sixty-day delay that perhaps indicated the Republican Roosevelt's personal unhappiness about welcoming into the Union a solidly Democratic state, the president announced the admission of Oklahoma as a sovereign and equal member of the Union.

The faith that the new state legislature would do the job that Theodore Roosevelt had prevented the constitutional convention from doing was not misplaced. At the same September 1907 election when voters approved the state's constitution, they also chose a solid slate of Democrats committed to a segregated society. Four out of five of Oklahoma's new congressmen were Democrats. All the new judges and state officials were to be Democrats. The state's first governor, Democrat Charles Haskell, won easily. As far as the all-important state legislature was concerned, the tally in the September 17 election was completely one-sided. When the lawmakers gathered in Guthrie, the Senate had 39 Democrats and 5 Republicans. The House consisted of 93 Democrats and 16 members of the GOP. The House promptly chose as its Speaker none other than that vocal racist who had so profoundly influenced the constitutional convention, "Alfalfa Bill" Murray.

The very first piece of legislation passed by both houses and signed by Governor Haskell on December 18 (one month after statehood) provided for the segregation of the races in public transportation. Railroad passenger cars would hereafter be devoted exclusively to one race or the other, and 540 depots around the state had sixty days to make provision for waiting rooms exclusively for travelers of each race. One provision of the law separating the races on railroads required separate but equal accommodations in coaches but permitted railroads to provide "luxury cars"—sleeping cars, dining cars, and so-called chair, or parlor, cars—for whites only. The legislature justified this initiative on the grounds that not many blacks would want or be able to afford such opulence. In

1914, this feature of the law was struck down by the U.S. Supreme Court, which ruled that "equality" required making available to even a single member of one race any accommodation made available to others.[40] Despite this setback, and despite massive and sometimes violent anti-segregation protests by black citizens,[41] the First Oklahoma Legislature plunged forward. A second law, finalized in May, strengthened the existing prohibition against intermarriage, making the act a felony and also making it a felony with a steep fine to be a clergyman who performed such a marriage.

Before the lawmakers headed home, they took the first steps toward another measure, a process not completed until 1910, establishing the so-called grandfather clause. It made voting dependent upon paying a poll tax and passing a literacy test, but stipulated that those requirements were waived for any person whose grandfather could vote. The law was an obvious attempt to limit black voting, and it was not merely an attempt to discourage blacks as political participants in a free society, but a shrewd Democratic ploy to damage the Republicans by denying them the votes of one of their most loyal constituencies.[42] Finally, in 1915, lawmakers authorized the Corporation Commission to make Oklahoma the first state in the Union to provide separate phone booths for black and white users!

Before long, Oklahomans had tightly fastened onto their state a system of racial separation that replicated the most extreme practices of the Deep South. Alongside the legislature's efforts to keep the races safely apart at school or while traveling or making a phone call, there were countless municipal ordinances and unwritten, quietly understood local customs that enforced the separation of blacks and whites in public facilities such as toilets and water fountains, in movie theaters and courthouses, in parks and other

40. *McCabe v. Atchison, Topeka, & Santa Fe Railroad Co.*, 235 U.S. 151 (1914).
41. Tolson, *Black Oklahomans*, 147–52.
42. In 1915, the U.S. Supreme Court struck down the Oklahoma law as an unconstitutional violation of the Fifteenth Amendment. *Guinn* v. *United States* 238 U.S. 347. However, this defeat did not stop Democrats and "lily-white" Republicans from attempting to deny the vote to blacks. For a general overview, see R. Darcy, "Did African Americans Vote between 1910 and 1943?" *ChO* 93 (Spring 2015): 72–98.

places of recreation, in residential neighborhoods, in restaurants and hotels, in hospitals, in cemeteries, and at public meetings.

And if law and custom were not enough to demonstrate to African Americans their subordinate place in Oklahoma society, there was always force. At the end of May 1921, the city of Tulsa suffered the worst race massacre in American history. It will never be known exactly how many died in that orgy of gunfire, arson, imprisonment, and murder; the thriving black neighborhood of Greenwood was burned to the ground.[43] The spectacular rise of the Ku Klux Klan after 1920, with its history of violence and coercion, was another manifestation of the belief in white supremacy at all costs. The *Tulsa Tribune* estimated the Klan's Oklahoma membership at 70,000 at the end of 1921.[44] There were probably more Klan members than members of labor unions in Oklahoma, and the Klan's numbers kept growing in the state through the first half of the 1920s. While it is true that the Klan of the 1920s had enlarged its targets beyond African Americans, the bloody organization remained a fearful enforcer of white supremacy. And finally there were the lynchings—the torture, hanging, or burning of victims, often with the acquiescence of local law enforcement officials. There were probably more than seventy racial lynchings in Oklahoma before the last recorded one in Chickasha in 1930.[45]

And then, as if all this were not enough, there was the crude little town of Norman, home of the state's university. One morning,

43. Scott Ellsworth, *Death in a Promised Land: The Tulsa Race Riot of 1921* (Baton Rouge: Louisiana State University Press, 1982); John Hope Franklin and Scott Ellsworth, eds., *The Tulsa Race Riot: A Scientific, Historical and Legal Analysis* (Oklahoma City: Tulsa Race Riot Commission, 2000).

44. Cited in Michael M. Jessup, "Consorting with Blood and Violence: The Decline of the Oklahoma Ku Klux Klan," *ChO* 78 (Fall 2000), 296, as *Tulsa Tribune*, March 6, 1922. See also Carter Blue Clark, "A History of the Ku Klux Klan in Oklahoma" (PhD diss., University of Oklahoma, 1976).

45. The Equal Justice Initiative's 2017 report, "Lynching in America: Confronting the Legacy of Racial Terror," counted seventy-six racial lynchings in Oklahoma, more than in any other state outside of the Deep South; see https://lynchinginamerica.eji.org/report/, Table 7 (consulted September 9, 2019). See also Dianna Everett, "Lynching," *OEHC*, https://www.okhistory.org/publications/enc/entry.php?entry=LY001 (accessed September 9, 2019).

sometime in the early 1890s, a young black man named Monroe Work got off the train in that town. He had come to see David Ross Boyd, the first president of the school. Before assuming the presidency of the university, Boyd had been school superintendent in Arkansas City, Kansas. Work, whose family was one of those Kansas Exodusters, had been a high school student there. In his early twenties, Work had told Superintendent Boyd that he would have to leave high school. Boyd, who claimed that his father had been part of the underground railroad back in Ohio, saw in Monroe Work (correctly as it turned out) a youngster of considerable intelligence and scholarly potential. Boyd loaned Work a hundred dollars so he could finish the school year, and he lent the young man his own wedding suit for the graduation ceremony. Now Work had come to Norman to repay the loan. He didn't know that Boyd was in Guthrie on university business. Mrs. Boyd was not at home either. So Work began wandering around the dusty town asking for the whereabouts of President Boyd. Within an hour the rumor spread that a black man had come to enroll at the university, and an agitated crowd gathered to make sure that would not happen. Meanwhile, Work boarded the Santa Fe and found Boyd in Guthrie. That evening a group of Normanites burned an effigy of David Ross Boyd.[46]

A few years later, in June 1898, a professional roofer based in Oklahoma City came to Norman on a job. He brought with him an African American helper. While the two were going about their work, a group of twenty-five citizens attacked them viciously. The roofer suffered a fractured skull and the loss of one of his eyes. He sued the town of Norman, alleging that there was a conspiracy of town officials and citizens to prevent by force black people from working there. He further alleged that the town's marshal was present during

46. The Monroe Work story was told by Boyd to Edward Everett Dale, who was planning a biography of Boyd. See Edward Everett Dale MSS, WHC, Box 212, Folder 7. A published version is Dale, "David Ross Boyd: Pioneer Educator," *ChO* 42 (1964): 17. By the time he died, in 1945, Work was regarded as a leading scholar of black history in America. See Linda O. McMurry, *Recorder of the Black Experience: A Biography of Monroe Nathan Work* (Baton Rouge: Louisiana State University Press, 1985).

the beating and that he had encouraged the others. In the roofer's testimony, he cited by name other blacks who had been beaten and driven out of town during the preceding three years.[47]

Norman was located in the southernmost county of Oklahoma Territory, and the great majority of its original settlers had made the land run from Texas through Indian Territory. They were southerners, many with ties to the old Confederacy. In August 1890, when it came time to assign their county a permanent name, the Republicans suggested calling it "Lincoln" in honor of their Republican hero, while the Democrats suggested "Cleveland," for the Democrat who had recently served as president and would do so again in 1893. The vote (809 to 405 in favor of Cleveland) indicates the extent to which southern Democrats dominated the town where the University of Oklahoma would soon be built.[48]

The racial prejudice that characterized Norman in the 1890s continued with unabated ferocity in the decades ahead. In the early 1920s, an Oklahoma City oilman, thinking that he would like to go to college, built an expensive home in Norman, near the university campus. He and his wife brought with them a black woman who cared for their two children and had been like a member of the family for many years. The woman lived in an apartment above the garage in back of the house. After enduring for a year the threatening messages and rocks hurled at their home, the family surrendered, sold the house to a sorority, and returned to Oklahoma City.[49] Not long thereafter, university president William Bennett Bizzell and his wife were visited by old friends from Texas. The friends were driven by a black chauffeur. President Bizzell naively thought that it would be all right to house the chauffeur overnight above the garage behind the president's home. By late afternoon, Bizzell had received so many threatening phone calls that it seemed wise to dispatch the chauffeur to Oklahoma City for the night.[50]

47. The case is described in detail in *BWC*, 6–8.
48. John Womack, *Norman: An Early History, 1820–1900* (Norman: privately printed, 1976), 79.
49. *BWC*, 8–9.
50. Ibid., 9–10.

One afternoon in the summer of 1934, George Cross, a newly hired professor of Botany who had just arrived in town, had a friendly chat with a local merchant. "During the course of our conversation," Cross recalled, "the man introduced the subject of racial relations, with the comment that I would never need to worry about the 'nigger problem.' He made the remark with obvious pride, explaining that there were no Negroes living in Norman or even in the vicinity of Norman. There was an unwritten law, he said, that a Negro could not remain within the city limits after sundown. This restriction had been in effect since the settling of Norman during the land rush of 1889." When Cross asked how such a "law" could be enforced, the merchant said that "there had never been the need for enforcement. The Negroes . . . understood the situation perfectly and knew better than to remain in the city after sundown."[51]

In fact, it was not until the outbreak of World War II that Norman allowed the presence of African Americans. The navy proposed creating two huge bases to the north and the south of the university's main campus, and the town's business and real estate leaders quickly understood that the arrival of thousands of newcomers would mean huge economic benefits. It was also understood that not all of the new arrivals would be white. There would be blacks in the military band, there would be black cooks and servers in the mess halls, black construction workers and black orderlies in the base hospital. Some officers living in town demanded that their black servants be permitted to stay with them. The choice for many Normanites—between the town's traditional racial purity or the prospect of millions of wartime dollars flooding into their sleepy little community—was a painful one. The *Norman Transcript*, representing the town's business community, frankly admitted that the presence of blacks "may change a situation that has prevailed ever since the day Norman was first settled in the run of 1889, that of having no negroes here." But in view of the opportunities the naval bases would bring, the newspaper urged the townspeople to

51. Ibid., 5–6. For the general phenomenon, which characterized thousands of American towns and suburbs outside the Deep South, see James Loewen, *Sundown Towns: A Hidden Dimension of American Racism* (New York: New Press, 2005).

behave "calmly, gracefully, and with no racial protests."[52] No doubt many Norman citizens quietly assumed and fervently hoped that once this awful war was finished, the blacks would pack up and leave, and the town would return to being as white as ever.

It must be apparent that any person, white or black, who had the temerity to challenge Oklahoma's tradition of segregation and white supremacy, was enlisting in a battle where the risks were high and the chances for success dubious. Embedded in a history that stretched back before statehood, back even before the invasion of whites and the creation of Oklahoma Territory, the separation of the races and the assignment of the lowest rank to the black race was an unquestioned fact of life. Segregation was established by custom, and sanctified by tribal, territorial, state, and municipal law. It was supported by the judicial system, the state's newspapers, and most of the state's white churches. It was sanctified by custom and enforced by social and economic coercion. And it was sustained, when it was thought necessary, by physical intimidation and unrestrained violence. And yet, somehow, from the very beginning courageous black men and women resisted segregation by whatever means they could.

George McLaurin surely understood what the odds were when he and five other African Americans came to Norman, a town notorious for its bigotry, and applied for admission to the University of Oklahoma. We cannot admire too much the courage such an act required. They must have known the risks, and yet they went ahead. But they were not the first African Americans who tried to breach segregated southern higher education. If they were given pause by the enormous resistance they faced, they must also have been emboldened and encouraged by the small handful of predecessors who had earlier made the same heroic decision to resist the oppressive tradition and pursue justice for themselves and others of their race.

<hr />

52. Cited in Breanna Edwards, "The Bases: The Story of Norman's Naval Bases during 1942," student paper, 2011, in WHC (University Archives), Vertical File: "Naval Air Training Center (South Base)," as "Negroes at Naval Bases," *Norman Transcript*, July 10, 1948, 8. See also Levy 2: 289–97.

CHAPTER 2

Pioneers on the Road to Desegregation

From the first day of its founding in 1909, the National Association for the Advancement of Colored People (NAACP) confronted a daunting array of injustices toward black Americans, and the new organization entered into the battle on half a dozen fronts. The NAACP attempted to resist outright violence against blacks by fighting for anti-lynching legislation. It fought against discrimination in employment and in the practices of labor unions. It opposed racial restrictions on residential covenants, public transportation, access to public accommodations, and the right to vote. Despite terribly limited financial resources and insufficient staff, the leaders of the NAACP did all they could to fight racism.[1] And alongside their other concerns, the problem of the abysmal lack of educational opportunities for African Americans began to assume increasing importance. By the mid-1920s the struggle against segregated and inferior education had become a major priority for the NAACP.[2]

The urgent focus on education arose in part from the realization that if black youngsters were not educated to the same levels as white youngsters, they were doomed to remain a permanent

1. Charles Flint Kellogg, *NAACP: A History of the National Association for the Advancement of Colored People* (Baltimore: Johns Hopkins University Press, 1967); Patricia Sullivan, *Lift Every Voice: The NAACP and the Making of the Civil Rights Movement* (New York: The New Press, 2010).

2. Mark V. Tushnet, *The NAACP's Legal Strategy against Segregated Education, 1925–1950* (Chapel Hill: University of North Carolina Press, 1987).

underclass in American society. A further incentive in the crusade for equal educational opportunities was the need, keenly felt by the activists in the offices of the NAACP, for a future supply of well-trained black leaders. Eventual equality in America would ultimately require the emergence of a substantial population of African Americans who could play prominent roles in the nation's political, professional, economic, and social life.[3] Fulfilling that requirement would depend upon vast improvements in the quality of education that African Americans received—from the earliest grades in elementary school straight through to collegiate, graduate, and professional programs.

Two things seemed obvious as the struggle to break down segregation in southern education gained momentum in the mid-1930s. The first was that the best chances for success would be in the so-called border states, states located on the edges of the old Confederacy, states that had allowed slavery but that had not actually seceded in the 1860s. It was clear that whites of the Deep South were so intensely committed to white supremacy and so fearful of any sort of social or political uprising by their black populations (which made up a much larger percentage of their citizenry than was the case in the border states) that, at least for the present, advances toward desegregation there were virtually impossible. The politics of places such as Mississippi and Alabama, Virginia and the Carolinas, Louisiana and Georgia were so single-mindedly devoted to keeping blacks in "their place," and the traditions of legal and informal Jim Crow separation so firmly entrenched, that any gesture even remotely threatening to segregation would be met with fierce resistance and probable violence. The second belief of those who thought about the coming struggle was that the best hope for success in attacking

3. This emphasis, of course, was an echo of W. E. B. DuBois's famous 1903 essay "The Talented Tenth." *The Journal of Negro Education* devoted its entire Winter 1935 issue to this matter. See, for examples, Charles H. Houston, "The Need for Negro Lawyers" (49–52); Paul K. Edwards, "The Need for and Education of Negro Business Men" (71–75); H. A. Callis, "The Need and Training of Negro Physicians" (32–41); and other articles in that issue.

segregation lay in graduate and professional education and not in schooling at the lower levels.

During the 1930s, seventeen states and the District of Columbia operated, by law, separate schools for black and white students at the elementary and secondary levels, and sixteen states excluded blacks from their state universities.[4] At every level there was abundant evidence of the grossly unfair treatment of black schools and their pupils. A study of the 1935–36 school year revealed that southern states were spending yearly an average of $49.30 for every white child in elementary or secondary schools but only $17.04 for every black child. In Mississippi and Georgia that second figure was closer to $9.00[5] Whether one considered per capita expenditures, the caliber and compensation of teachers, the length of the school year, the rates of attendance, the extent of academic offerings, the availability of classroom supplies, the money spent to transport children to school, or the quality and maintenance of equipment and buildings, the differences between white and black schools in the South were stunning.

Nearly every southern community, the Swedish sociologist Gunnar Myrdal reported in 1944, "has a substantial amount of discrimination coupled with segregation in the provision of education for Negroes. The buildings and equipment are inferior; in rural areas most of the schools are not run during the planting or harvesting seasons; the teachers get a lower rate of pay; Negroes have little control over their schools; many common academic subjects are not offered in the secondary schools in order to prevent Negroes from getting anything but a low grade vocational training."[6] Teachers in black elementary and secondary schools carried heavier teaching loads, taught more students in each classroom, and received much less pay than white teachers. So much for "separate but equal."

4. These sixteen states were: Alabama, Arkansas, Delaware, Florida, Georgia, Kentucky, Louisiana, Mississippi, Missouri, North Carolina, Oklahoma, South Carolina, Tennessee, Texas, Virginia, and West Virginia.

5. Gunnar Myrdal, *An American Dilemma: The Negro Problem and Modern Democracy* (New York: Harper & Brothers, 1944), 339.

6. Ibid., 632.

At the close of World War II, things had not improved. "In 1945," writes historian Richard Kluger, "the South was spending twice as much to educate each white child as it was per black child. It was investing four times as much in white school plants, paying white teachers salaries 30 percent higher, and virtually ignoring the critical logistics of transporting rural Negroes to their schools. In 1944, the segregating states spent a total of $42 million busing white children to schools; on transporting colored children, they spent a little more than one million dollars." The average white child in the South had 8.4 years of schooling; the average black child, 5.1. The percentage of white children finishing high school was four times the percentage of black children, and by one estimate of 1946, about a quarter of the black population nationwide was functionally illiterate, with blacks in the rural South especially handicapped in this regard.[7] Oklahoma was no better. In the late 1940s, the state maintained 101 accredited junior high schools for whites and only 2 for blacks. There were 656 accredited high schools for whites and 48 for blacks.

The situation at the college level was nothing less than scandalous. In 1940, postsecondary education for southern blacks was carried out in 117 all-black colleges. Of these, 36 were publicly funded and all but 7 of the rest were affiliated with a religious denomination.[8] Attendance at these black colleges was growing at a healthy rate,[9] but by 1940 only around 1 percent of southern African American youth had any college experience compared to around 8.5 percent of young southern whites. Even more important, with the exception of a small

7. Richard Kluger, *Simple Justice: The History of* Brown v. Board of Education *and Black America's Struggle for Equality* (New York: Alfred A. Knopf, 1976), 257. The estimate of illiteracy was made by Ambrose Caliver, senior specialist in Negro education in the U.S. Office of Education.

8. Myrdal, *American Dilemma,* 632.

9. See Fred McCuistion, *Graduate Instruction for Negroes in the United States* (Nashville: George Peabody College for Teachers, 1939), table 2, 17; "Enrollment in Negro Colleges and Universities," *School and Society* 50 (July 29, 1939): 141; and Marybeth Gasman and Roger L. Geiger, "Introduction," in Gasman and Geiger, eds., *Higher Education for African-Americans before the Civil Rights Era, 1900–1964* (New Brunswick, N.J.: Transaction Publishers, 2012), 6–8.

handful of fairly solid institutions such as Fisk, Howard, Atlanta, and the newly founded Dillard, the quality (even the adequacy) of the great majority of these black schools was dubious. Nearly all of them were starved for funds and had small or nonexistent endowments, inferior libraries, ramshackle buildings, and unkempt grounds. "Most of these colleges," wrote Myrdal, "did not have the teachers and school facilities to provide an adequate education."[10]

In 1943, the *National Survey of Higher Education for Negroes* concluded that "colleges for Negroes in general are below par in practically every area of educational service." Two years later, Charles Thompson, who had been the founder of *The Journal of Negro Education* and its editor from 1932 to 1963, complained that no black college "offers work that is even substantially equal to that offered in the corresponding state institutions for whites." When it came to accreditation, the record was dismal. No black college earned accreditation until 1930, and a decade later, the Southern Association of Colleges and Secondary Schools was accrediting only one in five black colleges, compared to accrediting almost half of southern colleges for whites.[11] In those institutions supported by public taxation in the South, around $86 million dollars went to white colleges and only $5 million to black ones.

The lone black college in Oklahoma was fairly typical of southern black colleges. Up through World War II, Langston University (formerly the Oklahoma Colored Agricultural and Normal University) had never been accredited. One student of the mid-1940s recalled that "the dormitories, classrooms, and administration buildings were old and outdated, as were the library and the university auditorium. There were almost no sidewalks, and the ones that there were went from nowhere to nowhere else." Any rain turned

10. Myrdal, *American Dilemma*, 951.
11. Ibid. For the condition of education in all-black southern colleges and universities in the 1930s and early 1940s, see the pages of Charles Thompson's invaluable *Journal of Negro Education*. In addition to Myrdal's monumental study, see also Horace Mann Bond, *The Education of the Negro in the American Social Order* (New York: Prentice Hall, 1934); McCuistion, *Graduate Instruction for Negroes;* and Gasman and Geiger, "Introduction."

the campus "into sticky mud, a form of cement that sucked a person's shoes off when he or she had to walk through it."[12] In December 1945, editor Roscoe Dunjee estimated that the state's unfair financing of Langston over the preceding forty years had robbed the college of $10 million dollars. As well as criticizing the deplorable physical conditions of the campus, Dunjee lamented the gross inequality in teacher pay, the scarcity of instructional materials, and the paucity of courses of study.[13] Thurgood Marshall would later claim that the library at the state prison in McAlester had more books than the library at Langston.[14] At the outbreak of World War II, Langston ranked in the lowest 6 percent among all American colleges and universities in the number of faculty members with doctorates and in the lowest 5 percent in its student-faculty ratio. The laboratories for chemistry, physics, biology, and home economics were stuffed into the upper floors of the Administration Building, and the Music Department was confined to a wing of the gym.[15] In 1945, the State Regents for Higher Education had $6,443,421 to distribute to Oklahoma's eighteen public institutions. Langston got a mere $186,000.[16]

While the provisions for black elementary and high school students in the South were clearly unfair and shamelessly unequal, and while the conditions for undergraduates in southern black colleges were, in general, deplorable, the opportunities for blacks to undertake graduate work or professional training were even worse. Fred McCuistion's 1939 study reports that of the nation's 117 black colleges only 7 offered any work beyond the bachelor's degree. Nine southern states provided absolutely no graduate work whatever for African Americans, and no black college in the nation offered work

12. *MBW*, 73. Fisher does, however, praise the faculty for its commitment to teaching.

13. Cheryl Elizabeth Brown Wattley, *A Step toward* Brown v. Board of Education: *Ada Lois Sipuel Fisher and Her Fight to End Segregation* (Norman: University of Oklahoma Press, 2014), 70–71. See also Patterson, *Langston University*, 146–47.

14. *DO*, November 12, 1948, 2.

15. Patterson, *Langston University*, chap. 13.

16. Donald Spivey, "Crisis on a Black Campus: Langston University and Its Struggle for Survival," *ChO* 59 (Winter 1981–82): 441–42.

beyond the master's degree.[17] At the end of World War II, there were 29 medical schools in the South for whites and 2 for blacks; there were 20 accredited pharmacy schools for whites and 1 for blacks; there were 40 accredited law schools for whites and 1 for blacks; there were 36 accredited engineering schools for whites and none for blacks.[18]

If the constitutional test for black elementary schools, high schools, and undergraduate colleges was "separate but equal" (a test which, had it ever been honestly applied, would have been failed miserably throughout the segregating South), what could be said in defense of the "separate but nonexistent" character of graduate and professional programs? Seven southern states, well aware of the dangers they would face in the event of a legal challenge, devised a mechanism that they hoped might satisfy the *Plessy* formula and preserve their white-only institutions. They began to offer scholarships to black students.[19] These awards would pay the tuition costs at northern colleges and universities that accepted African Americans and that offered graduate and professional programs not available to them in their home states. One of the states experimenting with this alternative was Oklahoma. In July 1935, the state legislature appropriated $5,000 for that purpose. A black student who wished to study a subject not taught at Langston, and who had lived in Oklahoma for the five years before applying, would be eligible for a $250 award and three cents per mile for travel. In 1941, the yearly appropriation for such awards was raised to $15,000; in 1946, to $45,000; and in 1948, to $50,000.[20] Around two thousand

17. McCuistion, *Graduate Instruction for Negroes,* 34.

18. Kluger, *Simple Justice,* 257. These inadequacies had serious outcomes for everyday black southerners. Each black dentist, each black doctor, for example, had to serve many more patients than their white counterparts. Myrdal reports that in 1930 there were 6 black lawyers in Mississippi and 4 in Alabama, compared to more than 1,200 and 1,600 white lawyers in those two states. In 1937, to take another example, about 35 percent of black babies were delivered by doctors, compared to 90 percent of white babies. Myrdal, *American Dilemma,* 326, 172.

19. The states offering these scholarships were: Kentucky, Maryland, Missouri, Oklahoma, Tennessee, Virginia, and West Virginia.

20. Hatcher, "Development of Legal Controls," 122–23.

black Oklahomans took advantage of these scholarships and left the state to study elsewhere.

But scholarships or not, the discrepancy in treatment throughout the South at these highest graduate and professional educational levels, the clear injustice of it, was so glaring that it made perfect sense for the NAACP to launch the attack on segregated education at these advanced levels of collegiate education. No one understood this better than NAACP chief counsel Thurgood Marshall. In June 1948, he wrote to Erwin Griswold, dean of the Harvard Law School, that "I believe that we have a better chance of breaking down segregation in professional schools and especially law schools than on any other level of public education." Besides the obvious injustice involved, Marshall sensed that "we will have the least amount of friction and opposition on that level."[21]

Unfortunately for the NAACP, the attempt to desegregate southern professional training got off to a sputtering—not to say disastrous—start. In North Carolina a 1933 effort to enroll a black man in the state university's School of Pharmacy quickly became embarrassing. Thomas Hocutt had mediocre high school and college grades, could not get a letter of recommendation from the North Carolina College for Negroes, and, according to Mark Tushnet, appeared "marginally literate when he took the stand in his lawsuit."[22] Some in the local black community feared that admitting blacks to white colleges would reduce funding for black schools; the local NAACP branch voted not to support Hocutt. The case was dismissed and not appealed.[23] Two Tennessee cases were also calamitous. In one, in August 1935, a black high school teacher said he wanted to go to law school but in the end decided to keep his job at the high school. In the other, inept local lawyers, trying to gain their client's admission to the University of Tennessee's pharmacy school, appealed directly to the president and board of regents, instead of going through the normal admission

21. NAACPPM, Reel 13, Frame 749.
22. Tushnet, *NAACP's Legal Strategy*, 53.
23. *Hocutt v. Wilson*, N.C. Super. Ct. (1933) (unreported). See Tushnet, *NAACP's Legal Strategy*, 52–53; and Kluger, *Simple Justice*, 155–58.

procedure. After a trial, but before a verdict, the applicant enrolled in Fisk University, where, writes Tushnet, "his work was an academic disaster."[24]

The North Carolina and Tennessee fiascos indicated the need for three improvements. First, more credible plaintiffs were required. Second, support from the local black community had to be secured. And third, first-class lawyers from the NAACP's national office in New York City had to get directly involved in trying the cases. Soon all these ingredients would be in place.

Donald Gaines Murray was born in Philadelphia but was raised in Baltimore by his grandparents. His grandfather was a bishop in the African Methodist Episcopal Church.[25] In June 1934, at the age of twenty-one, Murray graduated from Amherst College in Massachusetts. He returned to Baltimore hoping to become a lawyer. Tushnet says he was "the perfect plaintiff."[26] There was no law school for blacks in Maryland. On December 8, Murray requested an application form for enrollment at the University of Maryland School of Law, which was located in his hometown of Baltimore. A week later, he got an unceremonious letter from university president Raymond Pearson. He called Murray's attention to other educational opportunities for African Americans, including the possibility of "partial scholarships . . . at institutions outside of the State for Negro students who may desire to take professional courses."[27] Undeterred, Murray was able to secure an application form and submitted it on January 24, 1935, together with the required $2 money order. The

24. On the Tennessee cases, see Tushnet, *NAACP's Legal Strategy*, 53–54. A later Tennessee case (1939), failed because local attorneys misdirected a request for a writ of mandamus. Ibid., 55.

25. See Murray's obituary, *Baltimore Sun*, April 10, 1986, 4B.

26. Tushnet, *NAACP's Legal Strategy*, 56.

27. R. A. Pearson to Donald G. Murray, December 14, 1934. This letter and other primary source documents in the Murray case, quoted here, are made conveniently available online at *Archives of Maryland* (Biographical Series), "Donald Gaines Murray," MSA SC 352012494, https://msa.maryland.gov/megafile/msa /speccol/sc3500/sc3520/012400/012494/html/12494collect.html (accessed November 16, 2017). See also Kluger, *Simple Justice*, 186–94.

university's registrar sent Murray a second copy of President Pearson's letter, returned the money order, and added, "The University does not accept Negro students."[28] On March 8, Murray wrote directly to the university's Board of Regents: "I am a citizen of the State of Maryland and fully qualified to become a student of the University of Maryland Law School. . . . The arbitrary actions of the officials of the University of Maryland in returning my application was unjust and unreasonable." He asked the regents to review his qualifications and admit him. "I am ready, willing and able to meet all requirements as a student, to pay whatever dues are required of residents of the State and to apply myself diligently to my work."[29] Pearson replied by enclosing a third copy of his original letter and recommending that Murray apply to the fine law school at Howard University in Washington, D.C.[30]

By the time Murray applied to the Maryland law school, the legal department of the NAACP had become a force to be reckoned with. The organization's guiding spirit was a brilliant attorney, forty-year-old Charles Hamilton Houston. Born and raised in Washington, D.C., he (like Donald Murray) had gone to Amherst. Upon graduation in 1915, Houston was the only black student in his class, a member of Phi Beta Kappa, and the class valedictorian. During World War I, he was a lieutenant in the segregated army and saw service in France. Upon his return, Houston enrolled at the Harvard Law School, where he became a disciple of Felix Frankfurter. He was the first black student chosen as an editor of the *Harvard Law Review* and graduated with honors. Returning to Washington he practiced law and soon joined the faculty of Howard University. In 1929, Houston took over as dean of the law school and began to turn out a generation of able, civic-minded black attorneys. In 1935, the year of the Murray litigation, he became the NAACP's special counsel.[31]

28. W. M. Hillegeist to Murray, February 9, 1935, *Archives of Maryland*, "Donald Gaines Murray."

29. Murray to Board of Regents, March 8, 1935, ibid.

30. Pearson to Murray, March 8, 1935, ibid.

31. For Houston's early career, see Kluger, *Simple Justice*, chap. 5.

One of Houston's most promising students was a young Balti-more native named Thurgood Marshall. Marshall too had wanted to attend the Maryland law school but did not apply because of the school's all-white policy. After finishing first in his class at the How-ard Law School in 1933, he opened a practice in Baltimore and went to work for the NAACP. Like his mentor Houston, who was a dozen years older, Marshall was a dogged and tireless antagonist on behalf of civil rights for African Americans. Like Houston, he was a meticulous student of the law, an expert strategist and tactician, and a formidable and fearsome presence in the courtroom, sharp, quick on his feet, and capable of utterly destroying a hostile wit-ness.[32] In the spring of 1935, Houston, assisted by Marshall, came after the University of Maryland and its segregated law school on behalf of Donald Murray.

In April, the two lawyers filed for a writ of mandamus in the Baltimore City Court, and the case came before Judge Eugene O'Dunne on June 18. Marshall and Houston shared in the exami-nation of witnesses, and the two of them subjected President Pear-son and other officials to an uncomfortable series of questions. Kluger does not exaggerate when he writes that the defense was reduced to rubble.[33] A large part of Maryland's defense rested on the out-of-state scholarships. The NAACP attorneys showed that the 1933 act by the Maryland Assembly, which provided for those scholarships, had never been actually funded. An act of 1935 set aside $10,000 to provide $200 tuition scholarships for African Americans who wished to study fields not available to them in Maryland. Murray's attorneys argued, first, that providing only fifty such scholarships was inadequate and that the chances of any

32. Mark V. Tushnet, *Making Civil Rights Law: Thurgood Marshall and the Supreme Court, 1936–1961* (New York: Oxford University Press, 1994).

33. See "Stenographer's Record," a 142-page account of the proceeding in the Baltimore City Court. Baltimore City Court (Court Papers), Stenographer's Re-cord, Donald G. Murray vs. Raymond A. Pearson, et al., 18 June 1935, *Archives of Maryland,* https://msa.maryland.gov/megafile/msa/speccol/sc2200/sc2221/000011/000006/pdf/c174-2-12.pdf (accessed November 27, 2017); and Kluger, *Simple Justice,* 189.

Thurgood Marshall, circa 1960. Courtesy Library of Congress, Prints and Photographs Division, Visual Materials from the NAACP Records (LC-USZ62-120005).

individual black applicant receiving one was remote, and second, that covering tuition left students like Donald Murray in the position of having to fund themselves all other expenses involved in their studying away from home: transportation, room and board, living expenses.

Judge O'Dunne, who appeared sympathetic to Murray and his attorneys throughout the proceeding, had no difficulty in deciding the matter. Late in the afternoon of June 25, he directed his clerk to issue the desired writ, ordering the defendants to admit Murray in September as a first-year law student.[34] Before that could happen, the university, on July 31, appealed the decision to the Maryland Court of Appeals, the state's highest judicial body. After considering the briefs from both sides,[35] that court, on January 15, 1936, affirmed the lower court's ruling in no uncertain terms: "The case, as we find it, then, is that the state has undertaken the function of education in the law, but has omitted students of one race from the only adequate provision made for it, and omitted them solely because of their color. If those students are to be offered equal treatment in the performance of the function, they must, at present, be admitted to the one school provided."[36]

The University of Maryland chose not to pursue the case and admitted Murray to its law school. After graduating, Murray practiced in Baltimore until retiring in 1972. He undertook several government appointments and participated in some NAACP cases. In what must have been a satisfying moment for him, he was co-counsel in the 1949 case that ended segregation at the University of Maryland School of Nursing.[37] His co-counsel on that occasion was his own lawyer from 1935, Charles Hamilton Houston. When Houston was disabled by a heart attack (he was to die eight days after the nursing school decision), Donald Murray was joined in the courtroom by his other attorney of fifteen years earlier, Thurgood Marshall.

Because the university surrendered after the Court of Appeals ruling, Murray's case never entered the federal judicial system.

34. James B. Blake (Clerk of the Baltimore City Court), "Writ of Mandamus," June 25, 1935, *Archives of Maryland,* "Donald Gaines Murray."

35. Court of Appeals (Briefs), 1935, Nos. 47–53, No. 53, University v. Murray, MSA T 2088, MSA SC 22212445, *Archives of Maryland,* https://msa.maryland.gov/megafile/msa/speccol/sc2200/sc2221/000024/000004/000000/html/guide.html (accessed November 16, 2017).

36. *Pearson* v. *Murray,* 169 Md. 478 (1936) at 489.

37. *Esther McCready* v. *Harry C. Byrd, et al.* Md., October Term 1949, No. 139 [MSA S 393268, 1/66/6/18], *Archives of Maryland,* https://msa.maryland.gov/megafile/msa/speccol/sc2200/sc2221/000011/000016/pdf/s393-268.pdf (accessed November 21, 2017).

The decision, therefore, was not binding outside of the state of Maryland.

In 1936, the year that Donald Murray was admitted to Maryland's School of Law, the focus of the struggle against segregated higher education in the South moved from border-state Maryland to border-state Missouri. Lloyd Lionel Gaines was born in Mississippi in 1911, but when his father died in 1926, his mother moved him and his four siblings to St. Louis. Gaines was the valedictorian of his high school class and, upon graduating in 1931, spent a year at the all-black Stowe's Teachers College in St. Louis. He then entered Lincoln University, Missouri's black undergraduate institution, in Jefferson City. He was elected president of his senior class and, at the age of twenty-five, graduated with honors in June 1935.[38]

Lloyd Gaines's story was, in several ways, an echo of Donald Murray's. Like Murray, Gaines wanted to become a lawyer, and like Murray he was living in a state that had no publicly-supported law school for blacks. He applied for admission to the University of Missouri School of Law, and, to no one's surprise, was turned down solely on the basis that he was black and that the Missouri constitution mandated the separate education of the races.[39] On January 24, 1936, Gaines, aided by local attorneys and the NAACP's Charles Houston, petitioned the Boone County Circuit Court, in Columbia, for a writ of mandamus ordering the University of Missouri to admit him to its law school. In July, that court denied the request without issuing an opinion. Gaines then appealed to Missouri's supreme court. Houston sensed the outcome from the start. He told his friends back at the New York office that "it is beyond expectation that the court will decide in our favor, so we had just as well get ready for the appeal."[40] Houston's prediction was accurate; on December 9, 1937, the Missouri justices upheld the lower court's denial on the grounds that it was "contrary to the constitution, laws

38. Lucile H. Bluford, "The Lloyd Gaines Story," *Journal of Educational Sociology* 32 (February 1959): 242–46. On Bluford, see n. 52 below.

39. Constitution of Missouri, article 11, section 3.

40. Quoted by Kluger, *Simple Justice*, 204.

and public policy of the State to admit a negro as a student in the University of Missouri."[41] Gaines's attorneys immediately appealed to the U.S. Supreme Court, and on October 10, 1938, the High Court agreed to hear the case.

The state offered the two arguments that had persuaded the Missouri courts. First, Gaines should not have applied to the white university since it was obligated to refuse him in view of Missouri's legal and traditional policy of race separation. His proper remedy was to ask the curators of Lincoln University to provide him with a legal education substantially equal to the one given to white students at the University of Missouri. The state legislature had given the Lincoln curators discretion to expand the functions of that school as they saw proper. It was unreasonable to expect them to create a black law school until they were convinced that there was a demand for it. Let Gaines make that very demand, and Lincoln and the state of Missouri would respond. And second, if Gaines was unwilling to go through the proper procedure and seek his remedy through the curators of Lincoln, or if he was unwilling to wait while Lincoln created a law school for him, he was perfectly free to ask for an out-of-state scholarship. Missouri had a real (funded) scholarship program that, the state believed, would satisfy the Fourteenth Amendment requirement of equal protection of the laws. The Missouri scholarships enabled black students to attend schools in adjacent states (Kansas, Iowa, Nebraska, or Illinois), where they could study subjects that only white students were offered in Missouri. The awards provided the difference between Missouri's tuition and the higher tuitions of the neighboring states.[42]

The courts of two states had now passed differing judgments on these out-of-state scholarships: Maryland had deemed them inadequate to provide substantially equal education; Missouri had declared them sufficient to meet the separate but equal standard of *Plessy*. Until now the adequacy of the scholarships had never

41. *Missouri ex rel. Gaines v. Canada*, 113 S.W. 2d 783 (1938). S. W. Canada, the defendant, was the registrar of the University of Missouri School of Law.
42. Ibid., at 791.

been ruled upon by the Supreme Court. Arguments were heard on November 9, 1938, with Houston representing Gaines. He attacked both parts of Missouri's case. In the first place, a law school at Lincoln was purely a theoretical possibility for some time in the future. The state had not allocated funds for the purpose, and all of Lincoln's budget was needed to perform its undergraduate mission. It was, moreover, improbable that a law school quickly flung together at Lincoln could ever provide a legal education equal to the one that whites were getting at the well-established school of law at Columbia.

Houston's assault on the scholarship arrangement was devastating. In the first place, the scholarships provided only for the difference in tuition, not for the many other expenses someone studying out-of-state would incur (the argument made in *Murray* two years before). But Houston also insisted that Lloyd Gaines wanted to practice law in Missouri, his home state, and that the state university's law school was the appropriate place for him to study Missouri law and professional practice. Learning the intricacies of Missouri law, observing the local courts, making the acquaintance of other Missouri practitioners, and the acquisition of credibility and prestige among Missourians, his future clients, all were best accomplished not in Illinois or Nebraska, but in Missouri.[43]

On December 12, a month after hearing the arguments, the Supreme Court found on behalf of Gaines. The vote was 6–2, with the High Court's two most conservative justices dissenting.[44] The opinion was read by Chief Justice Charles Evans Hughes.[45] After praising Missouri's efforts to establish a measure of equality between

43. Missouri ex rel. *Gaines* v. *Canada*, "Petition of Certiorari," to the U.S. Supreme Court, at 20.

44. James Clark McReynolds, a staunch conservative noted for his bigotry and cranky personality, contended that educational policy was a state function and that state regulations should prevail. He was joined by Pierce Butler, another anti–New Deal opponent of what he considered federal overreach. The Court was still reeling from Franklin Roosevelt's attempt to "pack" it the year before. Two of the conservative "four horsemen" had quit and were replaced by more liberal justices. There was one absence on the Court at the time of the *Gaines* decision.

45. *Missouri ex rel. Gaines* v. *Canada*, 305 U.S. 337 (1938).

Lincoln and the University of Missouri at the undergraduate level, Hughes wrote: "But commendable as is that action, the fact remains that instruction in law for negroes is not now afforded by the State, either at Lincoln University or elsewhere within the State, and that the State excludes negroes from the advantages of the law school it has established at the University of Missouri. It is manifest that this discrimination . . . would constitute a denial of equal protection."[46] With respect to the state's claim that a law school for blacks would be built once the Lincoln curators were convinced that there was enough demand on the part of black aspirants, the chief justice asserted that "we cannot regard the discrimination as excused by what is called its temporary character."[47] Finally, Hughes, in a single sentence, brushed aside the state's assertion that the scholarships provided substantial equality to black students: "The basic consideration is not as to what sort of opportunities other States provide, or whether they are as good as those in Missouri, but as to what opportunities Missouri itself furnishes to white students and denies to negroes solely upon the ground of color."[48]

The Supreme Court's decision, reversing the Missouri Supreme Court and ordering that court to rehear the case, was a tremendous victory for the NAACP and for the cause of breaking down segregation in southern higher education. It would be cited in every future case touching upon the issue. *Gaines* seemed to leave only three alternatives for white southerners who hoped to maintain segregated higher education. They could, at enormous cost, construct for black students substantially equal, but segregated programs in graduate and professional education; they could discontinue their programs for whites; or they could admit black students to formerly all-white programs and institutions.

Unfortunately, however, the case of Lloyd Gaines had a bizarre aftermath, one that proved highly embarrassing to the NAACP. While waiting for the High Court's decision, Gaines was able to

46. 305 U.S. at 345. The chief justice cited and quoted at length the nonbinding *Murray* decision by the Maryland Court of Appeals.
47. Ibid., at 352.
48. Ibid., at 349.

earn a master's degree in economics from the University of Michigan in 1937, and he took a job with the New Deal's WPA in Michigan. On December 31, 1938, three weeks after the Court ruled in his favor, Gaines returned to Missouri. He told friends and newspaper reporters that he would wait in St. Louis until September and then begin his legal studies at the University of Missouri. He repeated this intention in a speech to the St. Louis NAACP branch in January. Meanwhile, however, the state of Missouri, desperate to maintain segregation, hastily manufactured a "law school" for blacks at an abandoned beauty school in St. Louis, hoping that it would satisfy the *Plessy* requirement of "equality." The NAACP, of course, set out to challenge in court the idea that this so-called Lincoln University School of Law was remotely equal to the operation in Columbia. While waiting for the challenge, Gaines worked in a gas station and gave speeches for the NAACP. After a speech in Kansas City, Gaines took a train to Chicago and sought refuge in the house of his Lincoln University fraternity, Alpha Phi Alpha. He had been talking more and more ambivalently about starting law school back in Missouri, and on March 19, 1939, he told someone at the fraternity house that he was going out in the rain to buy postage stamps. He never returned and was never seen again. Theories abounded. Many were convinced that he was abducted and murdered to prevent the desegregation of the Missouri law school. Others believed that he had simply gotten tired of the stress and celebrity and decided to disappear. Some suggested suicide; others thought that he might have been "bought off" to give up his effort. There were reports of his living quietly in Mexico.[49]

For the NAACP, Gaines's disappearance in the midst of its challenge to the Lincoln University law school was catastrophic. The organization needed Gaines as the only person being forced into the makeshift school, the only one with enough judicial "standing" to bring the case. The NAACP organized a frantic search for its

49. For retrospective reviews of the evidence, see Bluford, "The Lloyd Gaines Story"; Edward T. Clayton, "The Strange Disappearance of Lloyd Gaines," *Ebony* 6 (May 1951): 26–34; and David Stout, "Quiet Hero of Civil Rights History: A Supreme Triumph, Then into the Shadows," *New York Times*, July 11, 2009, A19.

missing client, asking local branches to keep an eye out for him, issuing press releases and advertisements.[50] When all efforts failed, Houston reluctantly dropped the case. "Since we cannot find Gaines we cannot go on," he wrote.[51] The Lincoln University School of Law continued until 1955, when it was shut down.

For ten years after *Gaines*, no major school desegregation case reached the Supreme Court.[52] The NAACP, suffering, as usual, from limited staff and resources, and absorbed by urgent matters arising out of World War II, brought litigation on a variety of other pressing concerns—the equalization of teacher's pay, restrictive housing covenants, voting rights, anti-lynching legislation, restrictions against blacks on juries—but the desegregation of higher education had to wait. Within weeks after the war's end, however, the battle was resumed. And it was resumed in Oklahoma.

As head of the Oklahoma NAACP and a member of the national board, Roscoe Dunjee was well acquainted with the big names in the New York office. He was "Roscoe" to them and they were "Walter" and "Roy" and "Thurgood" to him. In March 1940, Dunjee was eager to get a black student into the University of Oklahoma. He wrote Walter White, the executive secretary of the NAACP, informing him that the executive committee of the Oklahoma branch, at its meeting in Ardmore, "decided to attempt enrollment of a student, or students, at the University of Oklahoma this summer." They had located a promising young Oklahoma City man named D. B. Vance and were going to try to have him admitted to graduate work in chemistry. Dunjee asked White for help: "I am sure in the Maryland, Missouri and other attempts you learned something

50. TM to Bill Hanks, February 22, 1940, NAACPPM, Reel 13, Frames 329–30.
51. Cited in Tushnet, *NAACP's Legal Strategy*, 74.
52. Mention should perhaps be made of the effort of Gaines's friend, Lucile Bluford, who, with NAACP help, tried to enter the University of Missouri's School of Journalism. After her protracted attempts, the Missouri Supreme Court, in 1941, ordered her admission (*Bluford* v. *Canada*, 153 S.W. 2d 12 [Mo. 1941]). In response, the university temporarily shut down the Journalism School, blaming its action on the wartime shortage of staff and students. Bluford never attended.

regarding what has to be done which will be valuable. Let us have that information at once."[53] It is unclear what befell this prewar attempt on the part of Dunjee, but it appears to have quietly disappeared without leaving much of a trace. There would be a different outcome once the war had ended.

The trouble started on Saturday, November 3, 1945, when the Oklahoma NAACP held its annual meeting in McAlester.[54] The omnipresent Thurgood Marshall flew in from New York to attend the gathering, and upon leaving the meeting he told reporters that the NAACP would attempt to break down the color barrier in Oklahoma higher education. "This is the easiest case to me that ever entered the courts of Oklahoma," he told the cheering delegates. "I could win this type of case even down in Mississippi."[55] The story was sensational news in Oklahoma. The next day, an excited Dunjee wrote to Marshall that the *Daily Oklahoman* "called me five times last night" before writing its story.[56]

For the legal test, the organization quickly settled upon a bright and attractive twenty-two-year-old black woman named Ada Lois Sipuel Fisher.[57] Like Donald Murray in Maryland, she was a perfect choice: composed and courageous, quietly determined and patient in the face of numerous frustrating delays. Born in Chickasha, Oklahoma, she had graduated from Langston with honors in May 1945, and she wanted to become a lawyer. Oklahoma (like Maryland and

---

53. RD to Walter White, March 22, 1940, NAACPPM, Reel 13, Frame 333. For the attempt, see ibid., Frames 329–39, especially the general announcement (undated) to the Oklahoma NAACP membership, Frame 337.

54. For some reason, Cross (*BWC*, 30), Fisher (*MBW*, 76, 190), and Tushnet (*NAACP's Legal Strategy*, 120) all state that the NAACP meeting took place in September; only Wattley, *Step toward* Brown, correctly puts the date in November. For proof that the November 3 date is correct, see "State Negroes Plan Education Equality Fight," *DO*, November 4, 1945, 1; "State NAACP Conference Plans Bold Attack upon Education Inequalities in Sooner State," *Black Dispatch*, November 8, 1945, 1; and Levy 2: 344 n. 21. See also n. 59, below.

55. "State NAACP Conference Plans Bold Attack," 1.

56. RD to TM, November 4, 1945, NAACPPM, Reel 13, Frame 341.

57. Fisher's story is definitively told in Wattley, *Step toward* Brown; see also Fisher's autobiography, *A Matter of Black and White*. For the process of her selection by the NAACP, see Wattley, *Step toward* Brown, chap. 3; and *MBW*, 75–81.

Roscoe Dunjee, circa 1946. Courtesy *The Oklahoman.*

Missouri) had no law school for blacks. On Monday, January 14, 1946, nine weeks after the McAlester meeting and a few days before the start of the second semester, she appeared at the office of University of Oklahoma president George Lynn Cross, accompanied by Dunjee and Dr. W. A. J. Bullock, regional director of the NAACP.

The meeting in George Cross's office proved to be critical. It occurred against the background of an Oklahoma officialdom that had done everything it possibly could to protect the system of segregation in schools that had been its unwavering policy since well before statehood. In the mid-1930s, when segregation in southern higher education began to come under serious attack, Oklahoma, as we have seen, was one of those states that resorted to the expedient of out-of-state scholarships. But after the Supreme Court, in *Gaines,* declared these scholarships inadequate as a means of establishing "equality," Oklahoma officials scrambled to find some other way to preserve educational segregation. In 1941, the legislature addressed the problem by relying on harsh fines. The new law provided that any administrator who admitted an African American to a white school, or a white to a black one, was liable for a fine of up to $500, and that every day that the violation continued was to be regarded as a separate crime punishable by a new fine. The law also stipulated that any instructor who taught whites and blacks together was liable for a daily fine of up to $50, and that any student who agreed to receive instruction in a mixed-race classroom could be fined, every day, up to $20.[58] If this were not sufficient fortification, the university's Board of Regents, in a hastily called session in response to the NAACP's McAlester meeting,[59] unanimously directed President Cross "to refuse to admit anyone of Negro blood as a student in the University."[60]

Thus when Ada Lois Fisher and her two companions entered President Cross's office on January 14, 1946, they had no real expectation that Cross would comply with a request to admit her immediately to the School of Law.[61] That was not why they had come. They

58. 70 *Oklahoma Statutes* (1941), sections 452–64. The 1941 law repeated the constitutional definition of "colored" (article 23, section 11) to mean "all persons of African descent who possess any quantum of negro blood" and that "all other persons" (including American Indians) were to be considered "whites."

59. The panicked regents moved their regular meeting of November 14, 1945, to November 7, three days after Marshall's announcement in McAlester. See RM, November 7, 1945, 1932–33. The date of this session is more evidence that the McAlester meeting took place on November 3, not in September (see n. 54, above). It would have been astonishing had the regents waited two months (with three intervening meetings) to address Marshall's challenge.

60. Regent Lloyd Noble tried to soften the harshness of the action by offering a substitute motion that would have referred each case to the state's attorney general. When his motion was rejected by all the other regents, Noble joined in making the original motion unanimous.

61. Both Cross and Fisher left accounts of that meeting, and the two versions are in essential agreement. See *BWC,* 35–39, and *MBW,* 81–85.

had come for the purpose of asking Cross to write a letter clearly stating that it was her race—and her race *alone*—that disqualified her from admission and required her rejection. The meeting in Cross's office was cordial and respectful on both sides. The president and other university officials looked over Fisher's transcripts and quickly saw that, if she had been white, her admission would be perfectly routine. While his visitors sat across the desk from him, Cross called his secretary into the room and dictated the letter in exactly the terms they had hoped for. He was not required to comply with their request. He could have denied admission without giving an explanation. He could have denied it on the grounds that Langston, where Fisher had done her undergraduate work, had not been accredited.[62] But Cross, who had been raised in South Dakota, played college football with black teammates, and privately regarded the state's race policies as insane, was almost as eager as his visitors to give the applicants the court test they wanted. While waiting for the secretary to type the letter, Cross made his sympathies apparent to the three visitors sitting in his office. In a few minutes, the finished letter was brought in, and Cross signed it and handed it and a carbon copy across the desk to his guests.[63] Upon leaving the president's office, Dunjee praised Cross to reporters for dealing "forthrightly with the issue." A group of students and faculty members of the Equal Education Committee, affiliated with the campus YMCA and YWCA, had been waiting in the president's outer office. They took the visitors to a stand-up lunch, since no restaurant in town was available to them.

The next day, Dunjee wrote to Marshall: "Here is your case, and I think it's what one would call a 'natural.'" He told Marshall "confidentially," that he had gotten "a lot of cooperation" from George Cross. "He told me in the presence of Bullock and Miss Sipuel that he was sympathetic and wanted to cooperate with us in having just what we want to get into the federal court. . . . But the many [*sic*] was sincerely cooperative and told me openly that 'I'll put anything

62. Cross also realized that the university had, in the past, admitted a few white students who arrived with credentials from unaccredited colleges.
63. For the full text of the letter, see *BWC*, 37–38.

George Lynn Cross, circa 1946. Courtesy Western History Collections, University of Oklahoma Libraries (OU 71).

in this letter you feel will get you into court.'" Dunjee also cautioned Marshall that if Roy Wilkins, then a young attorney and publicist in the New York office, "uses any of this news story, tell him to not say anything that would compromise Cross with his board."[64] Two days later, Dunjee wrote Walter White, stating "the truth is that [Cross] wishes us to have a case, and exprest [*sic*] the hope that we would win. You of course cannot quote him on this, but that is the reason why he let down the bars and gave us an open and shut case."[65]

64. RD to TM, January 15, 1946, NAACPPM, Reel 13, Frames 342–43.
65. RD to Walter White, January 17, 1946, ibid., Frames 344–45.

Dunjee's confidence in the case, and Marshall's belief that it would be the "easiest" ever tried in Oklahoma, was based on their analysis of the legal issue. The Fourteenth Amendment declares that "No state shall make or enforce any law which shall abridge the privileges or immunities of citizens of the United States; nor shall any state . . . deny to any person within its jurisdiction the equal protection of the laws." What could be more obvious than that the state of Oklahoma was denying Ada Lois Sipuel Fisher, solely because of the color of her skin, the privilege of attending a law school that whites had been attending for decades, and denying her, thereby, the equal protection of the laws? This was not a case where a state law school for blacks might, or might not, be "substantially equal" to the one at the university. As had been the case with Donald Murray in Maryland and Lloyd Gaines in Missouri, there was simply no state law school in Oklahoma for blacks, and the old dodge of "separate but equal" did not apply. And yet, despite the compelling argument they were able to present, the case proved not to be as open and shut as Dunjee and Marshall predicted.

With Cross's "precious letter"[66] in hand, Fisher and her attorneys spent the next two years working their laborious way through Oklahoma's judicial system. On April 6, 1946, Amos T. Hall, serving as the NAACP's local attorney, asked the Cleveland County District Court for a writ of mandamus, ordering the authorities to admit her immediately to the University's School of Law.[67] Judge Ben Williams heard the arguments on July 9, and denied the writ on the grounds that the court could not order university officials to commit an act that violated state laws, namely the segregation laws. Two days later, Judge Williams rejected a motion for a retrial, and Hall, now joined by Thurgood Marshall, appealed to the Oklahoma Supreme Court.

On March 4, 1947, the courtroom was packed with spectators of both races, and the case was deemed so important that each side was given a full hour to present its arguments rather than the usual

66. *MBW,* 87.
67. "Petition for Writ of Mandamus," April 6, 1946, filed with the Cleveland County District Court.

half hour. Hall gave the opening argument on behalf of Fisher, and Marshall gave the closing. For the state of Oklahoma, Assistant Attorney General Fred Hansen repeated the argument that Oklahoma law required the separation of the races and, if the court granted the writ, the officials forced to execute it would be violating the law and subject to criminal prosecution. He was followed by Maurice Merrill, acting dean of the School of Law and a distinguished legal scholar, who argued that Fisher erred by pursuing the wrong remedy. She should not have sued the university in violation of state law; she should, instead, have asked the State Regents to establish a separate law school for her.

Cheryl Wattley has written that "to Ada Lois, Marshall's argument was so eloquent, logical, and morally compelling that she dared to dream that she might actually win her case before the Oklahoma Supreme Court."[68] It was a vain dream. On April 29, the court (seven of whose justices were graduates of the very law school the plaintiff was trying to enter[69]) affirmed the lower court's refusal to grant mandamus.[70] The NAACP lawyers were not particularly surprised by the court's denial. They may even have hoped for it. The way was now cleared for the case to be heard by the Supreme Court of the United States. The eyes and hopes of Oklahoma's black community now rested on this venue. No doubt one of those paying close attention was Professor George McLaurin of Langston University.

Sipuel v. The Board of Regents of the University of Oklahoma et al.[71] was argued before the nation's highest court on January 8, 1948, just one week short of two years since Fisher had first come to Norman asking

68. Wattley, *Step toward* Brown, 108.
69. Ibid., 107.
70. *Sipuel v. Board of Regents of the University of Oklahoma et al.*, 180 P.2d 135 (1947). The court also emphasized Fisher's failure to alert officials that she desired a legal education. This argument was used—erroneously, as Wattley shows (*Step toward* Brown, 109–10)—to distinguish the *Sipuel* case from the *Gaines* decision. It should be mentioned that Ada Lois Sipuel had married Warren Fisher on March 3, 1944, but the case went forward under "Sipuel" apparently because that was the name on her academic transcripts.
71. 332 U.S. 631 (1948).

for her chance to study the law. With the plaintiff sitting in the front row, her case was again presented by Hall and Marshall.[72] The justices listened quietly to Marshall, asking him only three or four polite questions. They were not so courteous to the attorneys from Oklahoma. Both Assistant Attorney General Fred Hansen and Acting Dean Merrill were pelted with hostile interruptions by the justices.[73] The *Washington Post* called it "a severe hazing," and Dunjee's *Black Dispatch,* "a severe grilling."[74] "One by one," reported *Time Magazine,* the justices "leaned forward to ask questions; and usually their questions were phrased to badger the attorneys from the State of Oklahoma."[75] The *Daily Oklahoman* headline summed it up: "High Court Caustic on OU Negro Ban." The story below the headline reported "a running fire of hostile questions."[76] Even the university's hometown newspaper acknowledged that "the Justices of the Supreme Court today ripped the attorneys for the state of Oklahoma."[77]

No doubt the verdict was predictable in view of the hostile remarks the justices directed at the state's attorneys. What was surprising was the astounding speed with which the Court rendered its unanimous decision.[78] Instead of the usual interim of weeks or months between oral argument and decision, the justices, in what the *New York Times* called "startling suddenness," spoke only four days later.[79] Citing their opinion in *Gaines,* they ruled that Fisher

72. Dillard Stokes, a lawyer and writer for the *Washington Post,* pointed out that "[Amos] Hall—himself a negro—rose to the bar of the Supreme Court without the advantage of law school training such as he demanded yesterday for Ada Lois Sipuel." Stokes, "Supreme Court Hears Negro's Schooling Plea," *Washington Post,* January 9, 1948, 1.

73. Wattley, *Step toward* Brown, 121–22; Levy 2: 349.

74. Cited in Wattley, *Step toward* Brown, 124, as *Washington Post,* January 9, 1948, 12; *Black Dispatch,* January 17, 1948, 1.

75. "Ada's Day in Court," *Time Magazine* 51 (January 19, 1948): 62–63.

76. *DO,* January 9, 1948, 1.

77. *NT,* January 8, 1948, 1.

78. The two arch-conservative justices that voted against Lloyd Gaines were no longer on the Court.

79. *New York Times,* January 13, 1948, 1. Some have speculated that the Court's motivation for acting so promptly was to permit Fisher to enroll for the spring semester, which was about to begin.

was "entitled to secure legal education afforded by a state institution," and that Oklahoma "must provide it for her . . . and provide it as soon as it does for applicants of any other group." The High Court's action received wide notice.[80] Dunjee told Marshall that the decision was "thrilling, and I do not know how to express myself I am so delighted over the results. Our entire state is in an uproar."[81] Fisher herself was ecstatic. "I'm going to become a lawyer," she said. "I am going to learn."[82] She prepared at once for her enrollment as the very first African American ever to attend the University of Oklahoma!

Not so fast. A *New York Times* editorial, three days after the Court had spoken, analyzed the ruling with somewhat greater clarity. It praised as "forthright" the justices' order that Oklahoma must accord Fisher a legal education. "So far so good," said the *Times*. "But not far enough. The Court again begged the issue as to whether state segregation laws are constitutional, whether establishment by Oklahoma of a School of Law for Negroes . . . comparable in faculty and facilities to that provided for white students, meets the tests of constitutionality under the Fourteenth Amendment."[83] Fisher and her allies had not reckoned with the fanatical determination of state authorities to keep the races apart. Five days after the High Court's decision, on January 17, the Oklahoma Supreme Court, to which the case was remanded for rehearing, directed the State Regents for Higher Education to provide Fisher a legal education, but ominously added that the regents must conform to Oklahoma's constitution and statutes "requiring segregation of the races in the schools of this state."[84]

The State Regents started working on the problem two days later, and on January 24, they announced the creation of "the Langston University School of Law," and two days after that, on January 26, proclaimed that the school was officially open, solemnly insisting that it

80. For national reaction, see Wattley, *Step toward* Brown," 124–25; and *BWC*, 47–48.
81. RD to TM, January 14, 1948, NAACPPM, Reel 13, Frame 532.
82. *MBW*, 124.
83. *New York Times*, January 15, 1948, 22.
84. *Sipuel* v. *Board of Regents of the University of Oklahoma*, 190 P.2d 437–38 (1948).

was "substantially equal" to the one in Norman.[85] The school was to be located in three rooms on the fourth floor of the state capitol in Oklahoma City. The students would have access to the state library. Three practicing lawyers were hired as "faculty," although each of them continued to work at his own law firm. The "miracle" of creating a law school in a week was denounced across the nation. Cross was informed that in view of this new law school for African Americans, Fisher must not be admitted to the white law school in Norman.[86] For her part, she and the NAACP regarded the new school as bogus, and Fisher said she would have nothing to do with so obvious a hoax.

Instead, on the same day as the State Regents' announcement, the NAACP petitioned the Supreme Court for a writ of mandamus ordering the admission of Fisher to the University of Oklahoma School of Law in Norman.[87] The attorneys argued that the justices could take "judicial notice" of the fact that the law school at Langston, created in a single week, could not conceivably offer Fisher a legal education equal to the one offered to white students in Norman, and that therefore the state's action in setting up the fraudulent school was in violation of the High Court's mandate of January 12. This time, however, on February 16, the Supreme Court found against Fisher.[88] The Court ruled that when it had heard arguments in January, the question of whether the state might satisfy the Fourteenth Amendment by creating a separate law school was not before it, and that it could not conclude that Oklahoma's action violated the justices' mandate.[89]

---

85. Chancellor M. A. Nash to GLC, January 23, 1948, copy in NAACPPM, Reel 13, Frame 547; Nash to Whom It May Concern, January 26, 1948, copy in GLCPP, Box 50, Folder: "Negro Question (#2)."

86. Chancellor M. A. Nash to GLC, January 23, 1948, copy in NAACPPM, Reel 13, Frame 547; Nash to Whom It May Concern, January 26, 1948.

87. TM to Thurman Hurst, January 26, 1948, NAACPPM, Reel 13, Frame 550. Hurst was the chief justice of the Oklahoma Supreme Court.

88. *Fisher v. Hurst*, 333 U.S. 147 (1948).

89. Two justices expressed their reservations about the decision. Frank Murphy thought that a hearing should determine whether the state of Oklahoma's action "constitutes an evasion" of the mandate (at 151). Wiley Rutledge argued that the state could not possibly be affording Fisher an equal legal education by "establishing overnight" a law school (ibid.).

For Fisher and her attorneys, that decision meant another wearisome round of litigation, back at the lower courts, to contest the preposterous notion that the new law school was, in fact, substantially equal to the one at the University of Oklahoma. On March 11, 1948, the NAACP filed a motion to that effect in the Cleveland County District Court. On May 24, after several postponements, Hall and Marshall made their intense and occasionally dramatic argument before Judge Justin Hinshaw. Marshall had painstakingly lined up an all-star parade of experts in the field of legal education. Traveling to Norman, at considerable inconvenience, to testify that the two schools could not possibly be considered equal were nationally known law professors from California, Chicago, Wisconsin, and Columbia. They pointed out that the Langston operation could offer no seminars, no moot court, no law journal, no substantial classes where a credible number of students might exchange ideas. The illustrious deans of the law schools at Harvard and the University of Pennsylvania took the extraordinary step of interrupting their duties and coming to Norman, Oklahoma, to plead with Judge Hinshaw that the two schools could not be reasonably compared. Harvard's dean, Erwin Griswold, for example, told the court that the schools were "not equal, not substantially equal, not so nearly that there is any fair basis for comparison."[90] A particularly telling moment in the proceedings was Thurgood Marshall's murderous mauling of Jerome Hemry, the newly appointed dean of the Langston law school. Fisher remembered that "Marshall tore him to pieces with such fury that it excited a little sympathy even from me." It came to the point where one of Marshall's co-counsels, Howard University's James Nabrit, leaned across the table and whispered, "Turn him loose, Thurgood." Marshall simply turned his back on the poor witness, waved his hand dismissively, and returned to his seat.[91] Afterwards, Charles Bunn, of the University of Wisconsin and one of the expert witnesses, wrote to Marshall that

90. Quoted in *BWC*, 83. For a thorough examination of the trial, see Wattley, *Step toward* Brown," chap. 6. See also *MBW*, 132–38, and Levy 2: 350–54.

91. *MBW*, 136. For a full account of the manhandling of the state's witnesses, see Wattley, *Step toward* Brown, chap. 6.

Ada Lois Sipuel Fisher with Tulsa attorney Amos T. Hall, Thurgood Marshall, and H. W. Williamston of the Oklahoma NAACP, 1948. Courtesy Western History Collections, University of Oklahoma Libraries (Ada Lois Sipuel Fisher 2).

"the case seemed to me as well tried on your side as any I have ever watched. Your cross-examination of Dean Hemry, in particular, was a masterpiece. My bet is that the ultimate result will show the case was won then and there."[92] The testimony went on for four days.[93]

All to no avail. Judge Hinshaw, saying that he would render a decision within two weeks, pondered the testimony for two months before announcing on August 2, with a straight face, that the two law schools were, in fact, substantially equal. "I sat there and looked at him," Fisher remembered. "I cannot say that I was shocked, nor even surprised. I was disgusted."[94] Cross would later

92. Charles Bunn to TM, June 8, 1948, NAACPPM, Reel 13, Frame 746.
93. The state offered a handful of witnesses that praised the qualifications of the three-man Langston faculty, the low student-faculty ratio, the number of volumes in the state law library, the proximity of the capital to the state Supreme Court, the small classes, and the close attention Fisher might expect.
94. *MBW*, 138.

call the decision "incredible," and historian John T. Hubbell wrote that Judge Hinshaw's conclusion "surpasses understanding."[95] For Fisher, of course, the ruling was a frustration and a setback, but she met it with her usual determination, patience, and courage. She and her attorneys quickly decided to appeal—first to the Oklahoma Supreme Court and then, if necessary, back to the Supreme Court of the United States.

There were others, however, who saw in that original Supreme Court decision, back in January 1948, the opportunity they were looking for. Ada Lois Sipuel Fisher was not to be the University of Oklahoma's first African American student. While she was tied up in the state and then the federal judicial system and waiting for further legal relief, other Oklahoma African Americans came forward, stating that they, like Fisher, wanted to do graduate work in fields not available to them at Langston. And in view of the ruling in *Sipuel v. Board of Regents,* they thought they had a good chance of actually being admitted. One of these hopeful candidates was George W. McLaurin.

95. *BWC,* 84; John T. Hubbell, "Desegregation of the University of Oklahoma, 1946–1950," 38.

CHAPTER 3

George McLaurin Brings the Color Barrier (Halfway) Down

Despite his importance in the struggle for civil rights, much about George McLaurin's life and career remains hidden in obscurity and contradiction. The following paragraphs attempt to piece together what can be known about him with a fair degree of confidence.[1] That he was born in Mississippi seems clear according to the consistent record of several United States censuses. It is very possible, therefore, that he was the son of former slaves and almost certain that he was the grandson of slaves. The precise place in Mississippi where he was born is not known.

There is also considerable confusion about the date of his birth and, therefore, about his age at the time of his enrollment at the University of Oklahoma. We may dismiss as an exaggeration the offhand remark that Thurgood Marshall once made to a group of reporters, stating that McLaurin was sixty-eight in 1948 (thus indicating a birth year of 1880 or 1881).[2] The *Social Security Death Index*

---

1. Some of the mysteries in McLaurin's life are mentioned and judiciously considered in Linda W. Reese's unpublished paper "Searching for George W. McLaurin, Forgotten Civil Rights Hero." Her paper can be found in University of Oklahoma Archives, WHC, Vertical File: "McLaurin, George." I am indebted to her detective work for several of the questions she raises and for leads that she suggests.

2. Kluger, *Simple Justice*, 266. That date for McLaurin's age is accepted in "'Reserved for Colored': Memories of Legalized Bigotry at the University of Oklahoma (1948)," *Journal of Blacks in Higher Education* 31 (Spring 2001): 75; and in "The Anita Hill Chair: A New Chapter in the Long Racial History of the University of Oklahoma College of Law," ibid., 11 (Spring 1996): 20. Marshall may have had an interest in exaggerating McLaurin's age in order to render absurd the racist

gives his birth date as September 16, 1887, and that date will be used in this account to indicate his age at various stages. There are solid reasons for trusting its accuracy, and several others have accepted it.[3] If it *is* correct, then McLaurin was sixty-one at the time he enrolled and took his first classes in Norman. When he registered for the draft in World War I, McLaurin gave 1889 as the year of his birth, and at various times thereafter he reported that his birth had occurred later—possibly in an attempt to present himself as being younger than he actually was. The most common date he would later give is September 16, 1894, and many writers mistakenly take that year to be the actual year of his birth.[4] That date is the one inscribed on his marker in the Oklahoma City cemetery where he is buried.[5] However, McLaurin regularly claimed a number of other birth dates from the early 1890s.

In September 1906, he had just turned nineteen and was living in Jackson, Mississippi. He enrolled for the academic year 1906–1907 at Jackson College (later Jackson State University), signing up for pre–high school remedial work in a "Ministers' Special Course."

---

claim that black men wanted to enter white colleges only so that they could hunt for white women.

3. *Social Security Death Index, 1935–2014*, genealogybank.com/doc/ssdi/news (accessed February 1, 2018, site discontinued). Among those who report McLaurin's birth date as being 1887 are Linda W. Reese, "McLaurin, George W.," in *African American National Biography*, edited by Henry Louis Gates, Jr., and Evelyn Brooks Higginbotham (New York: Oxford University Press, 2008), 5:531–33; Reese, "McLaurin, George W. (1887–1968)," *The Black Past Remembered and Reclaimed*, www.blackpast.org (accessed February 13, 2018); "University of Oklahoma's First Negro Student Dies," *Sacramento Bee*, September 7, 1968, 3; and Gene Curtis, "First Black Student at OU Still Faced Obstacles," *Tulsa World*, February 18, 2007. NAACP attorney Jack Greenberg writes that McLaurin was "then in his sixties" when the litigation unfolded; Greenberg, *Crusaders in the Courts: How a Dedicated Band of Lawyers Fought for the Civil Rights Revolution* (New York: Basic Books, 1994), 67.

4. Among the multitude of those who report that McLaurin was born in 1894 are George Cross in *BWC*, 85; Ada Lois Fisher in *MBW*, 143; the *DO* and the *Black Dispatch* (consistently); the *Omaha World Herald* (June 25, 1950, 50); and the *New York Times* (October 16, 1948, 4).

5. McLaurin is buried in the Trice Hill Cemetery, 5101 Coltrane Road, Oklahoma City, Memorial ID: 67995407.

The next year, 1907–1908, he prepared himself for entering Jackson College's high school by enrolling for eighth-grade equivalency work, and from 1909 to 1912, McLaurin, now in his early twenties, completed his high school education at Jackson. The U.S. Census for 1910 (in which his name is misspelled as George W. "McLausin") lists him as being in the grocery business, but it is likely that he was spending most of his time as a student.[6] He registered as a college freshman at Jackson for the 1912–13 academic year. Despite later claiming that he had earned a bachelor's degree at Jackson College, it seems that he did not.[7] After the 1912–13 year, he disappears from Jackson's records.[8]

As a matter of fact, we cannot even be sure that he actually attended that first collegiate year at Jackson in 1912–13, because on June 15, 1912, George McLaurin married Penninah S. Harlon in the little town of Vian in Sequoyah County, Oklahoma, and he indicated on the marriage license that his place of residence was Vian, not Jackson, Mississippi.[9] How and when George and Penninah first met is not known, but she was also born in Mississippi, in the town of Vaughan, about forty miles north of Jackson. She moved to Spiro, Oklahoma, in 1910, and taught school in both Spiro and Muskogee.[10] According to the marriage license, George was twenty-four and Penninah twenty-one. Thus as late as 1912, he was still giving his birth year as 1887.[11] Unfortunately, like her husband, Penninah was not consistent in reporting her age. If she was, in fact, twenty-one in 1912, she was born in 1891 or 1892; before

6. In 1910, McLaurin was still correctly giving 1887 as his birth year.

7. The claim is made in "Negro to Make Another Try," *El Reno* (Oklahoma) *Daily Tribune*, September 10, 1948, 1. Either the El Reno reporter misunderstood McLaurin, or McLaurin dissembled in saying that he had earned his B.A. at Jackson.

8. I am grateful to Darlita Ballard, the University Archivist at Jackson State University, for providing this information.

9. *Oklahoma: County Marriage Records, 1890–1995 (Sequoyah County, 1909–1913)*, 1291. Both her first and last names are spelled in different ways in various sources, but "Penninah S. Harlon" is the name given on the marriage license.

10. See the obituary articles "Mrs. McLaurin Ends Life Long Educational Fight in State," *Black Dispatch*, August 26, 1966, 1; and in *New York Times*, August 23, 1966, 39.

11. *Oklahoma: County Marriages Records*, 1291.

long, however, she was claiming to be four years younger and born in 1895.[12]

After their marriage, the McLaurins lived a wandering life, teaching in black schools in small Oklahoma towns. George might have begun his teaching career around 1915, because several accounts mention his retiring in 1948, after thirty-three years of teaching.[13] In 1915, the couple may still have been living in Vian—the birthplace of their first child, a son. In 1917, a daughter was born in Spiro. In 1920, when the McLaurins' second son was born, George was teaching at the new Banneker School in the black town of Brooksville, Oklahoma, fifteen miles south of the city of Shawnee. There is evidence that at some point McLaurin was the principal of the black high school in Holdenville, Oklahoma.[14] He may have taken some courses at Kansas State Teachers College in Emporia,[15] and beginning in 1922, he spent several summers at the University of Kansas. There he gave his birth date as 1893, and listed his residence (dubiously) as Parsons, Kansas. He took undergraduate courses in Lawrence during the summers of 1922, 1924, 1926, and 1929. In 1928, he also completed the requirements for a bachelor's degree at the Oklahoma Colored Agricultural and Normal University (the former name for Langston University).[16] Then, in the 1930s and early 1940s, he enrolled for graduate work at the University of Kansas and received his master's degree in Educational Administration and Supervision in 1943. His thesis was entitled "Data about Colored Schools in Oklahoma, 1924–1940."[17]

12. Although the *New York Times* obituary gives her age as seventy-four (i.e., born in 1892), her grave marker gives her birth date as July 7, 1895.

13. It is sometimes mistakenly claimed that he taught for thirty-three years *at Langston*. The thirty-three years represent his whole professional career as a teacher, however, with most of them spent teaching at lower levels.

14. "Holdenville Fine Given McLaurin," *DO*, June 27, 1950, 33.

15. See J. E. Fellows to MQW, undated, GLCPP, Box 50, Folder: "Negro Question (#2)."

16. Langston's *Bulletin* for July 1932 (7) lists McLaurin as an instructor in English grammar and indicates a bachelor's degree from "C. A. & N. University, 1928."

17. I am indebted to Rebecca Schute, University Archivist at the University of Kansas, for this information.

Exactly when the family moved to Langston, or when he began teaching at the college there, is not known, but the census of 1930 lists the McLaurins as residents of the town, and the Langston college yearbook for 1932 names McLaurin as an Instructor of English. Ada Lois Sipuel was a student at Langston in the early 1940s, and she mentions in her autobiography that McLaurin was a professor there during that time.[18] She also records a rather unflattering memory of Penninah: "One of the few local businesses [in Langston] was a bookstore run by Mrs. George W. McLaurin. The wife of a Langston professor, Peninah [sic] McLaurin sold used textbooks out of her front parlor at very competitive prices. Unsuspecting students who purchased her books often learned that their low costs had a reason: the school had discontinued using them. That did not mean that Mrs. McLaurin discontinued selling them, only that she discontinued refunding the purchase price once the book left her parlor."[19]

There can be little doubt about how strongly McLaurin and his wife, both of them teachers, felt about the importance of education. It was Penninah who felt this need for schooling most keenly and who exemplified it most thoroughly in her own life. Back in 1923, when she was in her early thirties, she herself had attempted to break the color barrier at the University of Oklahoma by applying for admission; naturally, her application was promptly and unceremoniously rejected.[20] According to one account, she had earned degrees in English and economics, and by 1950, had more than three hundred hours of college credit, and, as we will see, she wasn't finished yet.[21] McLaurin family members would later claim that Penninah was "the guiding force" behind her husband's climbing those stairs in Evans Hall a quarter century later.[22] Between the parents and their three children, the McLaurins would have earned, by

18. *MBW*, 70.

19. Ibid.

20. *New York Times*, August 23, 1966, 39; *DO*, August 21, 1966, 10. Some claim that her unsuccessful application for admission was made in 1921, not 1923.

21. *Omaha World-Herald*, June 25, 1950, 50.

22. *DO*, August 21, 1966, 10; "Mrs. McLaurin Ends Life Long Fight," 1.

1948, twenty-one college degrees or certificates—*Ebony,* the popular magazine for African Americans, may have been right when it labeled the McLaurins "the most educated family in Oklahoma."[23]

Given the limited educational, professional, and economic opportunities for African Americans during the first half of the twentieth century, the achievements of the three McLaurin children were quite remarkable. The star of the family was their youngest child, Dunbar Simms McLaurin. Graduating from high school at twelve, he earned a bachelor's degree at Southwestern College, in Winfield, Kansas, at seventeen and a master's degree in economics from the University of Kansas a year later. In 1941, at the astounding age of twenty-one, he received a PhD in economics from the University of Illinois. He served in the Philippines during World War II, rising in the segregated army to the rank of first lieutenant. While there, he saw that a lot of money could be made by buying up U.S. war surplus materials, especially vehicles, and selling them in Manila. He secured a $30,000 loan, stayed in the Islands after his discharge, and started the McLaurin Far East Trade Association. By the time he was twenty-seven, Dunbar had earned more than a million dollars, and *Ebony* was calling him a "business wizard." He moved to New York City, got a law degree from Brooklyn College, and soon became a prominent businessman and lawyer in the black community. Together with baseball great Jackie Robinson, and others, he established the first black-controlled bank in the city. He engaged himself in numerous projects to help blacks and Puerto Ricans in New York through his "Ghetto Economic Development and Industrialization Plan." He also served as a consultant on economic development projects in Nigeria and Ghana, and spent much time in Africa. Then the singular fairy tale of his extraordinary life came to a tragic end. He committed suicide in July 1973 at the age of fifty-three. The reason given was despondency over business affairs. When he died, he was undoubtedly better known than his father.[24]

23. *DO,* October 14, 1948, 2; "GI Business Wizard," *Ebony* 4 (December 1948): 43. See also *DO,* December 25, 1948, 24.

24. Copies of various vitae for Dunbar McLaurin can be found in the McLaurin Family Collection, at the Schomburg Center for Research in Black Culture, in the Harlem Branch of the New York Public Library. This two-folder collection is

Back when Dunbar was serving in the Pacific, his older brother, Joffre, was serving in Europe, and was promoted to the rank of major by the end of the war. Joffre then joined his brother in Manila, where the two ran the export-import business and also started a movie company featuring black actors. Back in the United States, Joffre earned a master's degree from the University of Kansas and did additional graduate work at Illinois and Colorado. He then settled in California and became a teacher.[25]

The McLaurins' daughter, Phyllis, was also a talented student. Following the example of her younger brother, she graduated from high school at twelve, and earned a bachelor's degree from Southwestern College at sixteen; a year later, she received her master's degree from Howard University. After a brief marriage, she moved to Los Angeles where her brother Joffre lived. She taught in the Los Angeles public schools for a decade and worked in the Los Angeles antipoverty program. Like her brother Dunbar, she died at the young age of fifty-three, after a long illness.[26] All three children outlived their parents.

No doubt George and Penninah looked on the success of their children with satisfaction and pride. By 1942, the couple had moved to a modest home in the black neighborhood of Oklahoma City, about forty miles from Langston,[27] and, probably in 1948, George retired from Langston.[28] He and his wife had attained a certain independence. Their three children were successful and gone, and

---

mainly a repository of newspaper clippings. On Dunbar McLaurin, see his obituary, *New York Times*, July 11, 1973, 44; "GI Business Wizard"; Joel Fishman, "This Banker Had a Heart," *Daily Argus* (Mt. Vernon, N.Y.), July 14, 1973; "Banker Dunbar S. McLaurin Suicide Victim in N.Y. Home," *Jet*, July 26, 1973; and affectionate tributes, poems, and photographs at his death in *The Sphinx* 59 (October 1973): 52–61. *The Sphinx* is the official journal of the Alpha Phi Alpha Fraternity.

25. *DO*, May 5, 1971, 5; "Oklahoma Honors McLaurin Family," *The Sphinx* 57 (December 1971): 37.

26. Ibid.

27. The move to Oklahoma City in 1942 is reported in the *Black Dispatch*, August 26, 1966, 1. Yet, as we have seen, Fisher, who graduated from Langston in 1945, reports that Mrs. McLaurin sold books out of her home in Langston. Did the McLaurins maintain two homes? I have not found a way to resolve this contradiction.

28. The *DO* insists that McLaurin merely took a leave of absence for the 1948–49 school year, but that he was not retired. See, for example, August 6, 1948, 1.

one of them, Dunbar, was quite wealthy. Over the years, George and Penninah had invested their spare cash in real estate, and they were comfortable in their retirement.[29]

The McLaurins must have known Ada Lois Sipuel when she was a student at Langston. It is unclear whether or not she actually took a class from George, but it is hard to believe that the professor was not aware of her. It was a small school and she was an excellent student and an energetic presence on the campus. Ada Lois was in the school choir, she acted in plays, and joined the debate club; she was a member of the "Women's Council," and a regular participant on panels and roundtables; she was an associate editor of the school newspaper.[30] Her comments about Penninah seem to suggest that she might have been an unhappy customer of Mrs. McLaurin's book-selling business. When George McLaurin died in 1968, Langston held a memorial service in his honor and it was Ada Lois who delivered the eulogy.[31]

Like so many others in Oklahoma's black community, McLaurin and his wife were probably paying attention to Fisher's frustrated attempt over the two years, since January 1946, to gain admission to the University of Oklahoma's law school. And George and his wife—who surely remembered Penninah's own rejection at the university a quarter century before—were no doubt heartened by the Supreme Court's ruling of January 12, 1948. In that ruling, it will be remembered, the High Court unanimously decreed that if any qualified black student wished to study a field that was not available at Langston, the state was obligated to provide instruction in that field or stop providing it to whites. Fisher, of course, had naively believed that the ruling would mean her speedy entry into the white law school in Norman, but she had underestimated the desperate determination of state authorities to maintain segregation and could hardly have foreseen their miraculous production of a bogus

29. *World Herald* (Omaha), June 25, 1950, 50.
30. Wattley, *Step toward* Brown, 75.
31. *Langston University Gazette*, September 1968, 1.

law school for African Americans. She and her lawyers were still enmeshed in lower court legal proceedings aimed at showing that the two schools were not actually equal. But it was that original Supreme Court ruling on January 12 that seemed to open the doors of the University of Oklahoma to the state's black citizens. Ambitious, education-hungry blacks wasted no time.

At about 2:00 P.M. on the afternoon of January 28, 1948, just two weeks after the Supreme Court had spoken and only two days after the State Regents had announced the creation of their black law school at the capitol, a group of six black men and women appeared at the office of University of Oklahoma president George Lynn Cross. It was the final day, almost the final hour, to register for the spring semester, and each of the six expressed a desire to enroll for graduate work in subjects that were being taught to white students in Norman, but which were not available to them at Langston. Two of them hoped to take graduate courses in social work, three others wanted to study business education, zoology, and architectural engineering. The sixth was George Washington McLaurin, who said that he hoped to earn a doctor's degree in educational administration. Each of the six was a citizen of Oklahoma, and each had earned at least a bachelor's degree.[32] Although the group was accompanied by an officer of the Oklahoma City chapter of the NAACP, both that official and the six insisted that the organization had nothing whatever to do with their applications. They were inspired and encouraged, they said, by the Supreme Court's January 12 ruling. In their view, the *Sipuel* decision covered their own situations precisely.

There is, however, some reason to doubt that the NAACP was not involved. For one thing, it was obvious that someone had carefully coordinated and orchestrated their appearance. The six arrived in

32. Ray Parr, "Six More Negroes Knock on OU's Door to Test Segregation," *DO*, January 29, 1948, 1; *NT*, January 28, 1948, 1; *BWC*, 65–67. The six candidates and the fields to which they applied were Mozell A. Dillon (Architectural Engineering), Helen M. Holmes (Commercial Education), Ivor Tatum (Social Work), Mauderie Hancock Wilson (Social Work), James Bond (Zoology), and George W. McLaurin (Education).

Six African American students, encouraged by the ruling in *Sipuel,* attempt to apply for admission to the University of Oklahoma, January 28, 1948. McLaurin is on the far right. Courtesy Western History Collections, University of Oklahoma Libraries (OU 2586).

Norman together accompanied by a reporter from the *Black Dispatch,* they posed for a group photograph taken on the steps of Evans Hall, and they had, the day before, alerted both Cross and other newspapers of their intentions.[33] Shrewdly choosing to make their appearance at the last possible moment of the three-day registration period is another indication of the sort of sophisticated strategic thinking that one associates with the astute lawyers of the NAACP. It would be highly unlikely that the politicians at the state capital or the State Regents, who had so quickly manufactured a black law school out of thin air, could, before the start of the spring

33. When the *Black Dispatch* reporter, Malcolm Whitby, entered Cross's office with the six applicants, the other reporters waiting in the outer reception area objected, and Whitby, at the president's request, "graciously agreed" to wait with the others while Cross conferred with the six.

semester a few days later, suddenly throw together at Langston "substantially equal" course work at the graduate level in all of the fields being requested by the six applicants. On March 5, moreover, Dunjee wrote Marshall urging legal action on behalf of "the other six persons *whom we offered for enrolment.*"[34] If the NAACP was not involved at the initial appearance of the six, though, the organization got involved quickly enough. Dunjee reported to Marshall that "I secured letters from all of the six students requesting enrolment asking the NAACP to represent them, and these letters have been in the hand of Attorney [Amos] Hall for the past two weeks."[35]

The meeting in Cross's office with the six was reminiscent of the meeting with Ada Lois Fisher two years earlier. Cross, who personally agreed with the applicants that the *Sipuel* ruling also covered their cases, greeted the visitors cordially and listened politely as each of them explained his or her academic ambitions. He understood that, given their undergraduate degrees, they were fully qualified for admission except for the color of their skins. But Cross was also mindful of state law and particularly of the enormous daily fines he, the faculty, and the students were liable to incur if he were to admit the six to the university. He told them that he would need to confer with the university's regents and, probably, with the State Regents for Higher Education and the state attorney general before arriving at a decision. He promised them that he would give them an answer very quickly and that, in their cases, he would waive the deadline for registration. As soon as they left his office, Cross telephoned the chair of the Board of Regents, Lloyd Noble (Ardmore), informing him of the new development. Noble said that he would alert the State Regents himself, and he instructed Cross to call an emergency meeting of the board for 10:00 A.M. the very next morning. When he had finished talking to Noble, Cross called the chancellor for higher education and asked him to certify to the fact that the programs requested by the students were, in fact, not available to them at Langston.[36]

34. RD to TM, March 5, 1948, NAACPPM, Reel 13, Frame 610. Italics added.
35. Ibid.
36. *BWC*, 67.

It is an indication of how seriously the matter was considered that, with only eighteen hours' notice, all seven of the university's regents appeared in Cross's office next morning.[37] The president began the meeting by reviewing the desires and credentials of each of the six applicants and certifying that each was a citizen of Oklahoma. He then "asked for directions as to what action he should take." As it happened, the board, at another special meeting eight days earlier (a meeting devoted largely to what to do about the *Sipuel* ruling and its hasty aftermath[38]), had directed Cross to ask Oklahoma attorney general Mac Q. Williamson "for advice and procedure to be followed upon any application by a person of African descent for admission to any department of the University."[39] Cross wrote to Williamson the day after that earlier meeting. In view of the emergency now created by the sudden arrival of the six new applicants, the attorney general and his staff worked through the night writing a response. It was delivered to the regents before their 10:00 A.M. meeting and immediately incorporated into the official record; it provided the basis for the regents' discussion.

Williamson's opinion was lengthy and technical. He began by summarizing the judicial history of the *Sipuel* case, adding that subsequent to Cross's request for an opinion, he had learned from the president orally of the appearance of the six new applicants. Williamson then reviewed the state's constitutional and statutory provisions that articulated "the long established policy of the State . . . prescribing segregation of the white and negro races, and providing penalties for violations thereof." The thrust of his opinion, however, was that the High Court's decision in *Sipuel* did *not* apply to the six newcomers. Why? Fisher had made known for two full years her desire to attend law school, and when the legislature and the State Regents

37. RM, January 29, 1948, 2589–96.

38. Ibid., January 21, 1948, 2585–88. Specifically, the regents were asked whether or not to accede to the request that University of Oklahoma law professors be allowed to teach at the newly created Langston law school. The regents declined to comply with the request, citing the already heavy teaching loads of the Norman professors.

39. Ibid., 2588.

did nothing to accommodate her, the Supreme Court stepped in. This new matter was entirely different, Williamson asserted (but not without allowing himself a gratuitous racist remark): "But here we have six people, evidently far above the average intelligence of their race, who could have made their educational wishes known in the spirit of reasonable advance notice, but who chose to wait until the closing hours of the last day of the regular 3-day registration period." The Supreme Court granted Fisher a right "long sought for." That was "a situation vastly different from 'eleventh hour' applications, without any previous notice." Because *Sipuel* was so different from the present case, Williamson concluded, "the Board of Regents . . . are and would be justified in declining the admission, at this time, of the six applicants." Williamson advised the university Board of Regents, however, to call the attention of the State Regents to these applications "for their consideration and action."[40]

The university's Board of Regents discussed Attorney General Williamson's opinion for at least six hours, and they found it vague and wanting. They desired a straight answer about whether or not to admit the six applicants. Regent Don Emery of Bartlesville (all along the regent most open to admitting black students to the university) offered a new motion:

> that the President of the University be authorized and instructed to request from the Attorney General . . . a supplemental opinion upon the following question: "Under the constitution of the United States and the constitution and laws of the State of Oklahoma, may the Board of Regents . . . lawfully admit, at this time . . . a Negro applicant qualified to receive the education for which he (or she) is applying if there is no institution for Negroes supported and maintained by the taxpayers of the State of Oklahoma that affords the education for which application is made?[41]

40. MQW to GLC, January 28, 1948, GLCPP, Box 34, Folder: "Negroes (#1)." The text of the letter may also be found in RM, January 29, 1948, 2589–95.

41. RM, January 29, 1948, 2595–96.

Next day, the headline in the *Daily Oklahoman* read: "Negro Question Is Tossed Back to Williamson; The University Regents Demand Attorney Say 'Yes' or 'No' Plainly."[42]

On Saturday, January 31, Mac Williamson again huddled with his staff for most of the day, and that evening he issued his opinion: under Oklahoma law, the six applicants must not be admitted to the University at this time.[43] Cross waited a day until he received the attorney general's opinion in writing. Then, on Monday, February 2, he directed Dean of Admissions J. E. Fellows to notify the six that their applications had not been approved.[44]

A week later, Governor Roy Turner summoned a group of the state's most influential legislators to discuss the implications of both the *Sipuel* decision and this more recent enrollment attempt by the six.[45] After "a night of debate," the group announced in a unanimous resolution that "we favor the maintenance of our separate school laws in both our common schools and our institutions of higher learning." Predicting where the attack on segregation was heading, the resolution also asked the State Regents for Higher Education to "take such steps as necessary to institute and maintain separate schools of higher learning for Negroes with functions and facilities substantially equal to those afforded white students." Six days later, the State Regents received the resolution and promptly established a committee to study just how this dual system of segregated higher education might be accomplished. The committee, to be chaired by the chancellor of higher education, M. A. Nash, consisted of three deans from the University of Oklahoma and three deans from Oklahoma A&M College in Stillwater.[46]

The deans did not dawdle. They announced their findings on March 22, and their conclusions must have stunned even the most

42. *DO,* January 30, 1948, 1.

43. Ibid., February 1, 1948, 1; *NT,* February 2, 1948, 1.

44. GLC to J. E. Fellows, February 2, 1948, GLCPP, Box 34, Folder: "Negroes (#1)." This was just six days after Cross told Fellows to tell Fisher that, in view of the Langston law school's creation, *her* application was denied.

45. *DO,* February 6, 1948, 1–2. The article gives the names of the key lawmakers in attendance.

46. Ibid., February 12, 1948, 2. The deans were from the two graduate colleges, the two colleges of Arts and Sciences, and the two colleges of Education.

vehement advocates of separate education.[47] The obstacles to providing separate and equal educational opportunities for black students at Langston were simply overwhelming. The deans pointed
out that there were, at present, more than fifty departments at
the university and the A&M that were providing graduate and
undergraduate work that was not available at Langston. Suppose
an enterprising young black student wished to become a nuclear
physicist or a dentist or an architect or a scholar of ancient Greek
or a journalist or an engineer. To create these programs at Langston would cost the state between 10 and 12 million dollars just for
buildings and other physical facilities—plus a half million dollars
per year for maintenance. Erecting these facilities would take at
least four years, and would inevitably and disastrously draw needed
dollars away from the other (white) institutions of higher education. And what about finding black teachers? In 1947, the deans
said, the United States produced a total of eight African American
PhDs. There were at least a hundred American colleges and universities that employed African American professors. What were the
chances of little, underfunded Langston attracting an entire faculty that could be considered even remotely equal to the faculties
teaching in Norman or Stillwater? And then there was the matter of
students. The deans' committee estimated that perhaps twenty-five
or thirty blacks would enroll in graduate work in any given year.[48]
Many departments and many buildings, created at great expense,
would be virtually without a single student much of the time.[49]

47. For the substance of the deans' report, see Otis Sullivant, "Legal Change
to Let Negroes in OU, A&M Proposed by Deans," *DO*, March 23, 1948, 1. See also
the helpful accounts in Hubbell, "Desegregation of the University of Oklahoma,"
41–42; and *BWC*, 75–77.

48. Their estimate was based on calculating the percentage of whites among
Oklahoma's population who were doing graduate work and then using that percentage to predict the number of blacks in the population who might apply.

49. The deans added as an aside a criticism of the utter inadequacy of Oklahoma's out-of-state scholarship program. Not only did the scholarships fail to satisfy
the Supreme Court's dictum, in *Gaines*, that what counted was what a state offered
to whites within its boundaries and denied to blacks, but that even in pure financial terms the money given to a black scholarship student was much too small to
pay for that student's basic needs.

The deans reached the only possible conclusion: "After considering the expense involved, the available funds, the decisions of the courts, the probable consequences of delay, the impossibility of securing adequate faculty, and the effect on other institutions of the state of attempting to develop and maintain a complete educational program, on both the undergraduate and graduate levels at Langston University, the committee had no alternative but to recommend that Negroes be admitted to graduate and specialized programs in all institutions in the state." The deans added that they had consulted with faculty and advanced students at both the university and the A&M and that "with very few exceptions" they agreed that the only reasonable thing to do was to admit blacks into existing, hitherto all-white graduate programs that were not available at Langston.

Advocates of desegregation were heartened by the committee's work. Royden Dangerfield, an astute political scientist who was one of President Cross's closest advisers, wrote to each of the six deans, calling their report "statesmanlike."[50] Perhaps predictably, opponents of desegregation were completely unmoved by the deans' views and no effort was made to implement any part of their report. The political reporter for the *Daily Oklahoman*, Otis Sullivant, reported that "legislative leaders are of an opinion that the legislature will not repeal the segregation laws."[51] If the segregationists thought that they could ignore the issue and that it would go away, however, they were poor judges of the increasing determination and mounting momentum that were propelling their opponents forward.

Due in part, perhaps, to Roscoe Dunjee's prodding, the national office of the NAACP took an interest in the situation sometime in the late spring or early summer of 1948. From his ongoing experience in the defense of Ada Lois Fisher, Thurgood Marshall was already familiar with the situation in Oklahoma and at the university. Why he chose George McLaurin from among the six is not known.

---

50. Copies of Dangerfield's letters are in GLCPP, Box 34, Folder: "Negroes (#2)."
51. Sullivant, "Legal Change," 1.

Perhaps it was because McLaurin was one of only two of the group who had already earned a master's degree, thereby presumably proving himself to be capable of advanced graduate work. Another reason, often suggested, is that Marshall was attempting to counter the racist allegation that black males wanted to attend white colleges only so that they could prey upon innocent and vulnerable white women. By selecting a mild-mannered, soft-spoken, married man of sixty-one, the father of three grown children, a former professor who never appeared without a suit and tie, that claim was almost automatically rendered ridiculous.

On June 17, McLaurin's lawyers began the appeal process by following the frustrating path they had followed with Fisher. They asked Judge Justin Hinshaw of the Cleveland County District Court for a writ of mandamus, ordering the University of Oklahoma to admit George McLaurin to the Graduate College immediately.[52] Judge Hinshaw set a date for hearing the arguments. But after five weeks, on July 26, the NAACP attorneys did something they had never attempted before in any previous case. They withdrew the petition for the writ,[53] and two weeks later went directly into the federal (not the state) judicial system, appealing to the three-judge Federal District Court for the Western District of Oklahoma.[54] Perhaps Marshall and his colleagues took the step because they felt sure they would get nowhere with Judge Hinshaw or even with the Oklahoma Supreme Court; perhaps Marshall was eager to expedite the process and to press the federal (constitutional) questions raised by the Fourteenth Amendment's Equal Protection Clause.

Marshall and Amos Hall now named as defendants the State Regents, the university's Board of Regents, President Cross, Graduate

---

52. *G. W. McLaurin v. Board of Regents, University of Oklahoma et al.*, "Petition for Writ of *Mandamus*," filed June 17, 1948.

53. Ibid., "Certificate of Dismissal without Prejudice," July 26, 1948.

54. "Federal Judges to Hear Negro's Plea August 23," *DO*, August 6, 1948, 1. See also Greenberg, *Crusaders in the Courts*, 66; and TM to Amos Hall, July 30, 1948, NAACPPM, Reel 13, Frame 768. The three federal judges were Alfred P. Murrah, of the U.S. Circuit Court of Appeals, and two district judges, Edgar S. Vaught and Bower Broaddus.

Dean Laurence Snyder, and Dean of Admissions J. E. Fellows. After arguing that McLaurin's situation, and that of "others similarly situated," fell properly under the jurisdiction of the federal court, they laid out their by now familiar contentions in a twelve-page "Complaint"[55]: George McLaurin was a citizen of Oklahoma and a fully qualified applicant for admission to graduate work in the university; he wanted to take courses that were unavailable at Langston, the state's only public college open to blacks; and he was denied admission solely on account of his color. The defendants, McLaurin's attorneys acknowledged, were insisting that they were prevented from admitting him because of the Oklahoma law of 1941, specifically Sections 455, 456, and 457, the three paragraphs that lay down heavy daily fines for administrators, teachers, and students who permitted or cooperated with the mixing of black and white students in Oklahoma schools. Those sections of the law, the NAACP attorneys argued, were unconstitutional because they denied their client (and others) the equal protection of the laws guaranteed by the Fourteenth Amendment.

The Federal District Court accepted jurisdiction and the three judges began their deliberations. After reviewing McLaurin's complaint, they informed the state, on August 23, that its duty was "unmistakably clear" and that McLaurin must be provided the opportunity to earn a doctorate in educational administration. The judges also warned that they would deliver their formal verdict at the end of September, in effect giving the university a little more than a month to prepare for his enrollment.[56]

On September 16, two weeks before the Federal Court was to announce its decision, McLaurin once again went to the University of Oklahoma to ask for admission to the Graduate College. He did this, presumably, to undercut the state's main contention that, unlike Fisher, he had not made known his desires before his last-minute application, thereby placing an unreasonable demand on state authorities to provide a comparable program for him in a black

55. "Complaint," *G. W. McLaurin* v. *State Board of Regents, et al.*
56. "No New State Move Is Likely in Negro Case," *DO*, August 25, 1948, 1.

institution. Arriving a few minutes before 5:00 P.M., with his wife and Roscoe Dunjee, McLaurin presented Cross, Dean of Admissions J. E. Fellows, and Graduate Dean Laurence Snyder with his transcript from the University of Kansas. All agreed that his credentials were in order and that the only thing preventing his enrollment was the state statute. His second application, like the first, was denied.[57]

On September 29, the Federal District Court decreed, to no one's surprise, that in view of the *Sipuel* ruling, George McLaurin was entitled to the graduate program he desired as long as the state of Oklahoma offered that program to white students in a public institution. Referring to those three controversial sections of the 1941 law, the court ruled that "insofar as any statute or law of the State of Oklahoma denies or deprives this plaintiff admission . . . it is unconstitutional and unenforceable." But then to this declaration the three judges added a troublesome additional sentence: "This does not mean, however, that the segregation laws of Oklahoma are incapable of enforcement."[58] The court obviously felt that— except in a case like McLaurin's, where those laws infringed upon an individual's constitutional rights—overturning the segregation laws of the sovereign state of Oklahoma was beyond its jurisdiction. Nevertheless, that added remark, Cross later wrote, "provided opportunity for more of the same kind of evasive action that had been so prevalent in the Fisher case."[59]

The only option now left to the university's Board of Regents was to delay McLaurin's entry for as long as possible, and the majority of the board, as we shall see, was not above this desperate tactic. Therefore, after the court's ruling, when George McLaurin doggedly appeared for the third time to ask for admission, the state had not yet surrendered. There would be another regents' meeting to see what could be done to avoid the inevitable. "I am sorry that circumstances are such that I cannot admit you," Cross wrote to McLaurin on October 5, but he added, "your case is to receive

57. "OU Still Says No to Negro," *DO*, September 17, 1948, 1.
58. 87 F. Supp. 526–28 (W.D. Okla. 1948).
59. *BWC*, 89.

consideration by the Regents of the University of Oklahoma at a meeting which will be held tomorrow, October 6, at 3:00 P.M. Immediately following this meeting we will notify you of the decision of the Regents by telephone and letter."[60]

At 3:30 P.M. on October 6, a week after the Federal Court had issued its decision, the university regents met in Cross's office to consider exactly what was to be done.[61] The importance of the occasion was indicated by the attendance, not only of every regent, but also of Governor Turner and Attorney General Williamson. The meeting began with a frank report by Williamson of the university's position after the District Court's pronouncement. This was, he said, "an entirely different situation from any that the Board of Regents has faced." This was the first time any court had declared those troublesome three paragraphs of the 1941 segregation law unconstitutional and the first time that any court had mentioned the University of Oklahoma by name. Further, Williamson predicted that if the board failed to adopt either of the two options (admitting McLaurin or ending that program for whites), McLaurin's attorneys would very likely seek an injunction and, in Williamson's opinion, it would be granted.[62]

After hearing the attorney general and after a long discussion (the meeting was to last for more than four hours), the regents went into an executive session, and Turner and Williamson departed. The majority of the board was determined to embark upon a last ditch effort to delay McLaurin's entrance. Regent T. R. Benedum (Norman) offered a motion that "further consideration of

60. Ibid.; GLC to G. W. McLaurin, October 5, 1948, GLCPP, Box 50, Folder: "Negro Question (#3)."

61. Technically, this was not a "special" meeting of the regents (as Hubbell claims), but a continuation of the regular meeting of October 2, four days earlier.

62. The district court had said: "We refrain at this time from issuing or granting injunctive relief on the assumption that the State will follow the law in the constitutional mandate. We retain jurisdiction of this case, however, with full power to issue such further orders and decrees as may be deemed necessary and proper to secure this plaintiff the equal protection of the laws, which, translated into terms of this lawsuit, means . . . equal educational facilities."

the application of G. W. McLaurin . . . be deferred until the next regular meeting of the Board of Regents." In the meantime, Benedum's motion continued, President Cross should figure out how "instruction on the graduate level can be afforded to the applicant on a basis of complete segregation" while, at the same time, providing McLaurin educational opportunities equal to those afforded any other student.[63]

Regent Don Emery immediately gave voice to a fact that everyone in the room knew very well: that the last possible day to enroll for the fall semester was October 13 and that the classes McLaurin wanted to take had been meeting since September 20. Passing the Benedum motion would mean buying the university at least another semester of segregation. Emery offered a substitute motion:

> That the Board of Regents . . . authorize and direct the President and the proper officials of the University, to grant the application for admission . . . in time for Mr. McLaurin to enrol at the beginning of the term, under such rules and regulations as to segregation as the President of the University shall consider to afford to Mr. G. W. McLaurin substantially equal educational opportunities as are afforded to other persons seeking the same education . . . and that the President of the University promulgate such regulations.[64]

Emery then proceeded to defend his substitute motion in an emotional speech: "I offer this motion because I believe, in taking my oath of office as a Regent, no other alternative is presented to this Board in view of the ruling of the court and . . . the advice of the Attorney General of Oklahoma. It is the ruling of the court that Mr. McLaurin be admitted now." Moreover, Emery continued, the attorney general gives us "only two alternatives in respect to Mr. McLaurin." We can admit him "on the same scholastic basis as other students until similar classes in substantially equal courses of

63. RM, October 6, 1948, 2880.
64. Ibid.

instruction are established and ready to function at Langston University," or we must not give those classes to white students. Emery's substitute motion failed by a vote of 6–2, with only Emery and Lloyd Noble voting in its favor.

Regent Benedum then said that he voted against the substitute motion because "I have concluded . . . that it was not the intent of the Court to require the immediate admission of the applicant," but "that the Court intended that the Board of Regents take necessary time to work out the details to admit McLaurin to the University on a basis of complete segregation." Benedum conceded that much study and planning had already been done about the matter, but "there are many details to be considered and policies to be made with reference to the instruction of McLaurin . . . on a basis of complete segregation." After all, the court had explicitly said that it was not breaking down Oklahoma's policy of segregation, and that admission implied the need to take some time "to arrive at a workable solution of the problem."[65] Benedum then reintroduced his original motion and it passed by a vote of 6–2, Noble and Emery again in the minority. In vain Emery reiterated his objection that "the time is past to further deny Mr. McLaurin his constitutional rights by now consuming time to promulgate rules and regulations for his admission on a segregated basis. To me the Court's opinion means that you may promulgate rules and regulations for his admission on a segregated basis afterwards, but you must admit him now in order to grant him his constitutional rights."[66] It was 7:40 P.M., the meeting ended, and the regents returned to their homes, most of them satisfied that they had delayed, at least for the time being, the entrance to the University of Oklahoma of a mild-mannered, sixty-one-year-old black man.

Then an extraordinary thing happened. The regents, having announced their delaying tactic on Wednesday, October 6, suddenly agreed to meet again on Sunday, October 10. "It was never quite clear to me," Cross later wrote, "why the decision was made to

65. Ibid., 2881
66. Ibid., 2881–82.

call this special meeting."[67] But what had happened was made clear enough by the minutes of that emergency session of October 10. The Sunday meeting was "called at the request of Attorney General Mac Q. Williamson," and when the regents gathered in Cross's office at 4:00 P.M, the attorney general took the floor. He explained that after word of the regents' decision to postpone McLaurin's admission reached the New York offices of the NAACP's Legal Defense Fund (probably sometime on Thursday, October 7), Thurgood Marshall telegraphed Williamson on the morning of Friday, October 8, saying that he intended on the following morning to telegraph Associate Justice Wiley Rutledge of the U.S. Supreme Court, asking for "a restraining order" in support of the District Court's ruling and "on the same date expect [to] file with U. S. Supreme Court petition for leave to file petition for writ of mandamus in same matter." After Marshall informed Williamson of his intention, Williamson immediately dashed off a telegram to Justice Rutledge, informing him that the regents would meet the next day and "will, in my considered judgment, bring about McLaurin's admission to said University . . . in ample time for him to be enrolled in the desired courses of instruction for the current or fall semester of the University." An hour later, Justice Rutledge telegraphed Williamson that in view of Williamson's assurance, "I have deferred until Monday any hearing or consideration of Mr. Marshall[']s application." Rutledge added that he "would appreciate your advising me Monday morning if possible concerning action taken tomorrow by Board of Regents."[68]

At the meeting of October 10, after the regents learned of the flurry of telegrams, Don Emery reintroduced his motion of October 6, and this time it passed unanimously.[69] Thus, under the threat of federal intervention and a court order, the Board of Regents

67. *BWC*, 91.
68. RM, October 10, 1948, 2893–94.
69. Lloyd Noble was not present at the October 10 meeting, but he had voted yes on the identical motion on October 6; Regent Joe McBride (Anadarko) voted no at the October 10 meeting, but at the next regents' meeting, he asked that his vote be changed from no to yes (RM, November 10, 1948, 2899).

finally did the right thing. Three days later, George McLaurin made that journey back to Norman and registered for his classes, and the day after that, he took his place in the alcove off of Room 104, ready to begin his studies.

But the District Court's opinion, with that troublesome added comment, left the university's administrative authorities with a perplexing problem: how to admit McLaurin to the university (as required by the District Court) and still maintain the separation of the races (as required by state law). This would prove to be far from a simple matter.

CHAPTER 4

Twenty-One Months of Hell

That Sunday afternoon meeting of the University of Oklahoma's Board of Regents was noteworthy for another reason. Sandwiched between Mac Williamson's telling the regents about the frantic exchange of telegrams between Thurgood Marshall, Justice Rutledge, and himself, and the final vote on Don Emery's reintroduced motion to admit George McLaurin as the school's first black student, the Regents received for their consideration one of the most bizarre reports ever presented in any American university. President Cross had asked his close friend and financial vice president Roscoe Cate to study and report on the matter that was on everyone's mind: how could the University of Oklahoma admit an African American student and still maintain segregation?[1]

After consulting with the administrators and teachers who would soon be dealing with McLaurin, Cate drew a crucial distinction between "complete" and "partial" segregation, and he came quickly to an obvious conclusion: the board could, if it wished, implement the complete segregation of McLaurin by the second semester; but if he were admitted for the present semester, "only partial segregation will be possible." Complete segregation would entail setting aside a classroom for his exclusive use and hiring a qualified teacher at the associate or full professor level. Cate pointed out that there were presently four faculty vacancies in the College of Education that the university was unable to fill, and that the remaining professors were already teaching loads so heavy that asking them to offer separate classes to a single student was impossible. And even if

1. For Cate's report, see RM, October 10, 1948, 2894–96.

that difficulty was somehow overcome, complete segregation would still be virtually impossible. For example, white graduate students had access to the book stacks in the library. To deny McLaurin that access was to invite further litigation on the grounds that he was not being treated equally. But how could he exercise that right and still be separated? Moreover, graduate students normally participated in seminars that were deemed an essential part of their education. How could McLaurin, the only black student in his College, avail himself of that opportunity under conditions of complete separation? Then there was the matter of the money involved. Hiring a qualified teacher (if one could be found) would require $6,000 a year, with another $1,000 needed to maintain separate facilities. These expenses had not been anticipated in the current budget; therefore, an appeal would have to be made to the governor's contingency fund. And then Cate raised the most harrowing possibility of all: "This cost is for McLaurin only. If other Negroes are enrolled in other departments, comparable professors at comparable salaries would have to be provided."[2]

Cate's report was almost too much for the regents to absorb. In the end, as has been seen, Emery's motion provided merely that McLaurin be admitted "under such rules and regulations as to segregation as the President of the University shall consider to afford Mr. G. W. McLaurin substantially equal educational opportunities . . . and that the President of the University promulgate such regulations."[3] In short, the regents, unable or unwilling to grapple with the intricacies of providing complete segregation, threw the responsibility to George Cross.

The arrangements (Cross called them "disagreeable details"[4]) that university officials devised were simple enough. All of McLaurin's classes would be held in Room 104, and for all of them he would sit at his own desk in the adjoining alcove. He could enter the library stacks at the same time as white graduate students, but

2. Ibid., 2896.
3. Ibid.
4. *BWC*, 92.

McLaurin's separated table in the library of the University of Oklahoma. Courtesy *The Oklahoman.*

he would have his own table in the library where no one else could sit, and he could sit at no other table. He was, similarly, assigned his own table in the Student Union. He could sit nowhere else and no white student could sit at his table. The "Jug," a snack shop in the Union, was open to him for lunch between noon and 1:00 P.M., and no white student could eat there during that hour. A toilet on the first floor of the Carnegie Building was set aside for his exclusive use. It was under such conditions that the first black student in the history of the University of Oklahoma began his studies.

McLaurin's enrollment for the first semester of the 1948–49 academic year led inevitably to the dire possibility mentioned in Cate's report. Other African Americans, eager for education and undeterred by the grotesque conditions imposed upon McLaurin, began to apply. By early February 1949, the university received five such applications for the second semester. Each was submitted by an Oklahoma citizen and each applicant was academically qualified for graduate work. Cross, obedient to the regents' directive, forwarded each case to Williamson for his opinion. The attorney general rejected two of the applicants, approved one, and left one to the regents' discretion.[5] Cross promptly admitted Orpherita Eugenia Daniels to the Social Work program and, once approved by the regents, Mauderie Hancock Wilson to study Sociology.[6] Both of them, naturally, were subjected to the same arrangements as McLaurin.

Williamson based his decisions on the controversial issue of prior notice. His stubborn contention was that black applicants must have made their educational desires known sometime in the past so that the state might have a reasonable opportunity to provide those fields at Langston. A sarcastic Thurgood Marshall wrote to Amos Hall in February 1949, as the new applicants were being screened, that Williamson "is still as wrong as ever" about requiring prior notice. "In all my life, I have never run across a lawyer who has deliberately misquoted the Supreme Court as much as Mac Q. Williamson."[7] Opponents of Williamson's criterion argued that it inevitably and unfairly delayed black students from starting their

5. MQW to GLC, February 4, 1949, GLCPP, Box 50, Folder: "Negro Question (#3)." Williamson did not discuss the fifth applicant, Helen Maxine Holmes, who wanted to study Commercial Education. Holmes had gone to court in July 1949 to secure a writ of mandamus, and her case was still being tried. Cross asserts (*BWC*, 108) that Williamson approved admission for *four* of the students. I rely here on Williamson's letter of February 4.

6. RM, February 9, 1949, 2991–92. Wilson's application was complicated because she sued after her rejection and her case was tied up in court, and because she later missed (by one day) the registration period, and, finally, because she elected to change from Social Work to Sociology. See MQW to GLC, October 22, 1948, NAACPPM, Reel 13, Frame 854.

7. TM to Amos Hall, February 10, 1949, NAACPPM, Reel 13, Frame 921. The issue went back to the *Gaines* case. Williamson had told the Oklahoma Supreme Court that *Gaines* did not apply to *Sipuel* because Gaines had given prior notice of his intention. Wattley (*Step toward* Brown, 109–10) shows that this distinction "was wholly false" because Gaines had never given notice of his wish to become a lawyer. Thus he and Fisher were "in the very same situation."

educations. Moreover, exactly how much notice had to be given was never made clear. And finally, since white students did not have to give prior notice of *their* plans, it meant that, contrary to equal treatment, only blacks had to jump this extra hurdle.

Cross, who regarded the procedure for admitting black students as "complex" and "absurd,"[8] was not alone in his criticism. A *Norman Transcript* editorial called the process "nonsense" and so technical that "action by the Legislature to clear up the situation is sorely needed."[9] At a meeting on January 29, the State Regents urged lawmakers to let qualified black students enter graduate programs in white schools if those programs were unavailable at Langston.[10] By April, even Williamson, tired of acting as the university's virtual admissions officer, was also ready to advocate change, and he too urged the legislature to modify the law.[11] Despite the mounting pressure to do something, the politicians delayed for as long as possible any action that would ease the path of blacks into white colleges and universities. Finally, at the end of the session, Edgar Boatman of Okmulgee introduced legislation. Cross and others at the university were initially heartened both by the willingness of lawmakers to address the problem and also by the provisions of Boatman's bill.

In its original form, House Bill 405 provided that qualified African American students, desiring a field of graduate study not available at Langston, could enter a state (white) college or university that offered that field. Boatman's bill did not change the segregation laws but only suspended them in such cases. Although black students could now enroll in white schools, they still had to be taught on a segregated basis. But importantly, the bill allowed authorities at the white institutions to decide precisely what measures

8. *BWC,* 108

9. "Abolish the Technicalities," *NT,* February 7, 1949, 4.

10. "Board Recommends End to Segregation in Graduate Schools," *DO,* January 30, 1949, 1.

11. MQW to Bill Logan and Walter Billingsley, April 6, 1949, GLCPP, Box 50, Folder: "Negro Question (#3)." Logan was president pro tempore of the Senate, and Billingsley was Speaker of the House. See also Hubbell, "Desegregation of the University of Oklahoma," 52–53.

constituted "segregation." Cross left for a trip to Chicago just before the scheduled vote for Boatman's bill. He was disappointed
that segregation was still required, but he thought that if he and the
regents could determine the actual arrangements, the university
could probably live with it.[12]

When Cross got back home, he learned to his horror that at
the last minute the legislature had disastrously amended House
Bill 405 under pressure from Senate president Bill Logan of Lawton. Instead of letting each white institution define what education on "a segregated basis" required, the amended bill defined
the segregation to mean "classroom instruction given in separate
classrooms or at separate times."[13] The amended bill was passed by
both houses and signed by the governor on June 11, 1949. Cross
saw instantly that it was unworkable. At least twenty-five black students were coming for the summer session. Finding both separate
rooms and the additional faculty for the dozens of classes involved
(most of them for only one or two students) was quite impossible.
He told the press that to comply the university needed $10,000 now
and $100,000 by September, funds to come, presumably, from the
governor's emergency fund.[14] Everyone knew that was unlikely.

A worried Cross turned first to legal adviser John Cheadle, who
had taught at the university's law school since it first opened in
1909. Cheadle's analysis of the new law was somber and sarcastic.
"I assume that it will be construed to mean separate class facilities,
separate living quarters, separate eating provisions (Negroes may
not be eaten by lions or tigers which heretofore have eaten only
white people), and separate rest rooms, etc." The astute Cheadle
summed it all up in eleven words: "This 1949 act will cause us a
great deal of trouble."[15] The president also asked Attorney General
Williamson for his opinion: "In your interpretation," Cross wrote,

12. *BWC*, 111.

13. 70 *Oklahoma Statutes, Supplement* (1949), sections 455–57.

14. "OU to Ask Extra Funds for Negro Instruction," *NT*, June 19, 1949, 1; "Separate Instruction Will Require $100,000," *OD*, June 21, 1949, 1.

15. John Cheadle to CMF, September 19, 1949, GLCPP, Box 66, Folder:
"Negroes."

"please indicate what constitutes a 'separate classroom.'" He also asked Williamson what the law required "with respect to eating facilities, library facilities, toilet facilities, University housing, attendance at athletic contests, and other campus activities."[16]

Cross was to call Williamson's response "most helpful,"[17] but it was more than that: it was a life saver for the university. The attorney general affirmed that House Bill 405 required that blacks had to be taught in separate classrooms or at different times. However, he added that "what constitutes a 'classroom' . . . is a matter which . . . can be more accurately determined by the governing board or other proper authorities of said institution than by this office."[18] Cross and his advisers promptly "determined" that if you used ropes or railings to mark off a part of an existing room, you magically created *two* separate rooms where only one had existed before! Cross had his doubts about whether the authorities would sit still for this ruse, but believing that the university had no other choice, he ordered that barriers and railings and "Colored Only" signs be placed where black students would be taking classes.[19] By calling these questionable classroom arrangements "temporary," the university hoped to ward off critics. The president was greatly relieved when, two weeks later, his actions were unanimously approved by the regents.[20]

Senator Logan was not fooled by this devious device of dividing rooms with rails and ropes. On June 18, a week after the law was signed, he wrote Cross a condescending ("Dear George") letter. He knew, he said, how hard it was to run a big university, and he only wished to offer some suggestions to be helpful and "to assist you in any way that I can." The politeness out of the way, Logan got down

16. GLC to MQW, June 11, 1949, GLCPP, Box 50, Folder: "Negro Question (#2)."

17. *BWC*, 112.

18. MQW to GLC, June 14, 1949, GLCPP, Box 50, Folder: "Negro Question (#2)." Williamson's opinion also gave governing boards authority to "adopt and enforce reasonable rules and regulations" as to eating, library, housing facilities, and so forth.

19. Ed Dycus, "Segregation Procedure Announced by Cross," *OD*, June 17, 1949, 1; "Railings Are Up at OU; Negroes Are Due Monday," *DO*, June 19, 1949, 38.

20. RM, June 29, 1949, 3179. One regent abstained.

to business. He learned, he said, that the university "is considering the placing of railings or ropes or some other such imaginary
division lines in classrooms." Such a scheme was "an insult to the
colored students" and an obvious "subterfuge." It revealed "scorn
and disrespect" for the legislature." Logan insisted that "there is
nothing ambiguous" about the law's requirement that instruction
occur in separate classrooms or at separate times. He shared with
Cross the definition of a "room" in Webster's dictionary, asserting
that "this is all so elementary that it should not require construction." The purpose of Logan's letter was to scold and threaten, and
anybody looking for the promised helpful "suggestions" would look
in vain. Nor did Logan explain why confining black students to
separate classrooms was less insulting than confining them by ropes
and rails to part of a space where whites were also being taught.[21] A
fierce response to Logan came from Edgar Boatman, the author of
the original bill. He accused Logan of unscrupulous politics "with
an eye on the 1950 gubernatorial race." Calling Logan "narrow
minded" and "foolish," Boatman charged that he would waste taxpayers' money "to build the white supremacy plank in his 1950 platform." In Boatman's view, Logan was guilty of "the worst example of
petty politics I have ever seen demonstrated by a public official."[22]

Nevertheless, it was clear to Cross, his assistants, and probably
to the regents that they were skating perilously on the edges of
legality. When the administration drafted a statement to assure citizens that the university was "making the strictest enforcement possible of segregation," Don Emery privately cautioned Cross that the
wording might create "an erroneous impression, especially in the
minds of those readers who know about the statutory proviso that
instruction will be in separate classrooms or at different times."[23] A
few months later, the attorney general asked Cross to write a letter

21. Bill Logan to GLC, June 18, 1949, GLCPP, Box 50, Folder: "Negro Question
(#3)." See also "Bill's Author Has Criticism for Cross," *DO*, June 18, 1949, 5; and
OD, June 18, 1949, 1.
22. "Logan Protest on Segregation Plan Produces Hot Words from Boatman,"
DO, June 19, 1949, 34.
23. Don Emery to GLC, September 16, 1949, GLCPP, Box 66, Folder: "Negroes."

"indicating the present status of segregation" at the university. Vice President Carl Mason Franklin advised the president not to do it: "The fact that the letter would eventually be made public would be detrimental," he warned, because it would reveal "that we are in direct violation of House Bill 405."[24]

It was a bold step for Cross to dodge the law's intent by resorting to the pretense that dividing a classroom with railings was enough to make two separate rooms. But since no additional funds for implementing the "different times" option were forthcoming, he could see no alternative, and he went ahead. As he remarked to a correspondent, we "have been walking a 'tight rope' in an effort to get the problem solved in a manner that would be just and at the same time legal."[25]

During the same week as Senator Logan's blast, Cross made another abrupt (and perhaps illegal) decision—and this one he did not make out of necessity He ordered that Ada Lois Sipuel Fisher be admitted to the university's law school even though the bogus Langston law school at the Capitol was technically still in existence. Because only one black student had ever attended the "school," the legislature decided to stop funding it as of June 30, 1949. When she got news of the school's impending demise, Fisher assumed the way was now clear for her to attend the university's law school, and on June 16, she attempted for the third time to enroll. The State Regents, however, refused her once again. The Langston school was still in operation (for another two weeks!), and the State Regents could not certify that the program she desired was not available to her at Langston.[26]

Cross learned of the denial the next day. He knew that if Fisher had to wait until the official closing of the Langston school, she would miss the summer session, further delaying her future as a lawyer. He decided that after three and a half years (1,251 days) of denying her the chance, further delay would be unconscionable.

24. CMF to GLC, February 3, 1950, ibid.
25. GLC to Fred McCuistion, October 19, 1950, ibid., Box 80, Folder: "Negroes."
26. Ed Dycus, "Ada Sipuel Fisher Denied Admission for Third Time," *OD*, June 17, 1949, 1.

"After reflecting for a few minutes on the possible consequences, . . . I decided it would be absurd not to permit the young woman to get under way immediately with her legal education."[27] Late that afternoon (he was to start his Colorado vacation the next morning), Cross phoned Vice President Franklin at his home and said, "Carl, it is time that we stop this foolishness and admit Ada Lois Sipuel to the OU Law School. I want you to do that in the morning."[28] Next morning Franklin phoned Page Keeton, dean of the law school. In view of the law, Keeton was reluctant to admit Fisher unless Franklin put the order in writing. Franklin wrote out the order, walked to Monnet Hall, and handed it to the dean.[29] Fisher got the news and rushed to Norman the next day to register for summer classes, and, at long last, it was done. "I will spend the rest of my life," she said, "trying to prove to Oklahoma that a mistake was made in the attempt to keep me from entering the school"[30]

On her first day of class, Fisher nervously entered the law building and found her classroom. It was "very large and built on a step-up incline. . . . In the back of the last row of seats was a single large wooden chair behind a wooden rail. Attached to a pole on the back of the chair was a large printed sign that said COLORED. The room was about half-filled when I walked in. I did not look about, just walked straight ahead and up the levels to the chair."[31] She had another shock awaiting her. "The door opened and in walked the instructor. I gasped. He was Maurice Merrill, the faculty member

27. *BWC*, 113.
28. When he was eighty-six, in 1997, Franklin wrote a long letter to then-president David Boren, recounting the episode. It is reprinted in full in David W. Levy, "The Week the President Went Fishing," *SM* 18 (Winter 1998): 26–30. See also CMF to J. E. Fellows, June 17, 1949, GLCPP, Box 50, Folder: "Negro Question (#3); and Oklahoma State Regents for Higher Education, "Minutes," June 27, 1949.
29. The situation was complicated because Franklin had come to the university in 1948 as both vice president and a professor of law. Therefore Dean Keeton was his superior as a professor but his subordinate when Franklin was acting as vice president. Franklin left the university in 1953 to teach law at the University of Southern California.
30. *NT*, June 19, 1949, 1.
31. *MBW*, 145.

who had represented the state in opposing my admission before the Oklahoma courts and the United States Supreme Court." As it happened, she had nothing to fear from her professor. He soon became "one of my favorite instructors," and the two became friends after her graduation from the law school.[32]

Fisher graduated in August 1951, passed the bar exam, and practiced law through the 1950s. In 1959, she returned to Langston to teach history and head the Social Sciences Department. In 1968, she came back to Norman to earn a master's degree in history. She retired from Langston in 1987. Four years later, the University of Oklahoma resumed, after a long hiatus, the practice of awarding honorary degrees. Two of the first four such degrees were bestowed upon Ada Lois Fisher and retired president George Lynn Cross.[33] That same year, Governor David Walters nominated Fisher to the university's Board of Regents in a widely praised act. The plaque in the garden dedicated to her on the Norman campus quotes Psalm 118, about how the stone that had been rejected by the builders became the cornerstone. Ada Lois Sipuel Fisher died of cancer on October 15, 1994, at the age of seventy-one.

Meanwhile, the new law of 1949 encouraged a steady stream of black students eager to pursue graduate work at the University of Oklahoma. The university kept careful records of the number of its African American students, and their names and areas of study. This was done, in part, because for each black applicant the university had to have written assurance from Chancellor Nash that the program requested was not being taught at Langston. Still, late enrollments and intermittent early withdrawals made discrepancies in the numbers inevitable. Some black students enrolled for study on the Norman campus, while others took classes at the Graduate Study Center in Oklahoma City. The Center, technically part of

32. Ibid., 146. See the oral interview with Merrill, in Herbert Hengst MSS, WHC. When Fisher taught at Langston, she became the adviser to pre-law students there, and her numerous contacts with Merrill were cordial and respectful on both sides.

33. The other recipients were Carl Albert and Helen Walton, widow of Sam Walton.

the university's Extension Division, specialized in various branches of Education, and the black students choosing the Oklahoma City option tended to be women teachers in black schools eager to improve their professional skills and work toward advanced degrees. Naturally classes at the Graduate Center were segregated.[34]

On June 4, 1949, Cross submitted to Chancellor Nash the names of 25 African American students who were seeking admission to the university. They would be joining the roughly 5,100 white students for summer school.[35] Among them were 3 of those 5 who had tried to gain entrance along with McLaurin in the fall of 1948. Another notable name on the list was that of Penninah McLaurin, George's wife, who had made the same attempt back in 1923; now, a quarter- century later, she wanted to take courses in Home Economics. Of the 25, at least 11 hoped to do graduate work in Education. The others wanted to study various fields from English to Sociology, from Engineering to Home Economics. Sixteen of the 25 were from Oklahoma City, and the others came from cities and towns across the state. Three additional black students were admitted on June 16, with 2 seeking master's degrees in Music Education and the third in Education.[36] The summer session began with 23 African American students, but soon their number grew to 31; they were enrolled in at least 40 classes.[37] It was no longer a rare and startling thing for white students to encounter a black face on the campus of the University of Oklahoma.

At the close of the summer session, a survey of those 31 black students indicated that at least 21 of them planned to continue into the fall semester of 1949–50. The majority of these (16) would

34. F. A. Balyeat to Laurence H. Snyder and CMF, August 25, 1949, GLCPP, Box 66, Folder: "Negroes."

35. GLC to M. A. Nash, June 4, 1949, GLCPP, Box 50, Folder: "Negro Question (#3)."

36. *OD*, June 17, 1949, 1.

37. *BWC*, 116; J. E. Fellows to CMF, August 1, 1949, GLCPP, Box 66, Folder: "Negroes." On June 29, Cross told the regents (RM, June 29, 1949, 3279) that there were 25 black students in the summer session. The *DO*, on June 19, fixed the number who were starting summer school at 26. On the same date, the *NT* reported the number to be 29. Two days later, the *DO* gave 30 as the correct number. The *OD*, on June 23, reported that 47 rooms were being used by black students.

be continuing their studies in Education at the Graduate Center in Oklahoma City.[38] The number of black students on the Norman campus at the start of the 1949–50 academic year (among the roughly 12,000 whites) was somewhere around 15 and about the same number were enrolled at the Graduate Center. At the start of the second semester, in January 1950, at least 64 black students were studying at the university—41 at the Graduate Center, 2 of them taking courses in Home Economics and the rest in Education. The breakdown by gender was significant: there were only 4 men as opposed to 37 women at the Center. In Norman, there were 23 black students, 7 men and 16 women. Of these, 19 were taking Education courses in Norman (including George McLaurin).[39] Looking back at the entire period from McLaurin's entry in October 1948 to the end of the academic year in May 1950, the university had enrolled close to 150 African American students. Among this number, there were nearly four times as many women as men (118 to 32), and of those women, the vast majority (probably around a hundred) were in various subfields of Education. There may have been as many as a hundred black students at the university in the summer of 1950, and in the fall semester of the 1950–51 academic year, as many as 64 could be found on the Norman campus. By October 1950, the university had accepted applications from 231 African Americans, and by July 1951 that number had reached 314, although many of those who were accepted never actually enrolled.[40]

In 1948, when McLaurin first arrived, nobody could have foreseen all the difficulties that lay ahead or imagined the contortions that would be required. As university officials moved forward, they improvised as best they could. But despite their best efforts and

38. "Survey of Educational Plans for First Semester 1949–50 of Negro Students Enrolled in 1949 Summer School," J. E. Fellows to CMF, August 1, 1949, GLCPP, Box 66, Folder: "Negroes."

39. GLC to Dean Bowden, March 15, 1950, GLCPP, Box 66, Folder: "Negro Enrolment." See also "Negro Enrolment for the Second Semester, 1949–1950," ibid., Folder: "Negroes."

40. GLC to Primus Wade, October 27, 1950, GLCPP, Box 80, Folder: "Negro"; Earnestine Beatrice Spears, "Social Forces in the Admittance of Negroes to the University of Oklahoma" (master's thesis, University of Oklahoma, 1951).

intentions, black students suffered. For twenty-one months, school officials had to invent policies that navigated between the demands of state law and those of decency and common sense. One thing is certain. John Cheadle's remark to Cross ("this 1949 Act will cause us a great deal of trouble") had been prophetic.

The basic physical adjustments that were needed cost considerable effort and some expense. "Will you please put a 'Reserved for Colored' sign on one of the cubicles in the women's restroom in the basement of the Administration Building," Vice President Franklin wrote to the head of the Physical Plant, Walter Kraft.[41] Kraft was also told to supply signs to every department and every classroom where black students might be present—no matter that most of the time there would be only a single black student. In nearly all the rooms to be used by black students during the summer of 1949, barriers, railings, ropes, and separated rows of seats had to be arranged. Usually it was the back row of the room that was separated for this purpose, and usually (as was the case with Ada Lois Fisher) only one student could be found sitting back there alone.

A problem arose immediately upon the admission of Orpherita Daniels, one of the two African Americans joining McLaurin for the second semester of the 1948–49 academic year. Her classes were to meet in Room 28 of the library. But, as Dean Fellows reported to Cross, that was "a small seminar room providing a maximum seating of twenty students around a large conference table. I feel that I should point out to you the difficulty of providing segregation similar to that used with Mr. McLaurin."[42] Some cases were easier than others. In response to a query at the start of the 1949–50 year, Arts and Sciences dean Edgar Meacham reported that the situation in the English Department was under control: "There is one student enrolled and he is seated on the back row in room K[aufman Hall]-140, K-132, and K-133 with no white students in these classes on these rows." Zoology, however, was "more complicated" because

41. CMF to Kraft, November 16, 1949, GLCPP, Box 66, Folder: "Negroes."
42. Fellows to GLC, February 9, 1949, GLCPP, Box 50, Folder: "Negro Question (#3)."

"there are three negro students and laboratories are involved." In the lecture hall, "the negro students sit in front on the right hand side of the teacher with no white students on that row." The labs, however, were a trickier proposition. In one of them a black student sat "on one side of the laboratory desk with three white students on the opposite side facing him." In the second "the negro student sits in an area surrounded by the wall and two tables forming an 'U' to separate him from the white students." And in the third, the desks "are arranged around the room against the wall with students facing the wall. The negro student in this class is separated from other students by the sink and a vacant seat."[43]

To comply with the "different times" option of House Bill 405, the university, in preparation for the 1949 summer school session, embarked on an earnest search for qualified instructors to teach classes composed entirely of black students. By a strenuous effort, the school was able to offer fifteen such classes.[44] The faculty who were hired to teach these classes were expected to be equal in their qualifications to those teaching the white students, and the university found some capable people, all of whom were white. Carl Cress, who was to teach a course for blacks on elementary education, had taught previously at the university and was completing his PhD at Stanford.[45] Both Thomas Tucker and William Lutker had also taught at the university before, and both had master's degrees and were finishing their doctorates in elementary education. Tucker's class on teaching reading attracted seven black students, while Lutker instructed two students on teaching mathematics.[46] Two members of the Modern Languages Department, one an associate professor and the other an assistant, were shifted into teaching all-black Spanish classes.[47] Elizabeth House was hired to teach a separate class in music forms and analysis; she had teaching experience and

43. Edgar Meacham to CMF, September 19, 1949, GLCPP, Box 66, Folder: "Negroes."
44. "More Separate Classes Ready," *NT*, June 26, 1949, 1.
45. John Pogue, "Cress Hired to Teach OU Negroes," *OD*, June 22, 1949, 1.
46. "More Separate Classes Ready," 1.
47. R. L. Schreiber, "Five Named to Instruct Negro Classes," *OD*, June 23, 1949, 1.

held a master's degree from the Eastman School of Music.[48] Thus the university was able, at least for the time being, to convince lawmakers and the public that it was doing its best to provide substantially equal educational opportunities, if not always in separate classrooms, at least, when it could, during different times.

Eating arrangements posed other difficulties. By a curious fact, neither the state constitution nor its statutory law required the separation of races at places where food was served. After conducting a study of the state's segregation laws, John Cheadle concluded that "there are no provisions forbidding the mixing of races in dining rooms and hotels." This omission, Cheadle believed, was "a sort of blind spot in our law."[49] Evidently, Cross and the regents were unaware of this, simply assuming that the mixing of races in public eating places was forbidden. In January 1950, their erroneous assumption was called to Cross's attention by a white undergraduate, Mary Kathryn Hickman. In a note to her, Cross confessed, "I find that, after investigation, you are right in your statement that there is no state law in regard to segregation in public eating places." Nevertheless, he wrote, "it was thought best, apparently, to provide segregation in regard to all activities associated with education, and not merely segregate with respect to classroom activities." Cross told Hickman that he hoped to discuss the matter with the regents soon and explore whether this might be a good time for changing university regulations.[50]

The plan that was devised to provide lunch for McLaurin during his first semester was continued for the second semester when he was joined by Orpherita Daniels and Mauderie Wilson. They were to eat at the "Jug" snack shop in the Union from noon to 1:00 P.M.

48. "Music Professor Named to Teach Negroes at O.U.," *NT,* June 24, 1949, 1.

49. John Cheadle to Roscoe Cate, April 20, 1948, GLCPP, Box 50, Folder: "Negro Question (#1)." State law segregated only four areas: transportation facilities, telephone booths, mines, and education. Most of Oklahoma's innumerable segregation practices were carried out by local regulations, municipal ordinances, and by widely understood but unwritten custom.

50. GLC to Mary Kathryn Hickman, January 6, 1950, GLCPP, Box 66, Folder: "Negroes." The board's minutes for the next few months fail to record such a discussion in an open meeting.

No whites could use the place during that hour, and they could not use it at any other time. That dining arrangement for black students was maintained during the summer session of 1949, but starting on June 30, it was necessary to set aside two tables in the "Jug" for black students. At first, the tables were separated by a chain, but after "constant publicity regarding rails and chains," the chain was removed and signs indicating that the tables were reserved for black students were added.[51] Finally, in early 1950, the "Jug" was closed, and black students were directed to eat either at the cafeteria in the Union or at the cafeteria at the Wilson Center dormitories. At both places, they were allowed to go through the lines with whites, but then they had to carry their trays to designated tables where no whites could sit. Anyone who thought that this simple arrangement would solve all the problems of providing food for African American students was naive. A string of incidents soon complicated the matter of human beings eating food.

On April 16, 1948, Roscoe Cate got a nervous letter from the director of University Housing. The woman in charge of the Wilson Center cafeteria reported that W. H. Smith of the Art Department brought into the cafeteria "a negro man as his guest today." Thankfully, "there was no incident or undue excitement" created by the students eating there. Nevertheless, the cafeteria's superintendent "was considerably perturbed over the affair since she hardly knew what to do about the matter." The director begged for a "definite statement of policy" because "it is entirely possible that the segregation laws of Oklahoma would prohibit our serving white people and colored people in the same room."[52] The problem was referred to Cheadle, who studied the matter and replied that the legislature prohibited the mixing of students, "but if the negroes are merely visiting the school or are there not as students but as invitees . . . that prohibition does not apply."[53]

51. W. H. Freeland to Paul MacMinn, January 9, 1950, GLCPP, Box 66, Folder: "Negroes."

52. Garner G. Collums to Roscoe Cate, April 16, 1948, GLCPP, Box 50, Folder: "Negro Question (#2)." But see n. 49 above.

53. John Cheadle to Roscoe Cate, April 20, 1948, ibid.

The hair-raising emergency caused by Smith and his guest occurred on school property. Most of the trouble, however, involved
use of the Memorial Student Union. That building had been erected
by a massive private fund-raising campaign in the mid-1920s, and
not a dime of public money was used for its establishment. The
building was governed by a nonprofit corporation, separate from
the university itself. Union policy was made by a Board of Governors consisting of prominent alumni living all over the country.
As a courtesy, and to enable the university to have a voice in the
board's deliberations, the school's president and the chair of the
regents were members. The day-to-day affairs of the building were
entrusted to a Board of Managers.[54]

There was strong sentiment on the part of some important
alumni, whether members of the Board of Governors or not, to
resist desegregation and keep things the way they had always been.
The board realized that there would be black students at the university but felt that they should be "furnished only such facilities
as are necessary for . . . obtaining an education."[55] Tom Carey of
Oklahoma City, a 1908 graduate and a respected and energetic
leader of the alumni association and twice its president, ventured
an opinion on blacks using the Union in a letter written the same
week as McLaurin's arrival for his first class. Carey emphasized
the independence of the Union from the university regents or
the state government, and he argued that the Union's governing
board should not defer "on this particular question." Because access to the Union depended on paying annual fees, "I would simply refuse to permit the collection or to accept fees collected for
the use of these premises by any persons other than white students
or students of Indian blood." Carey insisted that the absolute ban
he was proposing arose "not from any animosity of the Negro," but

54. Levy 2: 106–10. The corporation owns the building. With legislative approval, the Board of Regents leased the land on which the building sits for ninety-
nine years.

55. W. Hillyard Freeland to Paul MacMinn, January 9, 1950, GLCPP, Box 66,
Folder: "Negroes."

"because I believe the usefulness of the Union facilities will cease if it is opened to the Negro race."[56]

On December 11, 1946, a few years before McLaurin's arrival, the university had hosted a short course at the Union on the classroom use of audio-visual equipment. Among those attending were the director and two faculty members of Langston's Education Division. A dinner was planned to conclude the course and the three from Langston bought tickets. The Union refused to serve them. The incident was, of course, humiliating to the three teachers, but also to authorities at the university. When Cross learned of it, all he could do was tell the director of short courses that in the future he should "frankly explain . . . that the Oklahoma Memorial Union will not serve Negroes and that there are some luncheon or dinner meetings included in the conference to which Negroes cannot be invited." He also told the director to be more careful about selling dinner tickets to black guests and advised trying to find locations other than the Union where black people might be allowed to eat.[57]

In November 1948, the university's Student Senate hosted a statewide conference of student governments. A reception was scheduled for the end of the conference, and the Union management was advised "that there was a possibility of both colored and white delegates being present at the reception." The lounge was "tentatively" reserved, while the opinion of the Board of Governors was sought. "For your information," Union manager Ted Beaird wrote, "the mailed votes from the 17 members of the Board of Governors were tabulated [and]. . . . we have been instructed to advise you that by a majority vote . . . the booking has been denied. This is official notification that facilities of the Oklahoma Memorial Union

56. Tom F. Carey to Ted Beaird, October 18, 1948, GLCPP, Box 50, Folder: "Negro Question (#2)." Beaird was the secretary of the alumni association and manager of the Union.

57. GLC to John B. Freeman, January 17, 1947, GLCPP, Box 50, Folder: "Negro Question (#1)." Cross's letter was based on suggestions from his assistant, Royden Dangerfield, in ibid.

are not to be booked for assembly of white and colored students, under present regulations."[58]

In May 1949, Lawrence Rogers of the Health Education Department held a conference called "Spotlight on Health." After booking the Union, he told Beaird that one of the participants would be a professor from Langston. Rogers was told "that the colored professor would be required to take a seat aside from the white delegates at the conference." But that was not the end of it. What if Rogers and the others wanted to serve coffee or refreshments? Would it be possible, Beaird wondered, for the black professor to be served at a separate table in the conference room?[59] The answer returned to the manager of the Union was yes.

Finally, on October 11, 1949, the Union's Board of Governors gathered themselves in Oklahoma City for the purpose of "dealing with the colored student matters." They arrived at some definite decisions. The first involved the campus YMCA and YWCA, both of which had offices in the Union. The question was "Do negroes have access" to these offices for "mixed conferences" and counciling [sic]?" The Board of Governors ruled that "they do not. A colored student may go to the YM or YW offices . . . but not in mixed groups." It was next decided that black students who wanted to hold a luncheon or a banquet at the Union could do so "providing they meet the same priority, minimum number participating, etc., as do white students." The apparent generosity of that concession was somewhat mitigated by the governors' next decision: "It was definitely decided that rest room facilities could not be provided for colored students in the Union Building." In other words, they could have their banquet, but anybody needing to use a bathroom would need to leave the Union and scurry to the Carnegie Building or Evans Hall. The governors naturally decreed "that colored students could not attend social functions with white students" in the Union. It was, however, grudgingly conceded, and grudgingly

58. Ted Beaird to Gilbert Lincoln, November 17, 1948, GLCPP, Box 50, Folder: "Negro Question (#2)."

59. Ted Beaird to CMF, May 7, 1949, GLCPP, Box 50, Folder: "Negro Question (#3)."

expressed by Beaird, "that in case the negroes insist on participating in the use of the lounge facilities," a marked chair or divan could be set aside for them.[60]

Other areas of university life were also problematic. What about using the library? When McLaurin was the only black student at the university, it was agreed that, like other graduate students, he could have access to the stacks even if it meant mingling with whites. He would have to take his books to a special table off the main reading room. This arrangement might serve for one student, or even for half a dozen. But as the black population grew, it was no longer adequate. Blacks were then allowed to study in the reference room, but in November 1949, some of them complained that the noise and confusion inhibited their ability to study. Jesse Rader, who had been the university's librarian for decades, said he was aware of the situation and that "the complaint was justified," but limited space and the segregation policy meant that "there was little he could do." Cross weighed several options and then ordered that black students could study in the main reading room at tables marked for their use, even though Rader pointed out that reserving places for blacks would worsen already crowded conditions.[61]

What about black students who wanted to live on campus? The problem was complicated because virtually no landlord in town would rent to them. No African American student requested campus housing during the summer of 1949.[62] In September, however,

60. Ted Beaird to Paul McMinn [*sic*], October 12, 1949, GLCPP, Box 66, Folder: "Negroes." MacMinn was the dean of students. Beaird claimed that "our problem from the standpoint of Union management is *not* with the colored student, but with the white agitators who are causing 9/10 of the commotion that comes up." Perhaps it should be mentioned that the lounge under discussion is now named in honor of Beaird.

61. Paul MacMinn to GLC, November 30, 1949, GLCPP, Box 66, Folder: "Negroes"; and CMF to MacMinn, December 2, 1949, ibid. MacMinn noted that in the Law, Pharmacy, and Music branch libraries blacks and whites shared tables "with no undesirable incidents resulting."

62. Emil Kraettli to Board of Regents, July 30, 1949, GLCPP, Box 66, Folder: "Negroes."

Cross told the Board of Regents that a black male had done so, and the issue "was fully discussed." Once again, the regents were at a loss about what to do, and once again they threw the task to Cross, ordering him to "take such steps as necessary" to provide housing for black students in "units substantially equal to the facilities afforded to white students, but on a segregated basis." The board also asked Cross to request funds from the State Regents for such housing and, looking to the future, to explore the costs for two black dormitories—one to house fifty men and one for fifty women.[63] At the next regents' meeting, Cross reported that two such dormitories together would cost $300,000, and the board told Cross to ask the State Regents for that sum, suggesting that they pass on the request to the governor and to a special session of the legislature.[64] For the present, black students were assigned housing in the prefabs that had been built on the South Base to accommodate the flood of veterans flocking to the university after the war.[65]

As it happened, these events coincided with the start of the football era of Bud Wilkinson, who was appointed head coach in 1947. The fabled teams he put onto Owen Field were beginning their astounding string of fourteen consecutive conference championships, and enthusiasm for football reached a fevered pitch, even before the team won the national championship in 1950. It was inevitable that black students, like their white counterparts, would want to attend the games. But how on earth would it be possible to keep the races separated in the stadium? Cross raised the matter with the regents on July 13, 1949. Admitting that the problem was difficult because "people are in much closer proximity to each other in the stadium than in classrooms," he made his recommendations. Since the blacks were all graduate students, they were entitled to sit on the 50-yard line. Like the white students, each of them was allowed to purchase a ticket for a spouse. The president proposed

63. RM, September 14, 1949, 3227. See also GLC to Roscoe Cate, Walter Kraft, and CMF, September 15, 1949, GLCPP, Box 66, Folder: "Negroes."
64. RM, October 12, 1949, 3299; GLC to Oklahoma State Regents for Higher Education, October 15, 1949, GLCPP, Box 66, Folder: "Negroes."
65. *BWC*, 123.

that "a row or rows beginning at the top of the stadium . . . be designated as required by [the segregation] statute." These rows should
be separated from the seating for white students, either by leaving
empty a few rows in front of the black section or by "erecting a
temporary solid 'wall' behind the first top row of white students;
such wall to be as high as a person's head when seated on the row
in front of the 'wall.'" The regents voted for the wall. Cross noted
that separate restrooms in the stadium would be needed. He also
recommended that it would be a good idea to "privately instruct
the colored students that they should plan to arrive early and in this
manner try to avoid the surging crowds."[66]

That Cross and the regents were aware that they were doing an
embarrassing and perhaps disreputable thing in the stadium is revealed by another provision: "Provide for markers with adhesive backs
that may be put up the morning of the game and taken down soon
after the game and in this manner avoid as much as possible publicity and photographs." Cross hoped that his measures would solve the
problem "with the least possible adverse publicity."[67] By mid-October,
the separating barrier had been pushed back by whites in the row in
front of it by using it as a back rest. Blacks in the first row complained
(justifiably according to Vice President Franklin, who went to the
stadium to look) that it had become extremely uncomfortable for
them. Because there had been "no trouble whatsoever with respect
to Negroes attending football games," Franklin favored removing
the barrier and just marking the rows as reserved for blacks. Instead,
since the regents had expressed a preference for the wall back in
July, the plywood barrier was straightened and braced.[68]

It should be mentioned that the university refused to sell football
tickets to African Americans who were not students. The policy was
thought to be necessary "because of the rather free expression of

66. RM, July 13, 1949, 3184. Cross's recommendations were based on suggestions by Clee Fitzgerald, the business manager for the Collegiate Athletics Department. See Fitzgerald to GLC, July 1, 1949, GLCPP, Box 66, Folder: "Negroes."

67. RM, July 13, 1949, 3184.

68. CMF to Clee Fitzgerald, October 21, 1949, GLCPP, Box 66, Folder:
"Negroes."

emotions found in a football crowd." The authorities feared that "the presence of Negroes who are not students might encourage public demonstrations of racial prejudice," which might endanger the students and "reflect discredit upon the University . . . even though the disorder might be caused by persons not students in the University." Roscoe Cate held out the hope that "sometime in the future, after persons attending . . . football games have become accustomed to seeing Negro students in the crowd, . . . the regulation should be relaxed to permit the sale of tickets to non-student Negroes."[69]

In December 1946 (more than a year before the *Sipuel* case), a black man named Lawrence Lackey told the State Regents that he wanted to become a doctor. He gave notice to the governor in November 1947 and to Cross in March 1948. In May, he complained that "no medical college for Negroes has been established in Oklahoma" and that he had not been accepted at the University of Oklahoma's School of Medicine.[70] Not even the most rabid racist could propose the creation of a black medical school for one student in the same way a separate law school was attempted in the case of Fisher. The expense for the building and the equipment alone would have made such a project unimaginable. Presumably a separate hospital would have to be created so that a black student could gain the requisite training. And if blacks were permitted to enroll in the existing school, how could segregation be maintained during such aspects of the required training as going on "rounds" or observing in the operating room? In fact, it would not be until the year 1951–52 that an African American, Daniel Webster Lee, Jr., was enrolled at the School of Medicine. Lee had graduated from Langston the previous May and was an outstanding student.[71]

As with doctors, so also with nurses. In July 1949, Dianne Lowe, from Muskogee, was the first African American to apply to the university's School of Nursing. "As you probably realize," Cross wrote to

69. Roscoe Cate to GLC, September 23, 1950, GLCPP, Box 80, Folder: "Negro."

70. Lawrence Lackey to M. A. Nash, May 5, 1946, GLCPP, Box 50, Folder: "Negro Question (#3)."

71. Mark R. Everett and Alice Allen Everett, *Medical Education in Oklahoma: The University of Oklahoma School of Medicine and Medical Center, 1932–1964* (Norman: University of Oklahoma Press, 1980), 192.

the young woman's father, "there are many problems involved in offering nurse's training to a Negro under the provisions of the recent State legislation."[72] The dean of the School of Medicine, Mark Everett, thought that the difficulties "would be almost insurmountable." First, "it would be impossible to provide separate housing for the negro student." Second, while it would not be hard to segregate her in classes, "segregation would be an impossibility in the wards, in surgery and in other clinical assignments in which all student nurses must participate." And, finally, Everett frankly stated, "a repercussion by white patients who were attended by colored student nurses would probably be rather severe."[73]

Other difficulties were mentioned by Vernon Cushing, medical director of the University Hospitals. Since there were only thirty-six beds for black patients, no more than ten black nurses could be accommodated. In addition, the black students would be required to have the same number of surgical and obstetrical scrubs as the whites—but that would be possible only if the black nurses would serve white surgery and obstetrics patients. Also the black nurses would have to work in the white outpatient clinics since there was no outpatient service for blacks in the university hospital. If that were not daunting enough, Cushing mentioned two other problems "which would be quite difficult to solve." First, there were no eating facilities for blacks. Meals could not be staggered because the Dietary Department could not prepare more meals than it was already providing. Moreover there was no space for a separate dining room. And second, "we have no living quarters for Negro nurses, and until such quarters are made available, we would be unable to accept them."[74] Not until February 1951 were two African American women enrolled in the School of Nursing.[75]

Some of the difficulties university administrators confronted and some of the questions they had to decide were so bizarre and

72. GLC to C. G. Lowe, July 13, 1949, GLCPP, Box 66, Folder: "Negroes."

73. Everett's remarks were conveyed in a memo from CMF to GLC, August 6, 1949, ibid.

74. Vernon D. Cushing to Mark Everett, July 9, 1949, ibid.

75. Everett and Everett, *Medical Education in Oklahoma*, 192.

unforeseeable that they defy classification. These difficulties came
with the steadiness of hammer blows:

> *November 1946:* The American Veterans Committee, a rec-
> ognized student group, wanted to bring Roscoe Dunjee
> to campus to speak. Could this be permitted? Yes. Au-
> thorized student groups could hold meetings and invite
> speakers, and besides, state law did not prohibit black
> speakers from using university facilities.[76]
>
> *October 1948:* The director of the Guidance Service, W. B. Lem-
> mon, asked if he could "give the aptitude test for the
> American Council on Education to negroes" in school
> buildings? Yes, provided the test was administered on a
> segregated basis.[77]
>
> *October 1948:* Director Lemmon asked a second question.
> The Guidance Service (with the State Mental Hygiene
> Society) ran a "mobile psychological service." Black insti-
> tutions had asked for help. Could the university comply?
> Yes. Cross approved use of the psychological service in
> the black towns of Taft and Boley.[78]
>
> *March 1949:* Charles Wesley Qualls, a black sanitarian from
> Tulsa, wondered if he could audit classes there. Yes. But
> he would need to talk to the Tulsa authorities about class-
> room seating or field trips."[79]
>
> *March 1949:* While Orpherita Daniels was eating lunch in the
> "Jug," three white men and a woman entered the snack
> bar and asked for coffee and milk. They were told that the
> "Jug" was closed to whites between noon and 1:00 P.M.
> One of the men was allowed to buy a sandwich but was
> told not to eat it there. He complied, but the party then

76. Royden Dangerfield to GLC, November 8, 1946, GLCPP, Box 50, Folder:
"Negro Question (#1)."

77. W. B. Lemmon to CMF, October 14, and CMF to Lemmon, October 20,
1948, ibid.

78. Ibid.

79. F. A. Balyeat to Charles Wesley Qualls, March 8, 1949, GLCPP, Box 50,
Folder: "Negro Question (#3).

sat down and "remained at the table with Mrs. Daniels throughout the luncheon period."[80] If this should happen again, how should it be handled?

August 1949: Frank Balyeat was to teach a class for black teachers in Oklahoma City. He asked whether "the regular University application form would suffice for members of this class as it does for white enrollees," rather than using the special admission form for blacks as before. He was told that in keeping with House Bill 405 the regular form would suffice since graduate work in Education was not available at Langston.[81]

May 1949: The Summer Institute for Linguistics held annual sessions in Norman. Could black students be enrolled for these courses? Yes, but only if they found living quarters in Oklahoma City and commuted to Norman. "The Student Union building is prepared to provide segregated food service, but there is no provision in Norman for segregated housing for Negroes."[82]

October 1949: The university's American Legion branch brought Lionel Hampton, the famous jazz musician and composer, for a concert and dance after the homecoming game on October 29. The event was to be held at a building on the South Base. Ela Mae Reynolds, a black student who knew Hampton personally, wanted to attend the event. Could she? There were three options. One was to "exclude colored people from attending the concert." A second was to "rope off a section of the floor for them and allow them to participate in the dancing." The third (which was chosen), was to admit them to the balcony as "listeners."[83]

80. Ted Beaird to Paul MacMinn, March 18, 1949, ibid.

81. F. A. Balyeat to Laurence Snyder and CMF, August 25, 1949, GLCPP, Box 66, Folder: "Negroes."

82. Roscoe Cate to Eugene A. Nida, May 31, 1949, GLCPP, ibid.

83. Lois Brown to GLC, October 21, 1949, GLCPP, Box 66, Folder: "Negroes." Reynolds was to become one of the university's first three African American graduates.

November 1949: M. O. Wilson, chair of the Psychology Department, reported that a black student named Don White wanted to take the Graduate Record Exam. "Will you please indicate how I may handle this situation?" Yes, Mr. White could take the GRE along with white students provided that "as much segregation as possible be provided consistent with existing personnel and facilities."[84]

November 1949: Thirty-nine-year-old Malcolm Whitby, the first black naval veteran of World War II to enter the university, was an experienced musician and bandmaster. He wanted to play in the university's marching band. Was this possible? No. Cross told him that "your qualifications to participate in this activity are not questioned . . . but the state laws specify that instruction must be given to white students and Negroes under conditions of segregation which cannot be provided with respect to a marching band."[85]

December 1949: Mauderie Wilson, one of the university's first black students, was ready to undertake her student teaching. She applied to the School of Education and was told that "at the present time we are unable to send you a favorable reply." The director pledged that she would be told when it would be possible to accommodate her.[86]

February 1950: Professor Walter Campbell, who wrote under the name Stanley Vestal and taught a popular course in Professional Writing, had a question. A black student, already enrolled, wanted to take his course. That course, however, was listed at the undergraduate level (although

84. M. O. Wilson to J. E. Fellows, November 9, and CMF to Wilson, November 14, 1948, ibid.

85. GLC to Malcolm S. Whitby, November 3, 1949, ibid. There is much more to the Whitby case, and we shall return to it in the next chapter. Whitby was to be another one of the university's first three black graduates.

86. Carold D. Holstine to Mauderie Hancock Wilson, December 1, 1949, GLCPP, Box 66, Folder: "Negro Enrolment." Wilson was the third of the university's first three black graduates.

graduate students also enrolled). "Am I correct in believing that negro students are admitted only for graduate
work, and if so what action should I take on his application?" Also, if the student is admitted, is segregation still
required? "I have reason to believe that this is only the
first of several such applications coming my way," Campbell wrote. Vice President Franklin advised that the student be admitted. True, black students are admitted only
for graduate work, but "in a few areas, undergraduate
work has been certified by the Higher Regents" because
comparable undergraduate work was not offered at
Langston. It was also required of black enrollees that
the course in question be taken in connection with their
programs leading to a graduate degree. Regarding their
seating, "they should be given specially assigned seats
in order to provide as much segregation as is consistent
with the facilities available." Usually, "colored students
are seated either in the back or to one side."[87]

April 1950: Vice President Franklin had a question. Prior to
McLaurin's admission, the Graduate Study Center in
Oklahoma City gave Education classes for black teachers.
Back then, the black students "were more interested in
the courses than they were in the credits." Now, however,
some of them were enrolled in the university and they
wanted credit in those courses taken before the University admitted blacks. Can this be allowed? Yes. "Under
the circumstances . . . credit should be given if the work
done fully justifies it."[88]

June 1950: The director of the university's Extension Division, Thurman White, wondered if black visitors came
for short courses or conferences, could the university
feed and house them? Yes, it was once possible only to

87. Walter S. Campbell to E. D. Meacham, February 22, 1950, and CMF to
Campbell, February 25, 1950, GLCPP, Box 66, Folder: "Negroes."
88. CMF to John Cheadle, April 7, and CMF to L. H. Snyder, J. E. Fellows, and
J. R. Rackley, April 14, 1950, ibid.

feed, but not to house them. But as a result of a new judicial case, they could now be housed in buildings on the North Base.[89]

To modern readers, the whole business will seem perfectly insane, and to many Oklahomans of the time it must also have seemed so. But for twenty-one months black students at the University of Oklahoma endured almost unimaginable and degrading discrimination and numerous personal hardships. And officials at the university were required to wrestle with matters that might have been quickly solved by common sense. Meanwhile, thousands of men and women harbored strong feelings on one side or the other of this issue of race separation. Dozens of them were determined to have their say about the way in which the university was handling the matter. People from across the country, most of them with no formal connection to the school, along with Oklahomans from every corner of the state, and faculty and students on the campus itself poured forth their feelings. It will not be surprising that there erupted a vigorous debate about the necessity, the propriety, and the morality of segregation.

89. Thurman White to CMF, June 12, 1950, ibid.

CHAPTER 5

The People Speak

By deciding that George McLaurin and the African American students who came after him could be admitted to the University of Oklahoma, but only on a segregated basis, the state's lawmakers had stumbled onto a policy guaranteed to infuriate everyone. The steadfast defenders of segregation believed that letting blacks into the university was a despicable outrage and morally indefensible. Those opposed to segregation thought it despicable and indefensible to confine them to separated alcoves, roped-off seats, and proscribed tables and toilets. The former were not appeased when told that the admission of blacks was forced by the courts and the Constitution; nor were the latter mollified when reminded that state law left little choice in the way they could treat black students. With all parties in the discussion (if it can be called a discussion) incensed and all of them confident of being in the right, the rhetoric was inevitably inflated and harsh. The parties hurled stinging accusations against one another, filling the air with recriminations and insults. No compromise seemed possible, and no flags of truce passed between the combatants.[1]

1. Several scholars have studied the public dispute over desegregation at the university. See John T. Hubbell, "Some Reactions to the Desegregation of the University of Oklahoma, 1946–1950," *Phylon* 34 (1960): 187–96 (repeating chap. 4 of his master's thesis, previously cited); Michelle Celarier, "A Study of Public Opinion on Desegregation in Oklahoma Higher Education," *ChO* 47 (Autumn 1969): 268–81; William Bittle, "The Desegregated All-White Institution . . . The University of Oklahoma," *Journal of Educational Sociology* 32 (February 1959): 275–82; Earnestine Beatrice Spears, "Social Forces in the Admittance of Negroes"; and Julie Tart Hodo, "Fortifying a Divide: The Oklahoma Press and the Fisher Struggle" (unpublished student paper, 2005), WHC, Vertical File: "Desegregation."

The debate was also shaped and fueled by a pair of circumstances unfolding far from the borders of Oklahoma. First, at the same moment that Fisher and McLaurin were trying to gain entry to the university, the country was witnessing one of the most dramatic presidential campaigns of the twentieth century—the voting was to occur only nineteen days after McLaurin appeared for his first class. To many, it must have seemed as if the venerable Democratic Party was splintering apart and that it was splintering over the very questions raised by attempts to break down segregation at the University of Oklahoma: what was the proper place for black Americans in a democratic society and what was the role of the federal government in deciding the matter?

Many southern white Democrats viewed with alarm the recent attempts of party leaders to lure black voters away from their traditional home in the Republican Party. Blacks were now living (and voting) in heavily urbanized northern states—states with large numbers of votes in the Electoral College. Someone sent George Cross a tract by John U. Barr, of New Orleans. Entitled "For White Men and Women Everywhere," it called upon good southern Democrats to resist the "Negro loving New Dealers" and to hold their own convention "south of the Mason Dixon line."[2] President Truman's creation of a Committee on Civil Rights in December 1946 made many southern whites uneasy. The committee's report, published a year later, recommended far-reaching innovations in federal policy: the creation of a joint congressional committee and a separate branch of the Justice Department to be devoted to civil rights; federal action against lynching; abolition of the poll tax; desegregation of the military; and other measures.[3]

By July 12, 1948, when the Democrats gathered in Philadelphia for their convention, southerners were on edge. On July 13, the Democrats nominated Truman as their candidate and, on July 14, adopted a strong civil rights platform plank. Three dozen southern Democrats walked out of the convention. On July 17, southerners formed the States' Rights Democratic Party (soon known as the

2. A copy of the tract can be found in GLCPP, Box 34, Folder: "Negroes (#1)."
3. *To Secure These Rights, the Report of the President's Committee on Civil Rights* (Washington, D.C.: Government Printing Office, 1947).

Dixiecrats) and nominated Strom Thurmond of South Carolina for the presidency. On July 26, Truman enraged the white South with executive orders ending segregation among federal workers and in the military.[4] Thus many Oklahomans who were fighting against admitting blacks to the state university must have felt that they were part of a brave but beleaguered movement of opposition to federal interference, the erosion of states' rights, and the destruction of southern traditions of race separation and white supremacy.

While the storm over civil rights was the principal domestic matter facing the nation in 1948, the principal international issue was the Cold War confrontation with the Soviet Union. By the time McLaurin went to his first class, all hopes for friendly postwar relations with the Russians had evaporated, and the hostility between the two great powers developed quickly and with fearful intensity. In February 1948, the month when the initial applications of McLaurin and the other five were rejected, Communists took over Czechoslovakia and the last democracy in Eastern Europe swung into the Soviet orbit. Within a month plans were being developed in Brussels that would lead to the formation of NATO. In early April, Truman signed the Marshall Plan into law; its purpose was to shore up war-torn Western European economies in order to weaken the appeal of local Communist parties and stop the expansion of Soviet influence. At the end of June, the Russians cut all roads and rail traffic leading into Berlin, and the Allies launched the famous airlift to supply the besieged city. It was no longer possible to deny that the United States had entered into a serious competition with the Soviet Union. As will be seen, the specter of communism hovered over the debate about desegregation in Oklahoma as both sides appealed to popular fears of the red menace.

Those who favored Oklahoma's segregation policy made their views known—sometimes subtly in newspaper editorials, sometimes with

4. William C. Berman, *The Politics of Civil Rights in the Truman Administration* (Columbus: Ohio State University Press, 1970); Alonzo Hamby, *Beyond the New Deal: Harry S. Truman and American Liberalism* (New York: Columbia University Press, 1973).

less delicacy in letters to the editor or in the many volcanic fulmina-
tions that found their way to the desk of President Cross. Some of
the segregationists' views are striking for their extremity and irratio-
nality. S. N. Fox, from Marietta, Oklahoma, admitted that "all men
are equal in the sight of God," but, he insisted, that sort of equality
was strictly "spiritual." "No where [*sic*] do I find that Jesus taught
Social Equality with the negro, or mixing their blood." Among the
reasons Fox gave for separating black people was that "nature gave
him flesh and glands that throw off a stink to protect him against
moskitoes [*sic*] and insects so he could inhabit low swampy lands."
But, Fox warned, "nothing pleases the negro more than to mix his
blood with the whites. . . . Give the negro Social equality with whites
and he will degenerate and destroy the white race."[5] After the rejection of the six black applicants in January 1948, an anonymous
correspondent from Pekin, Illinois, wrote to congratulate the state
and the university for keeping them out. "I sincerely hope you will
positively retain this stand." This writer was particularly outraged
at the black women in her town "who are nothing but provoca-
teurs . . . going into exclusive shops and deman[d]ing the right to
try on expensive dresses."[6] On the same day, there arrived another
anonymous scrawl, notable for its wandering incoherence. It began
by recalling the trouble that occurred "when everlution [*sic*] broke
out." Apparently, the local banker's son "fell for it," until the writer
told him that "your folks may be monkeys, but I'm not [and] neither are my people. I got the Bible, in the first book in the Bible,
where God made man, & blew breath into his nostrils, never said a
word about a monkey. . . . Now here we are faced with the negro."
The letter writer remembered when a northerner moved to town
and ran for mayor. "He drove down the street, & tipped his big
hat to the negro women" and got elected. Immediately, "the buck
negroes & girls would push our white girls off the side walks." She
advised Cross to hold the line at all costs because "if you open up
the water gaps and let a little stream trickle through, then a big

5. S. N. Fox to J. E. Fellows, undated, GLCPP, Box 34, Folder: "Negroes (#1)."
6. Unsigned letter, January 28, 1948, ibid., Box 34, Folder: "Negroes (#2)."

gush of waves of water will come through."[7] An alumnus from the early 1930s told Cross that "after all, it hasn't been too long since the negro was wearing rings in his nose and practicing canabalism [*sic*] and it is my firm belief that the negro isn't ready to mix socially with our children. . . . I don't want some big black buck even close to my children." The writer asked Cross for advice "toward keeping our segregation in effect so we, as well as our boys & girls, will have a clean place to live."[8]

Other segregationists adopted a more measured tone, and several arguments regularly recurred. Some claimed to believe sincerely that students of both races were entitled to comparable high-quality education. But they insisted that this did not mean that instruction should take place in mixed-race settings. The editors of the *Stillwater News-Press,* for example, wrote that "we've always been convinced that because Negroes are American citizens they are entitled to equal rights. However, in Oklahoma and other states it has been the practice to extend equal rights through separate school facilities."[9] Someone from Earlsboro, Oklahoma, signing as "A Tax Payer," said that "I've two boys that plans [*sic*] to enter the University. Their [*sic*] not going to want to go" because of the presence of blacks. The solution was clear: build the blacks a university of their own. "My taxes are heavy but that's all right. . . . raise the taxes if necessary."[10] Although some were confident that black high schools and Langston were already as good as the comparable white schools, others recognized the inferiority of these institutions and advocated beefing them up until they were substantially equal. Both the *Daily Oklahoman* and the *Norman Transcript* blamed lawmakers for ignoring the warning signs and failing to improve

7. This anonymous letter, dated January 28, 1948, was sent to Chancellor M. A. Nash, who then sent it to Cross. Ibid. The writer refers to "my husband," thereby establishing her gender.

8. Jeff Pritchard to GLC, June 6, 1950, ibid., Box 66, Folder: "Negroes."

9. Cited in Celarier, "Public Opinion on Desegregation," 271, as "Supreme Court Decision," *Stillwater News-Press,* January 13, 1948, 7.

10. A Tax Payer to Regents of Norman University, November 15, 1948, GLCPP, Box 50, Folder: "Negro Question (#2)."

Langston. If they had financed quality programs there, the papers charged, this whole mess could have been avoided.[11] Thus a curious alliance developed between rabid racists and the officials of black schools who saw a chance for better funding for their institutions.

Others opposed to admitting blacks into white schools accused trouble-makers like Fisher and McLaurin of rank hypocrisy. They posed as sincere students, eager for knowledge and professional advancement, but their real purpose was to insinuate themselves into white institutions. A former housemother at the University of Oklahoma thought "these ambitious negroes" should go to black schools. "We do not want our white young people associating with black negroes." It is not education they sought, she said, but only "a step toward equality."[12] A letter writer to the *Daily Oklahoman* declared that from the start of Ada Lois Fisher's fight, "I have doubted her desire for a higher education . . . the only thing she cares about is to force her way into a school where Negroes have never gone."[13] A woman from Guthrie wrote to say that "it is not a desire for Higher Education that motivates, just an attempt to break the Segregation Laws. . . . Let them go to Langston."[14] No less a personage than that old racist and former governor, "Alfalfa Bill" Murray, asserted that "they are trying to break down segregation rather than secure an education."[15]

Many of these segregationists believed that forcing blacks upon the state university was the nefarious work of the NAACP, and that organization received severe criticism for meddling in the affairs of places far away from their New York City headquarters. Fisher, McLaurin, and the others were only pawns in the NAACP's crafty

11. *NT,* January 14, 1948, 4; and *DO,* February 2, 1948, 6.

12. Mrs. Walter Hadley to GLC, February 3, 1949, GLCPP, Box 50, Folder: "Negro Question (#3)."

13. Eunice Nolen, "The Real Reason?" *DO,* January 25, 1948, 6.

14. Nella D. Soward to GLC, February 8, 1949, GLCPP, Box 50, Folder: "Negro Question (#1)."

15. William H. Murray to MQW, August 24, 1948, ibid., Folder: "Negro Question (#2)." Murray suggested setting aside a room on the campus where all instruction of blacks would take place, and marking a section of the campus for the blacks, "with a rule that neither the Negroes nor the Whites shall cross the line . . . under penalty of dismissal from the University.

scheme. The suspicions of those holding this view were essentially "proved" when Fisher refused to have anything to do with the law school that had been created just for her. The same writer who was appalled at the black women in her town who wanted to try on dresses in exclusive shops wrote that what "rankles most of all" was that "some punk in New York is trying to ram this down the throat of Southern people."[16] An Oklahoma City correspondent echoed the allegation: "The McLaurin case and others spring not from a desire of these people to gain further education, but from a long range program of the NAACP to break down segregation." The *Norman Transcript,* which had always been hesitant about desegregation, also blamed the New Yorkers: "Refusal of officials of the NAACP to accept a separate law school for Negroes . . . makes it clear that the real objective of the association is to break down segregation laws in Oklahoma rather than to obtain a good law education for Mrs. Ada Lois Sipuel [Fisher]."[17]

The segregationists urged patience from the black community. Some were even willing to admit that the state's past failure to provide equal educational opportunities amounted to an injustice. The answer, however, was not for blacks to intrude themselves into white schools but to work with well-meaning whites to improve the black ones. The process would take time, as any reasonable person must realize, but much progress had been already made and more was on the horizon. An editorial in the *Daily Oklahoman,* entitled "Shall All This Be Sacrificed," warned that "all the good that has been accomplished [in race relations] in all these years of patient effort is being threatened to some extent by the intemperate courses of extremists in both races."[18] A student's letter to the *Oklahoma Daily* tried to put the state's segregation laws in a kindly way: those laws "are probably the most important set of legislated laws ever made to govern the regularity of the development of the Negro race. They allow the Negro to become educated, so he in turn can teach others of his race."[19]

16. Unsigned letter, January 28, 1948, ibid., Box 34, Folder: "Negroes (#2)."
17. *NT,* January 21, 1948, 4
18. *DO,* January 31, 1948, 4.
19. *OD,* February 3, 1948, 2.

As might have been expected, defenders of segregation found plenty of support in Holy Scripture. Marietta's S. N. Fox put it most directly: "The Bible teaches it is strictly again[st] God's will and a great sin for whites and negros [*sic*] to marry, and produce emalgimated [*sic*] races."[20] Fox laid it out in a printed tract he titled "Thy Will Be Done on Earth as It Is in Heaven": We see in the natural world, created by a wise God, that "birds of a feather flock together. Wolves go in packs, cattle and sheep, buffalos and most all animals go with their kind. Nature has designed it that way. God placed the negro in his countries and the white man and other tribes in their countries. So we see God planned segregation."[21]

As far as Cold War ideology was concerned, segregationists had been arguing for years that the Communists and their naive fellow leftists yearned for nothing so much as the "mongrelization" of America. Communists had been unashamed advocates of civil rights for blacks even before the war, and every organized effort to arouse blacks into making ever more dangerous demands was led, openly or in secret, by the "reds" and their friends. Some operated under direct orders of the Kremlin; others innocently cooperated, believing that they were actually doing good by undermining traditional race relations in America. The Russians engaged in those efforts partly to sow discontent and anger among the normally contented and docile black population and partly because they knew that America would be demoralized by diluting the Anglo-Saxon blood that had accounted for so much of the nation's strength and success. A Texas woman hoped that the South would "fight all the Communist or Socialist inspired negro demands for entrance to white Universities, not because the negro is interested in the subjects . . . but because he is the tool of the Communist-Socialist supported organization" the NAACP.[22]

Finally, segregationists put heavy emphasis on what they saw as two inevitable and terrifying consequences of allowing blacks and

20. S. N. Fox to J. E. Fellows, undated, GLCPP, Box 34, Folder: "Negroes (#1)."

21. A copy of Fox's tract can be found in GLCPP, Box 50, Folder: "Negro Question (#1)."

22. Bess McCullen to GLC, October 14, 1948, ibid., Folder: "Negro Question (#2)."

whites in the same classroom. First, they predicted that such mix-ing would produce enormous animosity. There would be confu-sion, friction, hatred, and the likelihood of violence. Oklahoma's assistant attorney general, Fred Hansen, argued that if Oklahoma's segregation laws were abrogated, "chaos would result." The woman who worried that the Communists were behind desegregation ef-forts sent Cross a newspaper report of a black man raping a white woman, asserting that this would be "a common occurrence if all state rights were taken from the South."[23] A letter writer named J. C. Landry warned Cross that "the south will never tolerate our children eating, sleeping & what not with the negro. We will have civil war—your city better get busy & protest."[24] A Tulsa woman, claiming to "speak for all Southern women of Oklahoma," warned that "the South fought one war over State's Rights and we will do it again if necessary."[25]

The second result of having the two races going to school to-gether was even more frightening. In fact, this fear was expressed so often and with such heightened urgency and extreme language that one suspects that this dread lay at the very heart of the re-sistance to desegregation. Paul Haggard, an Oklahoma City busi-nessman, laid out the danger: "If I had to sit by Negroes, pretty soon there would be Negroes sitting by grade school kids. They would start running around together, then they would start dat-ing, and that would lead to intermarriage. And that is wrong."[26] Put young blacks and whites together and social contacts would inevitably develop, and how then could intermarriage and mixed-race offspring be avoided? Once again, the laurel for direct sim-plicity must go to S. N. Fox: "Anti segregation laws mean the negro bucks are free to marry our Daughters."[27] A letter writer to the *Daily Oklahoman* claimed to support equal education for blacks, but, the writer added, "Wouldn't it just break your heart to see one of your

23. Ibid.

24. J. C. Landry to "Gentlemen," June 7, 1950, ibid., Box 66, Folder: "Negroes."

25. Mrs. E. B. Chaney to GLC, October 8, 1948, ibid., Box 50, Folder: "Negro Question (#2)."

26. *OD*, January 30, 1948, 1.

27. S. N. Fox to J. E. Fellows, undated, GLCPP, Box 34, Folder: "Negroes (#2)."

grandchildren with an entirely different color skin from your own? I'm afraid that's what it would come to."[28] The *Norman Transcript* was grudgingly ready to concede that desegregation might perhaps be feasible at the graduate level but only because persons of that age "could mingle freely without . . . development of a tendency for mixed marriages, which, after all, is the basic objection to free mingling of whites and Negroes."[29]

It must not be assumed that the racists held a monopoly on extreme language. Those who favored admitting blacks to the university and who opposed subjecting them to segregation were also capable of vituperation. John White of San Francisco began his letter to the university regents with these words: "Cowards all, You are the most contemptible yellow dogs under a tolerant God's sun. You ignorant currs [*sic*] are so full of hate. . . . I hope the government throws all of you in jail."[30] Another Californian wrote that he now understood "why your breed of Americans is called the 'Oakie-type' [*sic*], and called that with a mixture of genuine pity and strong contempt. . . . It is unfortunate that your kind is allowed to be a part of our nation." He closed his letter (in case there might be some doubt) "with the greatest condemnation."[31] A woman from New Jersey wrote that McLaurin was "probably far superior to those of you who in your stupid, arrogant, superiority plan to segregate him,"[32] and a Colorado high school student believed that "the way you are treating G. W. McLaurin . . . is one of the worst things I have ever heard of. . . . It[']s just plain rotten."[33] "You are really trying to make the state of Oklahoma look ridiculous," wrote another correspondent, "for you would take even such as Al Capone . . . but

28. *DO,* February 1, 1948, 14A.

29. *NT,* October 1, 1948.

30. John B. White to Board of Regents and Dean of the Law School, January 19, 1948, GLCPP, Box 34, Folder: "Negroes (#1)."

31. Richard L. Weed to Board of Regents, February 2, 1948, ibid., Folder: "Negroes (#2).

32. Margaret Brown to GLC, October 14, 1948, ibid.

33. Gordon White to GLC, October 15, 1948, ibid., Box 50, Folder: "Negro Question (#2)."

would reject George Washington Carver, or Marian Anderson, only because of an insignificant difference."[34]

The wide reproduction of those infamous photographs of McLaurin sitting at his desk as if he were carrying some fearsome disease sparked a flood of angry letters. One writer sent Cross a copy of the picture from his Seattle paper: "It's certain . . . that education in your college hasn't progressed since the founding of the college. Your policy of segregating negroes is ignorant and shameful."[35] Someone from New Jersey mailed Cross the item from the *New York Times,* asking, "Is this University which you head in the U.S.A., or in some Fascist Regime[?] The people in your state are ignorant and away out of line and you sir, are *not* a brave man or you would not tolerate having one of your students sit in an ante-room because his pigmentation happens to be dark."[36] D. K. Wallen, from Minnesota, thought that segregating McLaurin was "completely warped and unwarranted. As an institute of higher learning you have certainly sunk to lower darkness."[37] A woman who had lived in Tulsa during the Murray administration remembered being embarrassed for her former state back then: "But looking at the pictures of Mr. McLaurin, so hygenically segregated . . . I really reached a new low in civic pride."[38] There were others just as derisive.

Like some of the segregationists, some of those opposing segregation were able to marshal more reasoned and moderate language. Their principal argument was that the treatment of McLaurin and the other black students was contrary to American beliefs about democracy and Christianity, beliefs which were considered self-evident and beyond dispute. The typical letter writer would declare that he or she was a "believer in democracy" or "a Christian" or both, and then launch into the ways the university's practice was an affront to American principles or to the teachings of Jesus and the Bible. "As a Christian, a democrat and an American," wrote

34. Clarence H. Lee to University of Oklahoma, October 21, 1948, ibid.
35. L. E. Grunden to GLC, October 16, 1948, ibid.
36. [Name indecipherable] to GLC, October 20, 1948, ibid.
37. D. K. Wallen to Board of Regents, October 16, 1948, ibid.
38. Mrs. Fred Norton to GLC, October 24, 1948, ibid.

Alan Thomas of Stillwater, "it is my duty . . . to cry out against the senseless and criminal practice of segregation."[39] "I am a Christian," wrote Ruth Thomson, also of Stillwater, "and believe that we are all children of God and therefore brothers. I am an American. The American ideal that all races and nations can live together with equality of opportunity and equality before the law is very dear to my heart."[40] A Pennsylvania woman scoffed at Cross because he had no doubt "spouted pomposely [*sic*], many times . . . about the greatness of our country where all men are created equal."[41]

A writer from Minnesota reminded the university's Board of Regents of the words of Paul in Acts 17–26 and Galatians 3–28, where he asserts the unity of humanity.[42] Cornelia Raymond, at Vassar College, saw McLaurin's story in the *New York Herald-Tribune,* and wrote to pose a question. "Perhaps you can answer it using the enclosed stamped envelope. We all grant I suppose that negroes are Christians and will go to heaven. Must they there be admitted on a segregated basis?"[43] A woman from Norfolk, Nebraska, saw the picture of McLaurin in her local newspaper and echoed Raymond: "I'm sure he won't be obliged to sit at a special desk, or eat in a special room in the next world. Why should he here?"[44]

When it came to the imperatives of the Cold War, desegregationists were just as eager as their opponents to refer to the struggle with the Soviet Union. In their version of the contest, America was trying to portray itself to the world as the home of freedom, justice, and decency, while the Russians under Joseph Stalin were characterized as an enslaved people. But this picture was impossible to maintain as long as the United States was reducing black Americans

39. Alan Thomas to GLC, June 20, 1948, ibid., Box 34, Folder: "Negroes (#1)."
40. Ruth C. Thomson to GLC, June 22, 1948, ibid., Folder: "Negroes (#2)."
41. Margaret D. Brown to GLC, undated, ibid., Box 50, Folder: "Negro Question (#2)."
42. Acts 17–26 reads, in part, "God hath made of one blood all nations of men." Galatians 3–28 reads, in part, "There is neither Jew nor Greek—there is neither bond nor free . . . for all are one in Christ Jesus."
43. Cornelia Raymond to GLC, October 25, 1948, GLCPP, Box 50, Folder: "Negro Question (#2)."
44. Mrs. L. C. Barnes to "Dear Sirs," October 21, 1948, ibid.

to second-class citizenship and degrading segregation. It was clear, moreover, that a vital, perhaps even a decisive aspect of the competition between the United States and the Soviet Union would be in efforts to gain friendship and support among the dark-skinned peoples of Latin America, Asia, and Africa. But every time an African diplomat was denied service in a Washington restaurant or couldn't book a room in a Miami hotel, every report of physical abuse or of discrimination that implied the inferiority of nonwhites, every photo of a "colored only" water fountain in Georgia or of George McLaurin separated from his classmates in Oklahoma, meant that the Russians picked up points in the contest. Historian Mary Dudziak asked, "How could American democracy be . . . a model for those struggling against Soviet oppression, if the United States itself practiced brutal discrimination against minorities within its own borders?"[45] Several who protested what was happening in Norman noted the Cold War implications of Oklahoma's race policies. A woman from Stillwater regretted that those policies "furnish fuel for disparaging comments about our country by the Russian press."[46] A Californian lamented that Oklahoma's behavior gave a weapon to the Soviets "who accuse us of talking big about democracy and then repudiating it in practice."[47] Stillwater resident Alan Thomas thought that America "cannot hope to combat undemocratic forces outside its borders without correcting injustices within."[48]

Alongside the piles of letters that faulted the university for not living up to the tenets of democracy or ignoring the teachings of Christianity or giving the Russians ammunition with which to embarrass us, there were others that registered additional criticisms. Several referred to the hypocrisy of waging war against a racist Germany while adopting racist practices at home. "How can we tell the

45. Mary Dudziak, *Cold War Civil Rights: Race and the Image of American Democracy* (Princeton: Princeton University Press, 2000), 3.

46. Emma Louise Ellis to Board of Regents, January 14, 1948, GLCPP, Box 50, Folder: "Negro Question (#1)."

47. Clarence H. Lee to University of Oklahoma, October 21, 1948, ibid., Folder: "Negro Question (#2)."

48. Alan Thomas to GLC, June 20, 1948, ibid., Box 34, Folder: "Negroes (#1)."

world that Hitler was wrong in his race superiority when the highest institutions of Education at home force this program upon its people?"[49] Jacques Leiser, of Syracuse, asked, "If we are willing to cross an ocean to show these better ideals to foreigners, should we not have the responsibility of practicing them in our own country first?"[50] A number of critics warned that the university was becoming an object of national derision. One Oklahoman was sure that McLaurin's treatment "will be noted and ridiculed by newspapers all over the country."[51] A man from Illinois told Cross that "thousands upon thousands of people are ashamed for you," and a letter writer to the *Daily Oklahoman* warned that when the story of McLaurin's treatment gets around, "it will make Oklahoma the laughing stock of the nation."[52] Laurence Snyder, dean of the Graduate College, told Cross that because of the treatment of McLaurin, "in my travels I find the State, the University, and the Graduate College the target of much criticism."[53] Others mentioned the contradiction between the highest purposes of education and the practices at the university. Mrs. Frank Duffy, from Burlingame, California, telegraphed Cross on the day of McLaurin's first class that "your action of segregation . . . makes a mockery of all our colleges are supposed to teach."[54]

The crucial epicenter of the discussion, of course, was the campus. How did the various segments of the university community respond to the policies being enacted daily at their school? It is appropriate to start with the black students themselves, the young women and men who, in pursuit of educational opportunity, braved the

49. Mrs. Jen M. Lewis to GLC, November 27, 1948, ibid.

50. Jacques Leiser to Frank Balyeat, October 15, 1948, ibid., Box 50, Folder: "Negro Question (#2)."

51. W. E. Alspaugh to GLC, October 14, 1948, ibid.

52. Carl Barrs to GLC, August 12, 1948, ibid., Folder: "Negro Question (#1)"; A. E. Alspaugh to the editor, *DO*, November 28, 1948, 22.

53. Laurence Snyder to GLC, November 29, 1948, GLCPP, Box 50, Folder: "Negro Question (#3)."

54. Mrs. Frank Duffy to GLC, October 14, 1948, ibid., Folder: "Negro Question (#2)."

demands of the law, the attitudes and traditions of the town of Norman, and, to some extent, the prejudices they encountered at the university.

Thanks to Earnestine Spears's master's thesis of 1951, we have a fairly good statistical picture of the earliest group of black students.[55] For her thesis, she questioned 65 of her fellow African American students. The great majority of them came from urbanized counties surrounding Cleveland County, home of the university. Almost half (30) arrived from Oklahoma City. By 1951, some of these lived on the campus during the summer session. During the regular school year, however, most (being working teachers) commuted from the city for Saturday morning classes—the trip was about twenty miles each way and took forty minutes by car or bus. Nine of the 65 were from Wewoka, which had been founded a century before by a freedman and a group of black Seminoles. Seven came from Muskogee County, but only 3 were from Tulsa, probably because Oklahoma A&M in nearby Stillwater was, by this time, also starting to accept black students. Only 11 of the 65 came to the university directly, with no break after finishing their undergraduate work. Of the others, 39 were teachers, almost all of them pursuing graduate work in some field of Education.

Thirty-five of the 65 had been undergraduates at Langston. They had chosen that school because of its proximity to their homes and the low cost of attending. Those who could afford to go elsewhere rejected Langston principally because it was unaccredited. Interestingly, a few of the students attended out-of-state predominantly white schools, but all those who did so transferred to black institutions for their graduations. Those not from Langston chose undergraduate schools both because they were accredited and because they were close (7 students did undergraduate work in Texas and 5 others in Kansas and Arkansas). The students also chose schools on the basis of strength in fields they wanted to study. As undergraduates, they pursued a variety of majors. More than 20

55. The figures in these two paragraphs are derived from chapter 4 of Spears's thesis, "Social Forces in the Admittance of Negroes."

majored in Education, another 10–15 in the Social Sciences, and no more than 2 or 3 in the other possible major fields of study.

Starting with the summer session of 1949, every African American student attending the University of Oklahoma was handed a two-page statement outlining racial restrictions.[56] Signed by Vice President Carl Mason Franklin, the statement reviewed state law (quoting from House Bill 405) and listed the rules regarding the library and eating facilities. The handout also gave the locations of the five campus restrooms that black students could use. A general attitude among black students about these arrangements is difficult to discern. It is reasonable to suppose that most, if not all, resented both the rules and the racist attitudes that lay behind them. For the most part they remained silent, purchasing their chances for a decent education with patience and endurance of the indignities.

There were, however, some notable exceptions—black students who were willing to protest against and actively resist the oppressive conditions imposed upon them. Among these were students who complained about the inadequate arrangements in the library or the state of their set-aside space at the stadium. Others demonstrated their resistance in different ways. In January 1950, for instance, Cross got a note from his secretary: a staff member "phoned yesterday afternoon . . . to tell you that the three Negroes who eat at Woodrow Wilson Center at noon are not observing the rules about sitting at a certain table."[57] In August 1949, Dean Fellows asked all the black students who intended to enroll for the fall semester to indicate their home addresses, the dates they applied for admission, and their intended fields of study. Only one refused to answer any questions. She was none other than Penninah McLaurin.[58] We do not know if Orpherita Daniels conspired with the white students who broke the rules and sat with her at lunch, but she certainly did nothing to discourage them. These "troublemakers" tended to be older than the average, and three of

56. CMF, "Statement to Be Given to Each Student of the Colored Race Enrolled for Summer Term, 1949," GLCPP, Box 50, Folder: "Negro Question (#1)."

57. Lois Brown to GLC, January 12, 1950, ibid., Box 66, Folder: "Negroes."

58. "Negro Enrolment for 1st Semester, 1949–50," ibid.

them deserve special recognition on account of their bold determination to contest segregation.

One of them was Earnestine Spears, whose 1951 thesis has been mentioned. She was living in the prefabs on the South Base. In September 1950 she wrote a courteous but firm letter to President Cross. She claimed that she had applied for housing in the Women's Quadrangle (Cate Center) six weeks earlier and that she had paid her $10 deposit. She had heard nothing from the Women's Counselor, Dorothy Truex, but she knew that white women who had applied after her had already been assigned rooms; she also knew that there were vacancies. "Would you please advise me as to why I was not admitted to the Women's Quadrangle?"[59] Two days later she repeated her complaints to Roscoe Dunjee. She counted thirty-five ways in which the facilities for black women in the prefabs were inferior to those of white women in the Quadrangle. She mentioned, for example, the lack of facilities for ironing clothes. There was no such facility in the prefabs but one on every floor of every dormitory in the Quadrangle.[60] There were other complaints: "The white girls receive mail in their dormitories. Upon protest, the Counselor agreed that we could receive mail in the Lounge of the [Wilson] Center—still an inconvenience of walking from one to three blocks. To mail a letter we must walk to the Post Office approximately 10 street blocks from the housing. White women mail letters in the dormitories."[61] Spears registered another grievance in July 1950. A university class went on a field trip to Tinker Air Force

59. Earnestine B. Spears to GLC, September 29, 1950. A copy of the letter to Cross was sent to the NAACP. See NAACPPM, Reel 13, Frame 987.

60. A white friend let Spears use the iron on her floor, but then a sign appeared saying that nonpaying guests were not to use the ironing boards, bathrooms, or hair dryers. Spears paid no attention because she paid the same $240 fee as any student. Still, the dorm counselor told her that she could not use her friend's facility. Next morning, Spears went to see Truex, who backed up the prohibition and said that similar notes were posted generally. Spears and her friend canvassed "every floor of that dormitory and the other 16 dormitories" and found no other such note.

61. Earnestine B. Spears, to RD, October 2, 1950, NAACPPM, Reel 13, Frames 984–85.

Base and Will Rogers Airport. When they got to Will Rogers, black students were refused food service, and they, in turn, refused any of the makeshift eating arrangements they were hastily offered. Although the incident had nothing to do with university policy, Cross wrote Spears an apology and pledged to avoid such incidents in the future.[62] Spears was more vocal in expressing her feelings than many other black students but one can assume that she was probably expressing resentments common to many of them.

A second noteworthy student was Malcolm Whitby. He was the reporter sent by Dunjee to cover the story of the six applicants who appeared in Cross's office to seek admission in January 1948 Whitby was also the student who hoped to join the marching band but was prohibited from doing so. Whitby was thirty-nine when he entered the University of Oklahoma in June 1949, and was an extraordinary musician. Having taken up the clarinet at ten, he performed as a soloist throughout the Southwest while still in high school. He studied with the finest teachers in the country and had been bandmaster at Langston. In September 1942, he was inducted into the U.S. Navy as a musician and served for twenty-nine months. (He was the first black navy veteran to enter the university.[63]) After his discharge, he resumed his studies with a former member of the New York Philharmonic, joined the New York City Civic Symphony, and began writing a manual for teaching sight-reading using audiovisual materials. In October 1945, Whitby returned to Oklahoma to help his ailing father. He hoped to earn a degree in Education and then teach and become bandmaster at a black high school or college. He claimed that experience in the university's marching band would be vital for the career he hoped to follow.[64]

Dunjee wrote Cross, telling Whitby's story and emphasizing his wish to get into the band. Whitby's adviser endorsed the request and another instructor approved his enrollment. But when Whitby

62. Garold D. Holstine to GLC, July 20, 1950; GLC to Earnestine Spears, July 21, 1950, GLCPP, Box 80, Folder: "Negro."

63. Ron Logan, "Whitby Is First Negro Vet at OU," *OD*, June 22, 1949, 1.

64. Whitby reviewed his extraordinary career in a long letter to Marshall, November 5, 1949, NAACPPM, Reel 13, Frames 996–98.

reported to the band room with his instrument, the person in charge would not let him practice.[65] Instead of answering Dunjee's letter, Cross phoned him. Dunjee reported to Thurgood Marshall that he and Cross "talked for quite a time, during which [Cross] said he was in pretty bad shape and did not know what to do" because a couple of white students were raising questions about the university's non-compliance with the new segregation law. In response to the phone call, Dunjee drove to Norman for a private talk. He advised Cross to write a letter to Whitby, denying his request to play in the band "solely because it will violate the provisions of the segregation act." Cross said he "wanted to cooperate in any way that would bring the issue to a head, and he frankly said he would do anything to help us get the thing in the courts."[66] On November 3, Cross wrote Whitby just as Dunjee suggested. The next day, Dunjee urged Marshall and the NAACP to bring suit on Whitby's behalf because the case was "a natural." Marshall agreed that there was indeed "the basis for a good law suit," but advised delaying until two pending cases could be heard and decided by the High Court.[67]

A third black student whose resistance became a constant irritant for administrators and who deserves the prize for principled rebelliousness was Julius Caesar Hill, a forty-six-year-old man from Tulsa. He had graduated in English from Langston in 1932, and, except for four years in the navy, taught in high schools. He tried for admission to the University of Oklahoma in January 1949 but was vetoed by the attorney general because of Williamson's insistence on prior notice.[68] Hill waited until September, and the trouble started immediately. In filling out the application form for university housing, Hill came to the question asking his race. He

65. RD to GLC, October 22, 1949, GLCPP, Box 66, Folder: "Negroes." A copy can be found in NAACPPM, Reel 13, Frames 994–95. See also RD to GLC, October 29, 1949, GLCPP, Box 66, Folder: "Negroes."

66. RD to TM, November 4, 1949, NAACPPM, Reel 13, Frame 991.

67. TM to RD, November 8, 1949, ibid., Frame 1001. For the two pending cases, see the next chapter. Whitby was to graduate from the university in June 1950; he never played in the school's marching band.

68. "Negro Checks on Enrolment," *DO*, February 3, 1949, 4.

wrote "American" and sent in his deposit. When he got to campus and it was seen that he was not white, he was denied housing. He refused to accept the cancellation of his reservation: "I have all my belongings here, and I intend to stay tonight."[69] Finally, he agreed to live at the old Bachelor Officers Quarters on the South Base.

A month into Hill's first semester, Vice President Franklin got an anxious note from the chair of the Psychology Department: a student had told him "that Mr. Julius Caesar Hill, a colored student, refuses at times to occupy the space in the main reading room of the library reserved for colored students." This was not exactly news to Franklin. Librarian Jesse Rader had already informed him "once or twice" that Hill was not sitting where he was supposed to sit.[70] Three weeks later, Hill complained about eating facilities on Sundays— the university food services were closed, and unlike white men, Hill could not be served in town. Finally, the university installed a hot plate and a refrigerator in Hill's room.[71] A few days after that, another note from Rader to Franklin: "Mr. John March reports to me that on November 28th, Mr. Julius C. Hill was seated in the Reference Room at the wrong table. He has just reported to me . . . that he is again seated in the wrong room at the wrong table." On the next day, more of the same. "Miss Opal Carr has just reported to me that on this day, 11:00 o'clock A.M., Mr. Julius C. Hill was seated in the Reference Room at the wrong table." Dean of Students Paul MacMinn, promised to have a talk with him.[72] By January, Hill was repeating his library performance at the dining hall, sitting wherever he liked. Even worse, some white students would walk over and sit with him. MacMinn compromised. He told the staff to have the black students sit at the reserved table but "make no issue" if white

69. *Rocky Mountain News*, September 15, 1949, 11. From Colorado, Rita Devane sent the clipping to GLC, along with a denunciatory letter. GLCPP, Box 66, Folder: "Negroes."

70. M. C. Wilson to CMF, October 2, 1949, and CMF to Wilson, October 22, 1949, ibid.

71. GLC to Paul MacMinn, and MacMinn to GLC, both on November 9, 1949, ibid.

72. J. L. Rader to CMF, November 29, 1949, Rader to CMF, November 30, 1949, Paul MacMinn to CMF, December 2, 1949, ibid.

students came to sit with him. MacMinn promised another talk, "so that the policy can be more fully interpreted to him."[73]

In these ways, then, through quiet compliance, protest, and outright defiance did the first black students respond to the restrictions they faced at the University of Oklahoma.

The school's faculty and administration were heavily in favor of admitting African American students. No surveys of their opinions were taken, but there is strong evidence of their feelings. One hint of the faculty's view of racial matters came in May 1948, when the Faculty Senate resolved that "restrictions due to race in participation of athletics at the University be removed."[74] President Cross, whose own attitude is well documented, claimed that the faculty was "unanimous" in support of enrolling black students.[75] No doubt some in both the administration and the faculty still favored measures of segregation on the campus while endorsing the admission of black students (particularly after the courts had spoken). In contrast, there were some faculty who were vocal and uncompromising advocates of complete equality.[76]

Perhaps the most eloquent statement from the faculty and administration came from Laurence Snyder, dean of the Graduate

73. Paul MacMinn to GLC, January 17, 1950, ibid.

74. E. E. Hatfield to GLC, May 17, 1948, GLCPP, Box 34, Folder: "Negroes (#1)."

75. Dr. Cross shared this opinion with me in a conversation. When I expressed skepticism about a unanimous approval of desegregation among so large a group of people as the faculty (numbering more than seven hundred), he replied that he "knew of no exceptions."

76. Among the most energetic and outspoken in their advocacy were Royden Dangerfield (professor of Government and vice president of the University of Oklahoma until leaving in 1948 for the University of Illinois); his colleagues in Government, Cortez A. M. Ewing and John Leek; Paul David (Zoology); Henry Foster, Jr. (Law); M. O. Wilson (Psychology); Jens Rud Nielsen, Richard Fowler, and Gwyn Stone (Physics); Frank Balyeat (Education); Nathan Court (Mathematics); William Livezey (History); Carleton Berenda (Philosophy); and a handful of others. Two campus clergymen were also particularly visible in support of desegregation; they were Presbyterian minister John Thompson and Nicholas Comfort, director until 1946 of the university's affiliated School of Religion.

College since September 1947. Snyder was a world-famous geneti-
cist, the author of many books and articles. On February 23, 1948,
after only a few months on the campus, he delivered his first general
talk to 250 members of the Graduate Faculty. "If universities, which
are supposedly the epitome of culture and learning in our society,
cannot practice the principles of democracy and illustrate them by
example," Snyder declared, "where in the world will they be illustrated and practiced?" To the applauding crowd, he expressed the
hope that "in the very near future the Graduate College would be
open to every intellectually qualified Oklahoman" irrespective of
race.[77] *Time Magazine* noticed Snyder's speech and the audience's
approval of it.[78] A few months later, Snyder wrote to Cross, stating
that "Oklahoma and the University took a great forward step in the
direction of human rights and justice when they admitted a negro
to the Graduate College." But, he continued, that act was sullied
by two facts. First, it was done "under coercion from the federal
courts," and second, McLaurin's admission "was carried out on a
segregated basis." Nothing could be done about the first fact, but
Snyder, who expressed "great satisfaction" in the admirable attitude
of the administration, urged Cross and the regents to rectify the
second and remove the barriers to McLaurin's full participation
in collegiate life. "I have talked personally with many faculty members, and I find a very large majority of them in favor of removing
the segregation restrictions."[79] Cross assured Snyder that his personal views were "in agreement with your own."[80]

Student sentiments on admitting African Americans to the University of Oklahoma are difficult to assess. Of those who actually
articulated their views, some favored keeping the university an

77. Quoted in *BWC*, 79–80.

78. *Time Magazine* 51 (March 8, 1948): 86.

79. Laurence H. Snyder to GLC, November 29, 1948, GLCPP, Box 50, Folder:
"Negro Question (#3)." See also Snyder to Fred McCuistion, November 8, 1950,
GLCPP, Box 80, Folder: "Negroes." Snyder left Norman in 1958 to become presi-
dent of the University of Hawaii.

80. GLC to Laurence H. Snyder, December 20, 1948, GLCPP, Box 50, Folder:
"Negro Question (#3)."

exclusively white school by denying admission to any black applicant, some advocated admission of black students without any restrictions whatever, and still others were willing to admit blacks but only on a segregated basis. Those who took any of the three positions rejected absolutely the other two. Several surveys of student opinion were attempted, but none of them would pass modern standards of scientific validity. Thus, sweeping assertions about student opinion must be avoided. Nevertheless, at least three generalizations seem fairly sustainable.

First, it is important not to underestimate the extent to which many students—perhaps even a majority of them—were relatively indifferent to the entire matter. They went, as usual, to their classes, their dances, and their football games. They signed no petitions, participated in no demonstrations, attended no debates or panels, expressed no more than a bland pro or con opinion in conversations with their friends. They worried much more about the next exam or the next date or the next game or their future careers than they did about George McLaurin, Ada Lois Fisher, and the others.

Second, it seems apparent that those in favor of admitting blacks and eliminating discrimination were much more active than those favoring exclusion or the enforcement of segregation. On January 30, 1948 (two days after McLaurin and his five companions tried unsuccessfully to enroll), about 350 students who wanted to maintain segregation managed a feeble demonstration on the North Oval. About the same number signed a petition urging the Board of Regents "to uphold the racial segregation laws . . . and to prohibit the admission of Negro students."[81] But except for an occasional letter to the *Daily,* that demonstration and the petition were about the extent of organized opposition to admitting black students.

Meanwhile, advocates of desegregation undertook a whirlwind of furious activity on a dozen fronts. That weak pro-segregation gathering on January 30 was only a pathetic response to the more than a thousand students who had, the day before, braved freezing

81. The petition and signatures can be found in GLCPP, Box 34, Folder: "Negroes (#1)."

temperatures to demonstrate on behalf of admitting blacks. The earlier demonstration, organized by a student named Howard Friedman, was timed to coincide with the 10:00 A.M. regents' meeting. It culminated in burning a copy of the Fourteenth Amendment, dumping the ashes into an envelope, and marching to the post office to mail them to President Truman. Their action signaled the death of the amendment's Equal Protection Clause as far as Oklahoma was concerned.[82]

These desegregation activists joined or started energetic organizations. Especially effective were the Race Relations Committee of the YMCA-YWCA, the Student Christian Association, and the Interreligious Council. Some Norman students joined with others from Langston and Stillwater to form the Joint Committee for Equal Education.[83] These groups staged rallies, debates, and panel discussions; they invited outside speakers, including African Americans,[84] and circulated literature and reading lists. They allied themselves with the NAACP, the National Conference of Christians and Jews, and the Southern Conference of Human Welfare. The activist students took down the signs and dismantled classroom barriers; they made a point of walking over to greet and shake hands with newly arriving black students; they sat at the "Colored Only" tables in the Union, the Wilson Center, and the library. They also raised money for litigation—the Sipuel case cost approximately $26,000, and the McLaurin case, around $15,000.[85] A delegation of seven white students drove to Roscoe Dunjee's home in Oklahoma City to urge the NAACP to take action on behalf of a young black man who wanted to study petroleum engineering.

82. *BWC*, 67–69.

83. Spears, "Social Forces in the Admittance of Negroes," 30–34.

84. As early as February 1946, a group of students at the university invited Marshall to give a talk at John Thompson's Presbyterian church. Dunjee, in conveying the invitation to Marshall, said that he had himself spoken at that church "a half dozen times." RD to TM, February 18, 1946, NAACPPM, Reel 13, Frame 361.

85. Cited in Spears, "Social Forces in the Admittance of Negroes," 32, as H. W. Williamston to Spears, June 20, 1951. Williamston was president of the Oklahoma Conference of the NAACP. Ada Lois Sipuel Fisher gives his name (erroneously) as "Williamson."

Two white students, George Bassett and Edith Long, welcome McLaurin to the campus, October 1948. Courtesy *The Oklahoman*.

The student newspaper favored more liberal admission policies. On the day of McLaurin's first class, editor Alan Jenkins wrote that the "regents should get on their little scooters and catch up with the times. If present policies regarding Negro admission are continued, O.U. will be the last stronghold of an outmoded custom as ridiculous as wearing wind goggles in a [brand new] '49 sedan."[86] Some students suggested organizing a boycott of Norman merchants who refused to serve African Americans. (One administrator wondered if they wouldn't need "to boycott *all* the stores?"[87])

An early poll, conducted by the YMCA-YWCA Race Relations Committee and inspired by Presbyterian minister John Thompson,

86. *OD*, October 16, 1948, 4.
87. Lois Brown to GLC, February 24, 1950, GLCPP, Box 66, Folder: "Negroes."

queried fifty students about possibly mixing with blacks in classes, dorms, eating places, and at work. The findings, analyzed by Psychology Department chair M. O. Wilson, "were highly encouraging, in view of the results expected." Almost half of those questioned expressed "a mildly pro-Negro attitude."[88] A poll among law students found that 82 percent favored the admission of Ada Lois Fisher. ("I would take 82 percent any day" she would later write.[89]) In January 1948, the month when the High Court ruled in *Sipuel* and McLaurin and the other five were turned away, another poll was released. It was taken by a senior, Larry Stephenson, who interviewed five hundred students. He concluded that 43.6 percent favored admitting Fisher to the law school.[90] (A white student telephoned Dunjee to say that "his personal opinion is that at least 90 per cent of the student body would welcome Mrs. Fisher. He said the poll was a fake and that far more than 43 per cent favored her entry."[91]) One year later, after the campus had actually experienced the presence of some black students, the *Oklahoma Daily* conducted an extensive poll of 1,229 students. The paper reported that 79.9 percent of them favored admitting blacks on either a segregated or non-segregated basis, a stunning increase of thirty-five percentage points. Historian John Hubbell wrote that even considering the "foibles" of these polls, "this was a remarkable development."[92] A few weeks later, when asked whether state colleges and universities should abolish segregation, 385 students said no and 645 said yes.[93]

88. See the Vertical File "Desegregation" in WHC.

89. *DO*, January 13, 1948, 20; *MBW*, 122. The week after Fisher began attending classes at the Law School, the *DO* interviewed her fifteen classmates. "All favored the admission of Mrs. Fisher and said they saw no use for the railings." *DO*, June 21, 1949, 5.

90. Larry Stephenson, "The Sipuel Case," *SM* 20 (January 1948): 5, 26. Stephenson claimed that he was trained by Gallup pollsters and that he used Gallup methods.

91. RD to Walter White, January 23, 1948, NAACPPM, Reel 13, Frame 548.

92. *OD*, March 31, 1949, 2; Hubbell, "Desegregation of the University of Oklahoma," 71.

93. *OD*, April 21, 1949, 1.

Finally, it seems evident that the older and more mature a student was, the more likely it was that he or she would favor the admission of blacks to the university. World War II veterans, for example, were strong advocates of ending segregation. Stephenson's survey illustrated the phenomenon. He discovered that only 29.7 percent of freshmen were in favor of admitting blacks, but 40.8 and 49.5 percent of sophomores and juniors, and 54.0 of seniors were. Among graduate students, 63.5 percent were for admission.[94] The figures are obvious testimonies to the liberalizing effects of higher education.

In January 1948, Walter White, executive secretary of the NAACP, asked Roscoe Dunjee for his assessment of student reaction to the attempt to enroll Ada Lois Fisher. Dunjee wrote an ecstatic appraisal. "I can say without reservation that it is the most stimulating and inspiring aspect of this whole situation. I did not know until this case became red hot that there was so much social decency hiding around in the Sooner Hills of Oklahoma." While writing his response to White, Dunjee was interrupted by a phone call. When he got back to his desk, he told White that the call was from the student editor of the *Oklahoma Daily*, who had said "he will be in my office with a delegation at two-thirty (Saturday) to see what they can do." That wasn't all. Other students were planning a march on the capitol. The president of the Oklahoma City NAACP advised the students against it, but Dunjee thought they should go ahead.[95] Nineteen months later, in October 1949, with dozens of blacks attending classes in Norman, Dunjee was still pleased. "In the main," he wrote Cross, black students were telling him "that they are receiving good treatment and that their instructors and the student body have been unusually fine in their attitude towards them."[96] Cross told one correspondent, "The problem here is not one of persuading white students to accept

94. Stephenson, "Sipuel Case," 5. Among undergraduates, Stephenson reported, the most resistant to admitting blacks were in Business and Engineering, and the most favorable were juniors and seniors in Arts and Sciences.

95. RD to Walter White, January 23, 1948, NAACPPM, Reel 13, Frame 548.

96. RD to GLC, October 22, 1949, ibid., Frame 994.

Negroes in classes. As a matter of fact, the white students are quite willing to accept Negroes. . . . The difficulty has to do with our State laws."[97]

Perhaps inevitably, there were members of both the faculty and the student body who were impatient with the pace of the efforts that Cross and others in the administration were making to navigate the university through the uncharted waters of racial adjustment. As we have seen, there were plenty of conservative critics with whom Cross had to deal, but he also had to contend with those on the other side. They wanted faster and more decisive progress toward desegregation, and because they desired the same things that Cross desired, he must have felt that they were, in some sense, allies. But he must also have felt that they could be troublesome allies. Like them, he wanted very much to satisfy the demands for justice and decent treatment toward the African American students who had now become part of the university community. But unlike them, he had also to reckon with the law as it was written, with the suspicions and punitive powers of politicians, with the misgivings of some of the regents, with the attitudes of the citizenry of Norman, and with the prejudices and fears of Oklahoma public opinion. He must have felt, at least occasionally, that these critics on his left were not sufficiently sensitive to the full range of pressures impinging upon the university. In October 1949, for example, Vice President Franklin told Cross that "an unofficial faculty committee on negro problems" was being formed by law professor Henry Foster.[98] "Professor Foster seemed a little vague about the purpose of the committee," said Franklin, "except it purports to 'intervene on behalf of Negroes' who do not appear to be getting satisfaction" from the dean of students. Franklin reminded Foster that the president's office "always has its doors open" for such appeals and that unsatisfied students could come to him (Franklin) about any problems.

97. GLC to Orella D. Halstead, February 14, 1950, ibid., Box 66, Folder: "Negroes."
98. CMF to GLC, October 20, 1949, GLCPP, ibid. Earlier Foster had caused a stir by his testimony against the bogus law school created for Fisher. His comments were so fierce that the trial had to be recessed. There were some calls for his firing.

A number of especially active students also pushed against what they regarded as the lethargic pace of progress toward desegregation. Some of their names have come down to us, but many of them acted anonymously through various committees, organizations, or church groups. One outstanding voice belonged to "a small, quiet, even introvertish girl who doesn't look her 18 years." She was Mary Kathryn Hickman, the student who pointed out to Cross that there was no Oklahoma law segregating eating places. She was invited for an interview by the editor of the *Oklahoma Daily*. "I had to lean close to hear what she was saying. She whispers her headlines." Hickman created a sensation in November 1947 by saying that she would have no trouble whatsoever dating Ada Lois Fisher's brother. Some boys called her late at night with fake accents and insulting words, but she stood her ground.[99] Another intrepid crusader was Eva Sutton, who confronted Ted Beaird and Carl Mason Franklin, asking (unsuccessfully) to speak to the Union's Board of Managers about why members of the Equal Education committee could not eat at the Union with Orpherita Daniels.[100] Among male students who were especially active and vocal were Howard Friedman, Ben Blackstock, Maurice Schraeder, Larry Stephenson, Pat Richardson, Maurice Ogden, and several others.

A revealing episode occurred in May 1950. The Equal Education committee addressed a letter to Cross objecting to the "Reserved for Colored" sign in the Union cafeteria. The letter pointed out that segregation was not required by Oklahoma law, that such discrimination violated the Fourteenth Amendment, that several polls indicated that a majority of students opposed segregation, and that "our fellow Negro students are constantly humiliated and disgusted by this outrageous display of racism." The letter ended with a stern directive to the president: "We are convinced that since it is your desire to serve the best interests of the student body, you will exert your influence in having this sign removed as quickly as possible."[101]

99. "All the Way," *DO*, November 21, 1947, 2.

100. Ted Beaird to CMF, May 12, 1949, GLCPP, Box 50, Folder: "Negro Question (#3),"

101. Equal Education Committee to GLC, May 9, 1950, ibid., Box 66, Folder: "Negroes."

Cross's response displays his willingness to reason calmly with others. But it also exposes his irritation with the pressure from students who, he thought, were not fully aware of the complexity of the situation. He began his response by saying he was in general agreement with the points in the students' statement, and, he added (using the very wording of the students' demand), you may be "assured that the signs in the Union Cafeteria will be removed as quickly as possible." But, he continued, "by this I mean that they will be removed as soon as I think it is possible to do so without causing serious repercussions, as a result of which all of the progress that we have made in regard to the racial problem might be lost." While it was true that segregation was not required in eating places, "it is true, also, that there are State laws requiring segregation in classrooms. In regard to the latter we are clearly vulnerable." Cross was afraid, he said, that "racial feeling aroused as a result of removing all vestiges of segregation in our cafeteria might well lead to action which would require us to observe the State laws in regard to classroom segregation." Any single citizen of Oklahoma could bring a court action "which would cost him nothing," but could force the university to strictly segregate classrooms. "I would not want to let an error in judgment on my part bring this about." He closed with an eloquent but mild rebuke which indicated that (after twenty months of dealing with the pressures coming at him from all sides) he was not beyond getting annoyed:

I think you should assume that I am as interested in solving racial problems as is your group. I think, also, that I have a much greater knowledge of the social problems in our State which must be faced before this problem can be solved. Thus, though I appreciate having your expression of opinion concerning these matters, I believe that it would be best that I not be influenced in any way by any group, but that I use my own best judgment as to how these problems can be worked out at the University of Oklahoma.[102]

102. GLC to Ladies and Gentlemen, May 18, 1950, ibid.

Perhaps it was inevitable that a crisis would eventually arise from the political left. The first bombshell exploded when a sympathetic white student reported to Thurgood Marshall that a group of radical University of Oklahoma students had taken charge of the Joint Committee for Equal Education. These students, the accuser alleged, were at least Marxists or, even more terrifying, actual members of the Communist Party.[103] The Communists, with their forthright, vocal, and uncompromising advocacy of full equality for African Americans, were seen collectively by officials at the NAACP as a serious and dangerous competitor for the support of thousands of everyday blacks. Marshall claimed to have nothing against Communists personally, but he understood very well that in the America of 1948–50 any perceived connection between communism and the NAACP would be a public-relations catastrophe. He quickly asked a trusted friend in Oklahoma to investigate the allegations, and when the friend confirmed the story, the NAACP immediately cut ties with the radicals.[104]

To Oklahoma's political leaders, however, it did not seem to matter how strongly the university's administrators and faculty were opposed to excluding African American students or to segregating them once they were on campus. Nor did it seem to matter that white students were either indifferent to, or growing steadily more accepting of, the presence of blacks in the classroom. Nor did it seem to matter that all those dire predictions of chaos and violence had proven groundless as no such trouble ever occurred. Nor did it even seem to matter that the sheer cost of creating "substantially equal" programs at Langston or providing for segregation at the state university (building black dorms, for example, or hiring special professors) were going to be enormous. There was, apparently, nothing that could shake the view of the politicians that they were

103. Robert E. Lee to TM, December 17, 1948, NAACPPM, Reel 13, Frames 897–98.
104. TM to L. C. Pakiser, December 29, 1949, and Pakiser to TM, February 28, 1949, ibid., Frames 905–906, 924–25. Lou Pakiser was the Southwest Regional Chair of the American Veterans Committee.

following the views of their white constituents in insisting that black people and white people be kept separated. For those beleaguered officials at the university and those faculty and student activists who hoped for a fairer and more democratic arrangement, and those intrepid black students who every day endured insulting measures of prejudice and segregation, it appeared that there was only one hope. If relief was to come, it was to come in the courts of law.

CHAPTER 6

Mr. McLaurin Goes
to Court (Again)

George McLaurin's first class had been on Thursday, October 14, 1948. Late on Friday, October 15, Thurgood Marshall boarded a plane to Oklahoma City. Declaring that the arrangements the university had put in place to segregate McLaurin were "stupid," Marshall said that he had come to consult with local NAACP officials to see what could be done. McLaurin, he said, would not be abandoned "short of the abolition of segregation in the University of Oklahoma."[1]

Ten days later, on the morning of October 25, Marshall and Amos Hall appeared at the Oklahoma City Federal Courthouse. Also present were Attorney General Mac Williamson, his assistant, Fred Hansen, and some of the defendants, including President Cross, Dean of Admissions J. E. Fellows, and Dean of Education H. E. Wrinkle. Marshall and Hall brought George McLaurin, who, they hoped, would be allowed to testify. The plaintiff and his attorneys had come to seek a "modification" of the September 29 order that admitted McLaurin to the university. That order, by the three-judge federal court, required the university to admit McLaurin to its program leading to a doctorate in Education, but it also added that this did not necessarily mean that Oklahoma's segregation laws were "incapable of constitutional enforcement." The judges on that occasion declined to grant an injunction "on the assumption that the State will follow the law," but they did retain jurisdiction "with

---

1. "OU Asks Ruling on Entry Case," *DO*, October 16, 1948, 25.

full power to issue such further orders and decrees" to ensure that McLaurin received equal treatment.[2] Now the same three judges were ready to hear McLaurin's request that he be treated like any other student.

Marshall opened with a clever ploy. He argued that the three judges, in their September 29 opinion, had declared that the segregation provisions (Sections 455, 456, and 457 of the 1941 law) did not apply to McLaurin because they infringed upon his rights under the Fourteenth Amendment. Nevertheless, Marshall charged, the university's Board of Regents was segregating McLaurin in the classroom, in the library, and in his eating arrangements at the "Jug." In short, the regents "without a statute requiring them to do so, have undertaken the task" of segregating him. Judge Edgar Vaught interrupted: "Now just a moment. When did this Court say that the segregation statutes were void?" Marshall responded that "the ruling, sir, as I remember the journal entry, was that as applied to McLaurin they were void." Vaught insisted that they were void "only in so far as his admission to the State University was concerned," and that "this Court has never held that they were void or that they were unconstitutional." Marshall retorted by reading the journal entry from the September 29 decision: "If I may say, sir, the paragraph says that it is ordered and decreed that in so far as Sections 455, 456, and 457 are sought to be applied and enforced in this particular case, they are unconstitutional and unenforceable." Vaught repeated, "That has to do merely with his admission to the University." At that point, Judge Alfred Murrah intervened, stating that "we will construe our judgment in light of the facts which have transpired." Instead, he told Marshall to "tell us your position in the case, [and] what you expect to prove." An exasperated Vaught echoed Murrah: "What is it that you want? Just put it in plain English. What is it that you want?" Marshall replied that "we want McLaurin admitted just like any other student, take his seat in the same way as any other

2. *McLaurin* v. *Oklahoma State Regents for Higher Education, et al.*, Civil No. 4039, "Ruling of the [Federal District] Court [U.S. Western District of Oklahoma]," 39–40, and "Journal Entry of Judgment—October 6, 1948," 51–53.

student." Vaught: "In other words, you want him in the same room with the other students." Marshall: "Why, yes, sir. That is the only way he can get an equal education. That is our point."[3]

Actually, that was just one point. Marshall also contended that the state of Oklahoma and the university's regents had made a classification ("Negroes") and then imposed special regulations on McLaurin because he was a member of that class. Everyone understood that the Fourteenth Amendment did not prohibit making reasonable classifications. It was legal to make a "class" of young people with regard to voting or drinking or driving an automobile, or of felons with regard to carrying firearms, or (as was then believed) of women participating in combat. But, Marshall argued, such classifications had to bear some clear relation to the activity involved, and there was no reasonable ground for classifying "Negroes" in the area of schooling. "The position we take," Marshall told the judges, "is that classification . . . unless based on a rational basis connected with the purpose of the classification, violates the Fourteenth Amendment." The state has "not put on one piece of testimony . . . justifying this classification, so it stands as a classification without justification."[4]

Despite these arguments by Marshall, the thrust of the proceeding consisted of the judges probing the extent to which McLaurin was being treated "equally" to the white students. It was quickly acknowledged that he could freely choose his classes and teachers. Regarding the anteroom where McLaurin was situated, Murrah asked if the student could see the instructor. When Marshall agreed that his client could see the instructor, Murrah asked: "Do you agree that the physical conditions under which this plaintiff is admitted are equal to the physical conditions under which the other students attend the class?" Marshall insisted that McLaurin's separation, by itself, made the conditions unequal. When Marshall turned to the treatment of McLaurin in the library and how he had to sit at a separate desk in the stacks, Murrah asked if it was the same library as was used by the other students, and Attorney

3. Ibid., "Colloquy between Court and Counsel," 76–79.
4. Ibid., 140–41.

General Williamson asked if any of the white students had their own desks in the library. When it came to eating lunch at the "Jug," Vaught wondered whether McLaurin was being offered "the same food that is provided other students."[5]

Although the judges were reluctant to allow it, Marshall was permitted to put McLaurin himself on the stand. His testimony was lackluster, vague, and disappointing to Marshall:

> *Marshall:* I wonder if you would give to the Court in your own words the exact effect, good or bad, upon you of being in this anteroom . . . to the question of you getting the education you want. That is the only thing that this Court is interested in.
>
> *McLaurin:* Well, it hinders me from doing effective work as I have desired to do. That handicaps me and why of course I can't study and concentrate like I would want to do. Of course if I was just, you know, free without any handicaps to take a seat in the regular classroom where I wouldn't be conscious of anything else but got my mind right on my work.
>
> *Marshall:* Realizing, Mr. McLaurin, you are hearing the same professor and hearing the same students, and getting the same instruction from the professor why is it that you make the statement in your last answer that still you are impeded in getting the education you desire?
>
> *McLaurin:* I don't quite catch your point.
>
> *Marshall:* Just why is it that you cannot concentrate, I think is the word you used just why?
>
> *McLaurin:* Well, just different, just like now suppose that was the class over there, and then I am a member of the class sitting up here, so to speak, then you would have quite an effect on me, brings about a feeling that it is something irregular that I can't sit in the classes, which makes me conscious that something out of the ordinary or something out of the way where I can't sit in the class

5. Ibid., 84–85.

> just like the other ones, brings about that consciousness and so forth.
>
> *Marshall:* Does that have any effect on your studying, in your ability to take in what the professor is giving?
>
> *McLaurin:* Absolutely does.
>
> *Marshall:* How does it?
>
> *McLaurin:* Keeps me from taking in the knowledge that I should because those conditions will hinder me from learning and grasping things as fast as I should.[6]

Perhaps the verdict was predictable given the judges' questions. A month later, on November 22, they concluded that "the plaintiff is now being afforded the same educational facilities as other students." The judges found no "legal basis for the mental discomfiture which the plaintiff says deprives him of equal educational facilities." As far as Marshall's suggestion that segregation was based on an unjustifiable and irrational classification, the judges concluded that "the classification, based on racial distinctions . . . rests upon a reasonable basis, having its foundation in the public policy of the State and does not therefore operate to deprive this plaintiff of the equal protection of the laws." Moreover, "the Constitution from which this court derives its jurisdiction does not authorize us to obliterate social or racial distinctions which the State has traditionally recognized as a basis for classification. . . . The Fourteenth Amendment does not abolish distinctions based upon race or color, nor was it intended to enforce social equality between classes and races." The injunction that McLaurin sought, therefore, "is accordingly denied."[7] Attorney Hall announced that an appeal would be made to the U.S. Supreme Court as soon as the papers could be prepared.[8]

For half a century after the disastrous pronouncement, in *Plessy v. Ferguson*, that segregation was not unconstitutional if the facilities accorded to each race were substantially equal, those fighting

6. Ibid., 94–95.
7. Ibid., "Conclusions of Law," 64–65.
8. "Negro Seating Rushed," *DO*, November 23, 1948, 1.

discrimination against black Americans had to confront the doctrine of "separate but equal." In the mid-1920s, when the NAACP first began to attack the inequities of segregated education in the South, the almost reflexive strategy of the organization was to demand that the "equal" part of the equation be actualized, made real. There was ample evidence showing that in every conceivable measure—from dollars spent per student to salaries for teachers, from length of the school year to conditions of buildings and equipment, from the number of students in a classroom to facilities for transporting children to their schools—no southern legislature or local school board was taking seriously the *Plessy* requirement of equality.

To combat the inequities, one early strategy, favored by some NAACP leaders, was to initiate seven lawsuits in seven of the worst segregating states, demanding equalization in school expenditures.[9] Those favoring equalization litigation believed that such lawsuits would result in one of two salutary outcomes. White authorities would either have to pump huge sums of money into black schools to bring them closer to genuine equality, or, if the funds could not be found or if taxpayers rebelled, the authorities would be forced, however grudgingly, to relent and let blacks into white schools.

In 1930, the NAACP hired a thirty-two-year-old Jewish immigrant from Romania to map out a strategy to advance the cause of black rights. Nathan Ross Margold was a graduate of Harvard Law, where he was a disciple of Professor Felix Frankfurter. Margold applied his superb legal mind to the problem and concluded, in his important "Report" of May 1931, that a campaign of equalization lawsuits was hopeless.[10] In the first place, the sheer quantity of litigation would be enormous—there were thousands of southern school districts practicing discrimination against their black schools. Winning a victory in one district would have no binding impact on any of the others. In addition, as Kluger writes, efforts at equalization

9. Kluger, *Simple Justice*, 132. The seven were Alabama, Arkansas, Florida, Georgia, Louisiana, Mississippi, and South Carolina.

10. For excellent summaries of the Margold report, see ibid., 133–38; and Tushnet, *NAACP's Legal Strategy*, 25–28.

"would have to be waged not only district by district but also year by year, for such *mandamus* actions . . . might be directed only against the disposition of funds actually on hand at the time the proceeding was initiated."[11] Finally, Margold argued, the cost of any such campaign, even in normal times, would far exceed the resources available to the NAACP. In 1931, as the Great Depression worked its devastation and dried up donations to the organization, mustering up anything close to the needed funds would be almost impossible.

Instead, Margold recommended another strategy. Rather than bringing endless and ineffective lawsuits seeking equalization, the NAACP should directly attack the constitutionality of legalized segregation itself. Margold found support in a Supreme Court case ten years older than *Plessy*. In 1880, San Francisco adopted an ordinance requiring a permit to operate a laundry in a wooden building. Ninety percent of laundry workers in the city were Chinese, and 95 percent of the city's 320 laundries were operating in wooden buildings. But those who administered the ordinance consistently denied permits to Chinese laundry operators and consistently granted them to non-Chinese. (Of the two hundred Chinese applications for a permit, only one was granted; among the eighty non-Chinese who applied, only one was denied.) In an 1886 case, the Court ruled that despite the racially neutral wording of the ordinance, its racist *application* by administrators violated the Equal Protection Clause of the Fourteenth Amendment and was, therefore, unconstitutional.[12] Margold instantly perceived that the precedent applied directly to the segregating South. The wording of "separate but equal" might be racially neutral, but the statistics of southern school administration revealed that, virtually everywhere, segregation, *as practiced*, involved discrimination not compatible with the Fourteenth Amendment. Margold's report urged that the NAACP "boldly challenge the constitutional validity of segregation if and when accompanied irremediably by discrimination." In short, he urged a direct attack aimed at bringing down *Plessy v. Ferguson*.

11. Kluger, *Simple Justice*, 133.
12. *Yick Wo v. Hopkins*, 118 U.S. 356 (1886).

In 1933, Margold left the NAACP to join the Roosevelt administration as solicitor for the Interior Department. He was replaced by the brilliant and tireless black attorney Charles Hamilton Houston, another of Frankfurter's protégés at Harvard. The shift helped achieve a conscious NAACP goal: to replace very able white attorneys with very able black ones. Houston had reservations about immediately implementing the Margold plan. There was, of course, the always-present financial difficulty of mounting a direct attack on *Plessy*. Moreover, Houston believed that it was crucial to arouse local black communities to greater self-respect and militancy, and that local battles for equality were more likely to achieve that purpose than were remote and abstract efforts. Margold, the consummate legal strategist, was relatively indifferent to that aspect of NAACP endeavors. Houston thought that, for now, the organization should concentrate on going after likely victories and particularly in graduate and professional education, where the injustices were the most obvious and the resistance least vehement. The attack on *Plessy* could wait for the present.

In the early cases of *Murray* (1937) and *Gaines* (1938), any contention that segregation, in and of itself, was unconstitutional might have seemed pointless. Those cases were not about the evils of separating white and black students; they were about opportunities that were available to white students but entirely absent for blacks. Indeed, in *Gaines* the Supreme Court seemed actually to sanction segregation—provided that Missouri create a substantially equal law school at Lincoln University. By the fall of 1946, however, NAACP lawyers decided, after intense discussion and debate, that the time had come to launch the direct attack on *Plessy*. It first appeared in the effort of Ada Lois Sipuel Fisher to gain admission to the University of Oklahoma School of Law. Although that case appeared to echo *Gaines* (both were instances of "separate but nonexistent"), Marshall and others saw a chance to go beyond *Gaines* and attack segregation head-on. After all, her petition for mandamus had been denied in Cleveland County largely on the grounds that she had not asked the State Regents to make a law school for her at Langston. It seemed appropriate, therefore, in her appeal to the Oklahoma Supreme Court, to raise the issue of the segregation that would be established by the creation of such a school. The NAACP lawyers now, and for the first time, argued that the segregation that Fisher should supposedly have requested would, by itself, constitute a violation of the Equal Protection Clause of the Fourteenth Amendment.[13] Labeling "separate but equal" nothing but "a legal fiction," the brief to the state's Supreme Court was a resurrection of the Margold report. The court's opinion, despite the eloquence of Marshall, which had momentarily raised Fisher's hopes, made no reference to the contention that segregation, in and of itself, was unconstitutional.

The attack against segregated education and *Plessy v. Ferguson* was made at length in the brief accompanying Fisher's appeal to the Supreme Court. To be sure, her lawyers argued that the Oklahoma courts had erred in refusing to issue a writ that would have admitted her to the university's law school. But they devoted more than half of their fifty-two-page brief to the matter of segregation's constitutionality. Sections of their brief bore such revealing titles as: "This Court Should Re-Examine the Constitutionality of the Doctrine of 'Separate But Equal'"; "The Doctrine of 'Separate But Equal' Is Without Legal Foundation"; "Equality under a Segregated System Is a Legal Fiction and a Judicial Myth"; "The General Inequities in Public Educational Systems Where Segregation Is Required"; "On the Professional School Level the Inequities Are Even More Glaring"; and "The Doctrine of 'Separate but Equal' Facilities Should Not Be Applied to This Case."[14] Although, as we have seen, the justices treated Marshall respectfully while badgering the state's attorneys, their opinion—issued with unusual speed—rested entirely on their ruling in *Gaines* and ignored completely the matter of segregation's constitutionality. Their declaration that Fisher was clearly and immediately entitled to a legal education in the state of

13. Wattley, *Step toward Brown*, 106.
14. *Sipuel v. Board of Regents of the University of Oklahoma, et al.*, 332 U.S. 631 (1948), "Brief for the Petitioner," 1–52. Two *amica curiae* briefs in support of Sipuel were introduced by the American Civil Liberties Union and the National Lawyers Guild.

Oklahoma, could be, and was, hailed as a significant victory for civil rights. But careful students of the issues saw that the Court's desire to settle the case on the narrowest possible grounds disappointed hopes for a more sweeping decision. The astute legal writer for the *New York Times* said of the decision, "so far so good," but noted that the High Court had stopped short of what was needed.[15]

But now along came George McLaurin, who, it could be argued, was accorded full equality in the use of facilities at the University of Oklahoma. Indeed, the three-judge federal court had ruled as much in November 1948, when it denied his request for a writ that would order school authorities to treat him as any other student. In response, the NAACP attorneys, of necessity, but also with a sense that they were confronting a great opportunity, set out to make the argument that their client's segregation on the campus, despite the equality of the facilities, was a denial of the equal protection of the laws. They began intense work on the case they would make before the highest court in the land.

Six weeks after Ada Lois Fisher first came to Norman and announced that she wanted to enroll in law school, a thirty-four-year-old African American mailman from Houston appeared at the University of Texas and announced that he wanted the same thing. Heman Marion Sweatt was a small man (5'5" and 130 pounds), soft-spoken and dignified. He had graduated a dozen years earlier from Wiley College, an all-black private school in Marshall, Texas.[16] After teaching school for a few years, he went to the University of Michigan with plans to become a doctor. He happened to be in Ann Arbor at the same time as Lloyd Gaines, and the two were slightly acquainted. He performed respectably at Michigan but after a year decided to return to Houston, where he became a letter carrier, an

15. "Equal Rights in Education," *New York Times*, January 15, 1948, 22. For a review of public reactions to the Supreme Court's decision, see Wattley, *Step toward Brown*, 123–25.

16. One of Sweatt's teachers at Wiley had been Melvin Tolson, Sr., the acclaimed poet and father of Melvin Tolson, Jr., who was to become an esteemed professor of French at the University of Oklahoma after 1959.

Heman Marion Sweatt. Courtesy UT Texas Student Publications, Prints and Photographs Collection (di_01127), Dolph Briscoe Center for American History, University of Texas at Austin.

active member of the local NAACP, and a participant in several civil rights causes. Some of those campaigns awakened an interest in the law, and in early October 1945, he answered the Texas NAACP's call for a volunteer who would try to break the color barrier at the University of Texas School of Law. Like Oklahoma, Texas had no public law school for blacks. With aid from the NAACP, Heman Sweatt began his long march through the courts of Texas.[17]

On February 26, 1946, Sweatt and a delegation of black activists met with University of Texas president Theophilus Painter and a group of school officials on the Austin campus. After some polite but frank statements on both sides, Sweatt declared his wish to attend law school and handed Painter his Wiley transcripts. Painter said that he would seek the opinion of the state's attorney general.[18] On March 16, the attorney general, who was about to enter the race for governor, released his opinion. Praising Texas's "wise and long-continued policy of segregation," he came to a position similar to Mac Williamson's in Oklahoma: segregation at the Texas law school may not be abrogated unless and until the applicant makes a demand for legal training at Prairie View University, Texas's black college, gives the authorities reasonable notice, and is refused.[19] On May 16, Sweatt asked the Travis County District Court for a writ of mandamus that would require his admission to Texas's law school, and a month later the court heard arguments and issued its decision. The judge readily admitted that Sweatt had been denied the equal protection of the law. But rather than issuing a writ, he gave the authorities six months to provide Sweatt, in a segregated institution within the state of Texas, with law courses that were substantially equivalent to those provided at the university. The court would retain jurisdiction of the case during that

17. For the life and career of Sweatt, see Gary M. Lavergne, *Before Brown: Heman Marion Sweatt, Thurgood Marshall, and the Long Road to Justice* (Austin: University of Texas Press, 2010). The description of Sweatt's physical appearance is from p. 6.

18. Lavergne, *Before* Brown, 97–103. See also Charles H. Thompson, "Separate but Not Equal: The Sweatt Case," *Southwest Review* 33 (Spring 1948): 105–12.

19. Cited in Lavergne, *Before* Brown, 312, n. 37, as Grover Sellers to T. S. Painter, March 26, 1946, Opinion No. 0–7126.

period. If the state provided such an alternative legal education, the writ would be denied; if the state failed to do so, the writ would be issued. The judge set a hearing six months hence, on December 17, 1946.[20]

The state's response was to wait five months. Then, in November 1946, the Texas legislature passed a resolution to create a segregated law school in Houston, as part of Prairie View University.[21] On the basis of this pledge, the Travis County District Court, at its December 17 rehearing, declared the Houston operation to be substantially equal to the law school at the University of Texas, that the court's requirements had been met, that Heman Sweatt now had the opportunity to study law as he had requested, and that no writ would be issued. Kluger describes Prairie View in the late 1940s as "an academic hovel that offered college credit for mattress-making, broom-making, and other minimal vocational skills. . . . a university in name only."[22] Nevertheless, the state eventually rented a few rooms and hired a faculty of two Houston black lawyers, neither of whom had ever taught in the classroom. The Prairie View law school had no real library, no real faculty, no law journal, no moot court, and, since neither Sweatt nor any other black students came to enroll, no student body.

Recognizing the inadequacy of the Houston slapdash arrangement, the Texas legislature closed the facility and created a somewhat more plausible black law school, allotting $100,000 for the purpose.[23] This one was located in Austin, within yards of the capitol and a mile from the University of Texas campus. The school would be in a three-story building that also housed a newspaper and an oilfield services company. There would be four rooms, totaling

20. Cited in Lavergne, *Before* Brown, 314, n. 50, as *Sweatt v. Painter,* no. 74,945, Judgment of the Court, filed June 26, 1946, in the 126th District Court of Travis County, Texas.

21. Houston, forty miles southeast of Prairie View, was chosen because a ninth of all Texan African Americans lived in the metropolitan area and might provide students for a law school. Lavergne, *Before* Brown, 126.

22. Kluger, *Simple Justice,* 261.

23. The new law school was to be part of a new and ambitious "Texas State University for Negroes," for which the state legislature appropriated $3 million.

1,060 square feet, which the state would rent for $125 a month. Students would have access to the state law library, and three first-year instructors from the University of Texas were appointed as faculty. Sweatt received a letter from the new school informing him of his acceptance as a student (even though he had never applied!). By that time, Sweatt, the NAACP, and most black leaders in Texas had determined to reject this version of Jim Crow legal education and aim to have Sweatt admitted to the premier law school of the region, the one down the street at the University of Texas.[24]

To that end, Sweatt's quest for a writ of mandamus, ordering his admission to the University of Texas, proceeded. On March 26, 1947, the Texas Court of Appeals ordered a retrial, which, on June 17, 1947, resulted in a rejection of Sweatt's petition. In February 1948, the Court of Appeals affirmed the lower court's verdict and denied a motion for a rehearing on March 17. Finally, on September 8, 1948, the Texas Supreme Court affirmed the ruling of the Court of Appeals and six weeks later also denied a rehearing. Thereupon, Sweatt's attorneys asked the U.S. Supreme Court to hear the case. That request was granted on November 7, 1949.[25] The High Court linked the cases of George McLaurin and Heman Sweatt, and agreed to hear arguments on both of them together. After several postponements, the Court fixed Monday and Tuesday, April 3–4, 1950, for oral arguments.

Marshall and the others at the Legal Defense Fund recognized the unique opportunity that presented itself as the Supreme Court opened its October 1949 term, and they were poised to bring three cases (*Sipuel, Sweatt,* and *McLaurin*) that directly challenged *Plessy* and the doctrine of "separate but equal." *Sipuel* and *Sweatt* both raised the question of whether hastily fabricated law schools for blacks could satisfy the requirement of equality, and *McLaurin* was about to put forward the most crucial matter of all: Was segregation

24. Lavergne, *Before* Brown, chap. 12.
25. This judicial history is reviewed in the *Sweatt v. Painter,* 339 U.S. 629 (1950), "Brief for Petitioner," 2–4.

unconstitutional even if the physical facilities offered both races were equal? As Marshall put it, a month before the hearing, "His case is different from all other cases involving segregation in education and makes the clearest challenge to segregation in public education."[26] The stakes could not have been higher. What if the cases were lost? What if the Court ruled that the new black law schools were adequate, or that the matter was entirely within the sphere of state authority, or that the segregation on campus that McLaurin experienced was not detrimental to his right to an education? If any of those outcomes occurred, civil rights litigation would almost certainly be set back for a generation. In fact, there were spirited objections to bringing the McLaurin case forward by some black leaders and some elements of the black press. The critics feared that a loss would constitute a disastrous reversal in the battle against segregation and that the risks of proceeding to the Supreme Court outweighed any potential benefits to the cause.[27] Given both the extraordinary opportunities and daunting hazards, Marshall and his colleagues were determined to anticipate every contingency and to prepare for every possible pitfall.

Marshall's intention was to bring the three cases together, bombarding the High Court with a flood of arguments designed to overturn *Plessy*. As early as September 1948, he urged Amos Hall to see if the Oklahoma Supreme Court could be persuaded to "make an early decision" of the *Sipuel* case (about the supposed equality of the Langston law school) "so that it will get to the [U.S.] Supreme Court during the period when the Texas case and the *McLaurin* cases are there so we will have all of them there at the same time."[28]

26. Marshall's words came in a March 1, 1950, memorandum to Henry Lee Moon, the NAACP's publicity director. NAACPPM, Reel 16, Frames 623–26, at 624.

27. Robert Lee Carter, *A Matter of Law: A Memoir of Struggle in the Cause of Equal Rights* (New York: New Press, 2005), 86. Greenberg thought the *McLaurin* case was "dangerous because it allowed no victory on grounds short of overruling *Plessy*, which the Court might be reluctant to do." *Crusaders in the Courts*, 71.

28. TM to Amos T. Hall, September 7, 1948, NAACPPM, Reel 13, Frame 783. See also December 3, 1948, ibid., Frame 877; TM to Hall, February 10, 1949, ibid., Frame 921; and TM to Hall, March 3, 1949, ibid., Frame 942.

That plan, however, was shaken by upsetting surprises regarding both of the Oklahoma cases.

First, two unexpected occurrences threatened *McLaurin.* Sometime before the end of 1949, the University of Oklahoma modified its treatment of McLaurin and the other black students attending the school. McLaurin was released from his alcove and allowed to take a seat in the same room as the white students—his seat, however, was in a row reserved exclusively for black students. Moreover, black students were no longer required to eat at a special time, but, as we have seen, were permitted to use the university cafeterias, provided they took their trays to specially set-aside tables. Similar adjustments were made at the library. Marshall worried that these changes might weaken his case or even render it dismissible. "It is obvious that the Attorney General of Oklahoma will in some fashion raise the question as to whether or not the case is now moot," he wrote to the other lawyers.[29] Despite doubts and perhaps because they saw no choice, the attorneys elected to go forward anyway. Then another problem regarding McLaurin erupted: his poor academic performance. In September 1949, he failed his examinations for the doctorate.[30] He appealed to his committee, and was allowed to enroll "conditionally" in Education 599, a course required before he could start his dissertation research. He was told that he would have to pass a qualifying exam to remain in the course. At the end of March 1950, just days before his case was scheduled for oral arguments in Washington, President Cross informed McLaurin that he had failed the qualifying exam.[31] If that meant his withdrawal from the university, the case would certainly be moot. Marshall was nervous. He told Hall that he "would not want to see

29. TM to Lawyers on Sweatt and McLaurin Cases, February 8, 1950, ibid., Reel 16, Frame 553.

30. TM to Amos T. Hall, September 21, 1949, ibid., Frame 975. Marshall wrote: "I assume that you have checked to determine whether or not he really failed or was failed because of prejudice." Since there was no claim of bias, it must be assumed that McLaurin's performance was unsatisfactory.

31. TM to Amos T. Hall, October 18, 1949, ibid., Frame 977; GLC to McLaurin, March 30, 1950, GLCPP, Box 66, Folder: "Negroes."

the case moot under any circumstances because it is too important a case and the issue is too large to be made moot at this time."[32] Fortunately, the university let McLaurin take a few courses despite his failure. His standing as a student was thereby maintained, and the case could proceed.

Yet another unexpected disruption of Marshall's strategy occurred on June 17, 1949, when Cross admitted Sipuel Fisher to the university's law school. That act did, in fact, render her case moot—she was arguing that the law school created for her at Langston was not equal to the one at Norman. Now she was without any standing in the case, any personal stake in the question, and her attorneys had no choice but to withdraw the case from consideration.[33]

Meanwhile, a new segregation case, having nothing to do with the NAACP and nothing to do directly with education, was working its way up to the Supreme Court. Like *McLaurin* and *Sweatt*, it also aimed at overturning *Plessy*. The case involved segregation on interstate railroads.[34] The policy of the Southern Railway, approved by the Interstate Commerce Commission (ICC), was to equip each of its dining cars with ten tables for white passengers and, at the end of the car and covered by a curtain, one table for blacks. If all the white spaces were taken before a black person appeared, whites could be seated at the Jim Crow table and the curtain removed. On May 17, 1942, Elmer Henderson, an African American government employee, bought a first-class ticket for a trip from Washington to Birmingham. At 5:30, he went to the dining car. He was informed that since all the white tables were filled, three white passengers were seated at the Jim Crow table. The steward told him he could not be seated. Henderson returned to the dining car twice, but to no avail. He later filed a complaint under the auspices of the black fraternity Alpha Phi Alpha. Section

32. TM to Amos T. Hall, October 18, 1949, NAACPPM, Reel 13, Frame 977. See also TM to Charles E. Cropley, October 25, 1949, ibid., Frame 979. Cropley was Clerk of the Supreme Court.

33. TM to Amos T. Hall, June 9, 1949, and TM to Hall, August 4, 1949, ibid., Frames 961 and 974.

34. *Henderson v. United States et al.*, 339 U.S. 816 (1950).

3 (1) of the Interstate Commerce Act of 1887 made it illegal for an interstate railroad "to subject any particular person . . . to any undue or unreasonable prejudice or disadvantage in any respect whatsoever."[35] Henderson charged that the railroad had violated the law, and that the very practice of such segregation was unconstitutional. The ICC and the railroad admitted that Henderson had been treated shabbily but that this was the result of poor judgment by an employee. The railroad's general arrangement for dining cars (slightly modified after the incident[36]) was justified by the lower courts in terms of *Plessy* (blacks, after all, were served the same food in the same cars as whites). The case was appealed to the Supreme Court and was scheduled to be argued on the same day as *McLaurin* and *Sweatt*. Although Marshall played no part in preparing the *Henderson* brief, he thought that it was "a good job on the *Plessy v. Ferguson* doctrine as well as a good brief against segregation in public facilities."[37] Marshall did write an amicus brief for *Henderson* on behalf of the NAACP.

To ready the two NAACP cases for the all-important April 3–4 oral arguments, Marshall, his colleagues, and legal experts from around the country went to work with high hopes and enthusiasm, meticulously scrutinizing every possible argument. In June 1949, forty-three attorneys and numerous officials from various NAACP chapters held a strategy session in New York to weigh approaches to the upcoming cases.[38] There was a shared recognition that April 3–4 would present a golden opportunity to end racial segregation in public education at the professional and graduate level. But everybody also understood that a victory would have critical implications for education at lower levels as well. This time the aim was not

35. 54 Stat. 902, 49 U.S.C. § 3 (1).

36. The Southern Railway's modified arrangement provided that the Jim Crow table would be exclusively reserved for black passengers and permanently separated by a curtain.

37. TM to Thomas I. Emerson, November 15, 1949, NAACPPM, Reel 16, Frame 508.

38. Carter, *Matter of Law*, 84–85.

merely to "equalize" facilities available to blacks; this time the aim was to challenge the constitutionality of segregation and dispute the validity of classifying black Americans for purposes of public education. As soon as the Supreme Court scheduled the arguments for the spring of 1950, individual lawyers were assigned to research topics likely to occur at the hearings.[39] The NAACP attorneys were, for the most part, African Americans, and they were quite young, and superbly talented. Many of them were connected directly to the invigorated law school at Howard.

For both cases, Marshall was assisted by the hardworking and efficient Robert Lee Carter. After graduating from Howard Law in 1940, and earning a Master of Laws degree at Columbia the next year, Carter joined the Army Air Forces, where he created considerable fuss by insisting that black officers be allowed in the officers' club on the same terms as white officers. In 1944, at the age of twenty-seven, he joined the Legal Defense Fund, and Marshall soon came to rely on his steadiness and competence. Carter would eventually succeed Marshall as general counsel of the NAACP, where he won more than twenty civil rights cases before the Supreme Court. He ended his career as a federal district judge for the Southern District of New York.[40]

Among the other high-powered strategists working on the briefs was William Hastie, a kind of elder statesman among black lawyers (Carter was to call Hastie his "role model"[41]). After an illustrious undergraduate career at Amherst, Hastie enrolled in Harvard Law, where he graduated in 1930. He was persuaded by his second cousin, Charlie Houston, to teach at Howard. One of his students there was Thurgood Marshall. In 1939, after several positions in the Roosevelt administration, Hastie assumed the deanship at Howard Law. From 1946 to 1949, he served as the territorial governor of the American Virgin Islands, and shortly after his work on

39. Ibid., 85. For the topics and the lawyers assigned to research them, see NAACPPM, Reel 16, Frames 506–507. The list and assignments were the work of Robert Carter.

40. Carter, *Matter of Law*, especially chap. 4

41. Ibid., 23.

Attorney Robert Lee Carter, circa 1950. Courtesy Library of Congress, Prints and Photographs Division, Visual Materials from the NAACP Records (LC-USZ62-126948).

the *Sweatt* brief, President Truman named him the country's first black appellate judge.[42]

Three other first-rate legal minds were soon helping with the cases. William Robert Ming, Jr., a graduate of the University of Chicago School of Law, taught at both Chicago and Howard. Bob Ming was thirty-nine when he worked on the briefs. James Madison Nabrit Jr. was a Texas attorney who moved to Washington in 1936 to

42. Gilbert Ware, *William Hastie: Grace under Pressure* (New York: Oxford University Press, 1984).

teach at Howard. He eventually became dean of the law school and, in 1960, president of the university.[43] The only white legal counselor at the NAACP was Jack Greenberg. He became conscious of prejudice against blacks while serving in the navy in the Pacific. He graduated from Columbia Law School in 1948 and, at twenty-five, joined the Legal Defense Fund in 1949. He possessed a sharp mind and would argue dozens of civil rights cases in the coming years. He eventually succeeded Marshall as director of the Legal Defense Fund, a job he held for two dozen years.[44] Handling matters of Texas law in *Sweatt* was attorney William J. Durham, who had been fighting racism in the state for more than twenty years; and serving the same purpose regarding Oklahoma law for *McLaurin* was Amos Hall. There were others, including two women, Constance Baker Motley, a legal assistant fresh from passing the bar in 1948,[45] and Annette Peyser, a young consultant who specialized in sociological and economic research and who had been with the Legal Defense Fund since 1946.

In addition to the formidable team of in-house lawyers at the NAACP, Marshall was able to enlist the services of some impressive legal scholars from the leading law schools in the United States. Among them were Thomas I. Emerson (Yale), Erwin Griswold (dean at Harvard), Max Radin (University of California), Earl Harrison (dean at the University of Pennsylvania), Malcolm Sharp (Chicago), Milton Konvitz (Cornell), and Walter Gelhorn (Columbia), who also enlisted some of his students in the cause. Some of these scholars had testified in Norman about the absurdity of thinking that the law school created for Fisher was equal to the one at the University of Oklahoma. Also worthy of mention is Robert Redfield, the renowned anthropologist at the University of Chicago, who testified in the *Sweatt* case, refuting purported differences in learning abilities between blacks and whites.[46]

43. See Nabrit's obituary, *New York Times*, December 30, 1997, B8.
44. Greenberg, *Crusaders in the Courts*, chaps. 6–7.
45. Constance Baker Motley, *Equal Justice under the Law: An Autobiography* (New York: Farrar, Straus, and Giroux, 1998), chap. 3.
46. Kluger, *Simple Justice*, 264–65.

The actual writing of the *Sweatt* brief, putting together the research and suggestions of the others, was done by Carter and Greenberg.[47] It was a mixture of boldness and caution. As Greenberg later said, the brief "flatly attacked the constitutionality of segregation. Yet it made arguments that could bring victory while allowing decision on grounds short of overruling *Plessy*."[48] The first two sections of the brief asserted Sweatt's rights under the Equal Protection Clause and the error of creating an unwarranted classification of "Negroes" for educational purposes. The third section devoted fifteen pages to *Plessy:* "If this Court considers *Plessy v. Ferguson* applicable here, that case should now be reexamined and overruled."[49] The final section pointed out the terrible inequalities between educational facilities for whites and blacks in Texas, drawing special attention to the contrast between the University of Texas's law school and the one recently created for blacks.[50]

Originally Marshall was to write up the *McLaurin* brief, but in the end that duty was handed off to Carter.[51] Not surprisingly, there were similarities between the *McLaurin* and *Sweatt* documents. Most of the wording in their sections attacking *Plessy* was identical.[52] The arguments against the classification of blacks for purposes of education also shared many of the same words and quotations.[53] Both briefs stressed the harmful effects of segregation on both races; the system prevented members of each race from knowing the other, increased unhealthy suspicions, weakened democracy, hampered genuine education, and accentuated and exaggerated imagined differences. Of necessity, the *McLaurin* brief placed less emphasis on exclusion (McLaurin, after all, was in the same university and the same classes as whites) and more emphasis on the social, psychological, and educational effects on the segregated individual.

47. Carter, *Matter of Law*, 88.
48. Greenberg, *Crusaders in the Courts*, 70.
49. *Sweat v. Painter*, "Brief for Petitioner," 52.
50. Ibid., 71–75. The section compares the two schools' physical plants, libraries, faculties, and student bodies.
51. Carter, *Matter of Law*, 88.
52. Compare *Sweatt v. Painter*, 52–67, and *McLaurin v. Board of Regents*, 44–53.
53. Compare *Sweatt v. Painter*, 8–26, and *McLaurin v. Board of Regents*, 15–35.

McLaurin's "uncontradicted testimony," read the brief, "shows the effect of racial segregation upon him in his effort to obtain an education. . . . The very fact of segregation establishes a feeling of humiliation and deprivation to the group considered to be inferior." The psychological results of enforced separation were innumerable, permanent, and dire. "Probably the most irrevocable and deleterious effect of segregation upon the minority group is that it imposes a badge of inferiority upon the segregated group. This badge . . . is recognized not only by the minority group, but by society at large." Indeed, the real purpose of enforced segregation, its very intent, is "the establishment of an inferiority status."[54]

Both briefs were heavy with citations to nonlegal authorities: the books and articles of sociologists, psychologists, historians, educators, and religious leaders. In the *McLaurin* brief there were more than forty such nonlegal citations. Alongside references to fairly standard works by Kenneth Clark, Franklin Frazier, Ashley Montague, William James, and Gunnar Myrdal, there were citations to and quotations from little-known studies with such titles as *Race Attitudes in Children*, "The Psychological Effects of Enforced Segregation," "Psychogenic Hazards of Segregated Education of Negroes," *The Protestant Church and the Negro*, and many others.

Both sides in the contest, knowing what was at stake, rounded up support in the form of amicus briefs. Those not directly involved in the proceedings, but feeling an interest in the outcome, presented supporting briefs for the High Court's consideration. Eleven southern states (including Oklahoma) submitted amicus briefs endorsing segregation. Supporters of Sweatt and McLaurin countered with briefs (some of them taking stronger positions than the NAACP was willing to venture) on behalf of such organizations as the American Civil Liberties Union, the American Federation of Teachers, the American Veterans Committee, the American Jewish Committee, the Congress of Industrial Organizations,[55] and the Japanese American Citizens League. At Marshall's urging, Yale law

54. *McLaurin v. Board of Regents* brief, 24–27.
55. The CIO's amicus brief was written by the organization's general counsel, Arthur Goldberg, who would one day be a member of the Supreme Court himself.

professors Thomas Emerson, John Frank, and David Haber entered a particularly noteworthy brief. Calling themselves the "Committee of Law Teachers Against Segregation in Legal Education," they produced a statement signed by 187 of the most distinguished law professors from the most distinguished American law schools. The professors, many of whom must have been personally well known to the justices, denounced the classification of Negroes, demanded that the Court face the question of whether segregation in education was reasonable, and closed with a ringing insistence that for the sake of the nation's conscience, the Court must, at long last, do justice to America's black citizens.[56]

Finally, Ada Lois Sipuel Fisher submitted an affidavit. Eager to refute the segregationists' claim that even if blacks were admitted, white students would treat them badly, she testified to the cordial treatment she was receiving from her fellow students. Mentioning the "Reserved for Colored" signs, she wrote that they "did not keep my classmates from coming back to talk with me and exchanging class notes. . . . From the first, my classmates were friendly. Now I am accepted as any other member of the class. . . . Not only am I accepted in the School of Law, but I have been treated very kindly by white families in Norman who have invited other Negro students and me to their homes for dinner."[57]

Another critical element favored Sweatt and McLaurin as their hearings grew closer to the fateful day: the suddenly outspoken attitude of the United States government. Generated both by the growing need to earn the votes of northern blacks and by the exigencies of Cold War competition with the Soviet Union, the new climate in Washington was palpable. It was exemplified by the Fair Employment Practices Committee, the desegregation of the military and the civil service, anti-lynching and anti-poll tax measures, and the

56. John P. Frank to TM, November 18, 1949, and Thomas I. Emerson to TM, November 18, 1949, NAACPPM, Reel 16, Frames 915, 916. Part of the amicus brief was written by Dean Erwin Griswold of Harvard. See also, Kluger, *Simple Justice*, 275–76.

57. *Sweatt v. Painter*, Appendix D: "Report of First Negro Student to Enter the Law School, University of Oklahoma."

strong civil rights positions of the Democratic Party. This novel at-
titude must certainly have buoyed the hopes and expectations of
those fighting for racial equality. Both NAACP briefs cited *To Secure
These Rights*, the 1947 report of the President's Committee on Civil
Rights.[58] Even more telling, the Justice Department, led by Solicitor
General Philip Perlman and Special Assistant Philip Elman, entered
a fourteen-page amicus brief on behalf of Sweatt and McLaurin in
January 1950.[59] "These cases, together with . . . *Henderson v. United
States*," they began, "have great importance to the Government and
the people of the United States." "They are significant because they
test the vitality and strength of the democratic ideals to which the
United States is dedicated." The government's brief also made a
sidelong reference to the Cold War competition between democracy and totalitarianism: "It is in the context of a world in which
freedom and equality must become living realities, if the democratic way of life is to survive, that the issues in these cases should be
viewed."[60] In another important gesture of federal support, the attorney general of the United States, J. Howard McGrath, was ready
to appear before the High Court, ready, when the time came in
April, to advocate the reversal of *Plessy*.

Meanwhile, the NAACP launched a tremendous public relations campaign, issuing frequent and detailed press releases that
carefully explained the cases and the issues involved in them. These
releases were sent to dozens of editors, black and white, all across
the country. In addition, Marshall and Henry Moon, the NAACP's
publicity director, courted favorable coverage from some of the
country's leading journalists. Copies of the *McLaurin* and *Sweatt*
briefs and personal letters went to such key opinion-makers as
Edward R. Murrow, Drew Pearson, Max Lerner, Benjamin Fine of
the *New York Times*, Ralph McGill of the *Atlanta Constitution*, Bruce

---

58. See *Sweatt v. Painter*, 20, 27, 74, and *McLaurin v. Board of Regents*, 26.

59. Philip Elman to TM, February 7, 1950, and Constance Baker Motley to
Elman, February 8, 1950, NAACPPM, Reel 16, Frames 554, 555.

60. *McLaurin v. Board of Regents*, and *Sweatt v. Painter*, "Memorandum for the
United States as *Amicus Curiae*," 1–2, 13.

Bliven of the *New Republic*, Jerry Tolliver of the *Nation*, Virginius Dabney of the *Richmond Times Dispatch*, and many others.[61]

Marshall summoned all the participating attorneys to Washington on Friday, March 31, for strategic discussions. He also arranged for a dress rehearsal on the evening of April 1, "a full and complete discussion of the argument" before faculty and students at the Howard Law School. This would give the legal team all day Sunday to consider criticisms and comments and, as Marshall put it, "to iron out the kinks."[62]

On Monday morning, April 3, the Supreme Court was jammed with spectators of both races. After disposing of a few routine matters, the justices heard arguments in the *Henderson* case.[63] The first to speak was Attorney General McGrath, who condemned the Southern Railway's policy in the strongest terms. The nation's chief attorney declared that the Constitution does not permit racial segregation by law and that "segregation signifies and is intended to signify that a member of the colored race is not equal to a member of the white race." The doctrine of "separate but equal," he continued, was a mistake, "an anachronism which a half-century of history and experience has shown to be a departure from the basic constitutional principle that all Americans . . . stand equal and alike in the sight of the law."[64]

61. Copies of the press releases can be found in the NAACPPM, as can correspondence with numerous journalists. See for examples Reel 16, Frames 635–48.

62. TM to W. J. Durham, March 16, 1950, NAACPPM, Reel 16, Frame 596; and TM to George M. Johnson, March 16, 1950, ibid., Frame 593.

63. *New York Times*, April 4, 1950, 60.

64. Lewis Wood, "Bar Segregation, High Court Asked," *New York Times*, April 4, 1950, 41. The best account of the hearings in the Supreme Court on April 3–4 can be found in *United States Law Week* 18 (April 11, 1950), 3271–81. In the following paragraphs I rely on that source, and I have taken the liberty of putting into quotation marks *both* passages that are quoted from the mouths of the participants *and* passages taken from the *Law Week*'s summaries of what was said. I realize that some may object to this practice, but I have chosen to do so partly to avoid the complexity and awkwardness of indicating which is which, and partly because if we are to trust the reporter's direct quotations from the participants as being accurate, I see no reason to doubt the accuracy of the same person's unquoted summaries of what was said.

McGrath was followed by Solicitor General Perlman, who described Henderson's dining car experience and criticized the railroad's means of calculating potential black demand for service. He echoed the attorney general, asserting that segregation, however practiced, violates the Constitution. After responding to questions from Justice Stanley Reed about previous cases, Perlman said that equal conditions could never be provided under segregation and that Justice Harlan's eloquent dissent from *Plessy,* in 1896, had been correct because it reflected the Constitution's intent. Henderson's attorney, Belford Lawson, Jr., praised the attorney general and the solicitor general on behalf of "all of us who have lived under the iron heel of . . . Jim Crow." An exchange, suggestive of the outcome, then occurred between Lawson and Justice Frankfurter. Lawson argued that in a case of 1941, *Mitchell v. United States,* the Court had ruled that discrimination against black passengers on railroads was illegal.[65] Frankfurter interrupted, asking whether Lawson thought that Henderson's case was covered by the *Mitchell* ruling. Lawson: "That is right. We go one step further." Frankfurter: "You don't have to go one step further." Lawson: "We want to go one step further" (i.e., to attack *Plessy*). Frankfurter then reiterated his well-known view that the Court should avoid constitutional issues if at all possible.

The rest of the morning and most of the afternoon was devoted to arguments made by lawyers for the Interstate Commerce Commission and the Southern Railway. The former argued that the ICC only cared about relatively equal treatment and that it left the question of segregation to the judgment of each railroad. The latter defended segregation and contended that Congress had the power to regulate interstate commerce and over many decades had condoned (or at least had not condemned) segregation. The arguments on both sides having been heard, at 4:05 P.M. the Court turned to the matter of George McLaurin's treatment by the

65. 313 U.S. 80 (1941). Mitchell, who bought a first-class ticket for a Pullman car, was forced, because of his race, to leave the first-class car and ride in a second-class one. The Court ruled that Mitchell's treatment was illegal under the Interstate Commerce Act.

University of Oklahoma. There was less than a half hour before the Court's 4:30 adjournment.[66]

The original plan was for Amos Hall and Thurgood Marshall to argue the McLaurin case, but Marshall changed his mind and Robert Carter was given the assignment. Hall spoke for about ten minutes. He wished to answer briefly two contentions in the state of Oklahoma's brief. First, he denied the state's assertion that the imposition of segregation on McLaurin and the other black students was never intended to humiliate them. The policy, he claimed, carried with it a burden of implied inferiority. Second, Hall denied the state's argument that the policy was needed in order to avoid disorder and protect black students from hostility. The presence of McLaurin and the other black students on campus had caused no animosity and certainly no trouble. Then it was Carter's turn. It was his first appearance before the Supreme Court and, as he later recalled, "I was very nervous . . . and very worried that my nervousness might overwhelm me.[67] But it had been a long day and the justices seemed eager to head home. In the few minutes left that afternoon, Carter was not interrupted as he explained the facts of the case, asserting that McLaurin "met all the requirements except that he was colored." Upon adjournment, all the attorneys supporting McLaurin and Sweatt retreated to the lawyers' lounge in the Supreme Court Building for a critical review of the afternoon's proceeding. It was the general consensus that Hall and Carter had done extremely well and that the case was off to a good start. "My confidence was given such a boost," Carter was to remember, "that when I began the argument the next day, I was completely at ease, to the point of arrogance. The questions came fast and furious, but I was able to deal with all of them with composure and assurance."[68]

Next morning, as he continued the argument for McLaurin, Carter was asked whether the initial conditions of McLaurin's

66. Carter, *Matter of Law*, 89.
67. Ibid.
68. Ibid., 89–90.

segregation on campus had changed since he was first admitted. Carter acknowledged the changes that now governed McLaurin and the other black students. Frankfurter queried, "There are no railings?" Carter: "None. It was taken down. They can use the library and cafeteria but at a segregated table." Carter then argued that the Fourteenth Amendment had been adopted to protect blacks from unfriendly state actions, and the Equal Protection Clause was intended to assure that all persons were treated alike. Frankfurter pressed again: "There isn't any argument that the content of the education he gets isn't the same?" Carter: "No controversy." Frankfurter: "It is simply the physical seating." Justice Hugo Black asked, "Are those rules enforced that way now?" Carter replied that the signs were taken down, but "Negro students must conform to the rules and are required to sit in certain seats." Frankfurter commented that "when the litigation started the question was quite different." Carter acknowledged that this was true. There were then more queries about classroom seating and whether or not white students were also assigned seats. Carter replied that only black students were singled out in this way. After "considerable discussion" of the physical arrangements, Carter had his opportunity to bring up *Plessy v. Ferguson*, arguing not only that it was bad law but also that it was not relevant to this case, because regulating railroads was not the same as regulating education, and in the field of education, the Supreme Court had not upheld segregation.

Oklahoma was represented by Fred Hansen, the state's assistant attorney general. Marshall had contempt for Hansen's boss, Oklahoma Attorney General Mac Williamson, but he and Hansen had developed a cordial and mutually respectful relationship over the past months.[69] Hansen's presentation to the justices was remarkably moderate. According to the *Law Week* reporter, Hansen conceded that "the demand for segregation is disappearing [in Oklahoma] and pointed out that the cost of maintaining segregated schools

---

69. See for example, Fred Hansen to TM, April 9, 1949, and TM to Hansen, April 13, 1949, NAACPPM, Reel 13, Frames 1009, 1011.

would solve the problem." Justice Sherman Minton, referring to the new rules on the campus, said that "when a policy of segregation has broken down to this extent, there isn't much point to segregation, is there?" Hansen replied "Not, possibly, on the graduates' level." Hansen was at pains to defend the motives and the character of state and university officials. When Chief Justice Vinson offered that "this policy is just sort of an out for the officials under the statutes of Oklahoma," Hansen agreed: "These officials are thoughtful men and good men doing the best they can under difficult conditions." The strongest argument the assistant attorney general offered was that *Plessy v. Ferguson* ought to be enforced, and he pointed out that at the very time when the Fourteenth Amendment was written and adopted, Congress was providing for segregated education in the District of Columbia, indicating that the amendment was not seen, at the time, as a bar to such segregation. After a brief rebuttal by Carter, the arguments in *McLaurin* ended and the Court turned to *Sweatt v. Painter.*

Texas attorney W. J. Durham began by reviewing the complicated history of Heman Sweatt's attempt to enter the University of Texas School of Law. When he finished, Thurgood Marshall rose to continue the argument. In remarks that applied almost as much to *McLaurin* as they did to *Sweatt*, he insisted that the Court deal with the large question of segregation. "They can build an exact duplicate [of the law school at the University of Texas], but if it is segregated, it is unequal." To the claim that separation was preferred by members of both races and that even if a black man were admitted to the white school, it was likely that the white students would have nothing to do with him, Marshall replied forcefully. Suppose some whites decided to shun a black student. "There would be nothing wrong. We want to remove governmental restriction—if they want to, they can keep their prejudices." "Texas has an integrated bar," he added. "All lawyers are admitted. There is nothing in the law requiring segregation. Why can't they study law together?"

Representing Texas was Price Daniel, the state's attorney general. Kluger writes of him that he would "subsequently serve as

United States Senator for three years and governor of Texas for eight—and prove a white-supremacist throughout all of them."[70] He made the expected arguments: that the classification of Negroes was reasonable; that segregation was favored by both races; that separate schools had been approved in many northern states; and that "in certain states it is necessary to have separate facilities." He closed by describing the new black law school in Houston in fulsome terms. "It has a fine building, a five-man faculty, 23 students, and a good library." Daniels was at a handicap, of course, because he was trying to persuade a group of men who had attended law schools themselves, and if they knew nothing else, they knew what constituted a good law school and what constituted an inferior one. Carter offered another quick rebuttal, and the hearing was adjourned.

Thurgood Marshall was forty-one years old, and this was his eighth appearance before the Supreme Court. He was at the height of his powers. One of those fortunate enough to hear him that day was Charles Henry Thompson, the founder and longtime editor of the *Journal of Negro Education* and dean of the graduate school at Howard University. When the Court adjourned, Marshall was surrounded by friends and admirers, and Thompson did not get the chance to speak to him. The next day, however, he sent him a letter: "What I wanted to say to you was this: I have heard you upon numerous occasions in the lower courts and several times before the Supreme Court. But I think that your presentation yesterday surpassed all of your past performances. Your presentation possessed a clarity, a cogency and a degree of persuasiveness which you have never equalled before, and was not equalled by any of the counsel in these three cases."[71]

Certainly Marshall had done his best. All of them, on both sides of the question, had done their best. Everyone involved understood the importance of these two days in determining the future of race

---

70. Kluger, *Simple Justice*, 262.

71. Charles H. Thompson to TM, April 5, 1950, NAACPPM, Reel 16, Frame 609.

relations in the United States, and in these three cases both sides had now had their say. All the participants probably left Washington feeling that, whatever the outcome, they had presented their views as thoroughly and as convincingly as they could. There was nothing to do now but await the Court's decisions. "We have had our day in court," Marshall replied to Thompson, "and all we can do now is wait with our fingers crossed."[72]

72. TM to Charles H. Thompson, April 12, 1950, ibid., Frame 608.

CHAPTER 7

The Decision—Yes and No

As they considered the records of the nine justices who had read the briefs and heard the arguments, Marshall and his colleagues might have permitted themselves some cautious optimism while they waited for the rulings. The Supreme Court of 1950 was one of the most volatile in American history. Gone were the troglodytes who, a dozen years earlier, had dissented in *Gaines*. Now the Court was composed of five men named by Franklin Roosevelt and four chosen by Harry Truman. Although, as Michael Klarman notes, both of those presidents picked justices primarily on the basis of their sympathy for New Deal economic measures, it happened that "civil rights litigation enjoyed unprecedented success in the Court during this era," and even though it was "not by design," the men chosen by Roosevelt and Truman "proved remarkably supportive of civil rights."[1]

One of the justices who heard *McLaurin* and *Sweatt* was Felix Frankfurter, who, back when he was a professor at the Harvard Law School, had been a legal adviser to the NAACP. It was Frankfurter's disciple, Nathan Margold, who had devised the organization's strategy of directly attacking segregation, and another disciple, Charles Hamilton Houston, who had engineered important victories in

---

1. Michael J. Klarman, *From Jim Crow to Civil Rights: The Supreme Court and the Struggle for Racial Equality* (New York: Oxford University Press, 2004), 173, 194. For helpful analyses of the civil rights views of the Supreme Court justices on the bench in 1950, see ibid., 193–96, 292–312; and Lavergne, *Before* Brown, 269–71. For a general look at the Court, see Melvin I. Urofsky, *Division and Discord: The Supreme Court under Stone and Vinson, 1941–1953* (Columbia: University of South Carolina Press, 1997).

the 1930s. Another of the nine was Hugo Black, who, despite his membership in the Ku Klux Klan in the early 1920s, had compiled a solid record as a champion of civil rights. Black was also a close personal friend of the NAACP's executive secretary, Walter White.[2] William O. Douglas, a staunch liberal on social and economic matters, had been on the Court since 1939. He was to earn a notable record on civil rights issues. At his death in 1980, Thurgood Marshall, who had been his colleague on the Court, said that "every ounce of his boundless energy was directed to the protection of personal rights," and the *Washington Post* called him "a fierce defender of civil rights."[3] Tom Clark was a newcomer to the Court, having been confirmed in August 1949. But he had been Harry Truman's attorney general and, in that capacity, proved himself to be an effective proponent of the rights of black Americans on several fronts.[4]

Of more conservative bent were two Truman appointees, Sherman Minton and Harold Burton, but both of them were "ardent Cold Warriors" and were open to making decisions that advanced "the Cold War imperative for racial change."[5] Robert Jackson, back from his work as chief prosecutor at the Nuremberg Nazi trials, was also more conservative than some of his colleagues, and was somewhat of an uncertainty regarding civil rights. No doubt the most conservative of the nine were two Kentuckians, Stanley Reed and Chief Justice Fred Vinson. Their positions were unclear at this point, but the NAACP attorneys could take some comfort from the fact that both had voted in favor of Sipuel. The attorneys might have been a good deal less optimistic if they had known that at their conference about whether or not to hear the *McLaurin* case, three

2. Howard Ball, *Hugo L. Black: Cold Steel Warrior* (New York: Oxford University Press, 1996), 100–104. As early as 1941, White invited Justice Black to address the annual conference of the NAACP.

3. Spencer Rich, "William O. Douglas Dies at 81," *Washington Post*, January 20, 1980, A1.

4. For Clark's civil rights record as attorney general, see Mimi Clark Gronlund, *Supreme Court Justice Tom C. Clark: A Life of Service* (Austin: University of Texas Press, 2010), 106–12.

5. Klarman, *From Jim Crow to Civil Rights*, 194–95.

of the justices (Burton, Reed, and Vinson) had voted to affirm the lower court's ruling.[6]

Adding to the uncertainty, the Supreme Court of 1950 was hardly a cordial band of brethren. Bitter feuds, rampant animosities, and considerable distrust among its members marred its deliberations. Perhaps this was the inevitable result of having such brilliant, egotistic, and domineering personalities as Frankfurter, Black, Jackson, and Douglas working under a relatively weak chief justice. But, writes Supreme Court historian Herbert A. Johnson, the chief justiceships of Harlan Stone (1941–1946) and Fred Vinson, his successor, "share the unenviable distinction of being perhaps the least collegial and most internally vindictive periods of the Court's history." Indeed, Johnson continues, "one wonders how the Stone and Vinson Courts conducted any business whatsoever given the animosity and personality clashes among its members."[7] According to constitutional historian Melvin I. Urofsky, "Vinson had neither the intellectual nor the political skills to lead the Court."[8] The central tension, as much personal as ideological, was between Hugo Black and Felix Frankfurter. Black was eventually joined by Douglas.[9] Meanwhile a feud, just as bitter, simmered between justices Black and Jackson.[10] That hostility erupted upon the death of Chief Justice Stone in April 1946. There were strong rumors (perhaps untrue) that Black threatened to resign from the Court if Truman named Jackson (then in Nuremberg) as chief justice position,

6. Jan Palmer, *The Vinson Court Era: The Supreme Court's Conference Votes* (New York: AMS Press, 1990), 3.

7. Herbert A. Johnson, "Editor's Preface," in Urofsky, *Division and Discord*, ix.

8. Urofsky, *Division and Discord*, 8.

9. Wallace Mendelson, *Justices Black and Frankfurter: Conflict in the Court* (Chicago: University of Chicago Press, 1961); Melvin I. Urofsky, "Conflict among the Brethren: Felix Frankfurter, William O. Douglas, and the Clash of Personalities and Philosophies on the United States Supreme Court," *Duke Law Journal* (February 1988): 71–113. For the philosophic differences, see Jeffrey D. Hockett, "Justices Frankfurter and Black: Social Theory and Constitutional Interpretation," *Political Science Quarterly* 107 (Autumn 1992): 479–99.

10. Dennis J. Hutchinson, "The Black-Jackson Feud," *Supreme Court Review* (1988): 203–43.

and that Truman chose Fred Vinson as a compromise candidate.[11] It is appropriate that Urofsky called his study of these years *Division and Discord.*

There was simply no telling, in advance, how these internal divisions within the Court would impact not only the verdicts in the three civil rights cases but the important matter of exactly how far the justices would be willing to go in addressing the question of the constitutionality of segregation. Would the terrible factionalism among the justices result in crippling compromises in the decisions or a vote so divided as to water down its effectiveness? During the previous (October 1948) term, after all, the individual justices had dissented from the majority 272 times in 126 opinions.[12] In short, Marshall and the others might have been encouraged by the social attitudes of most of the justices and by the unanimity of the *Sipuel* decision two years earlier, but given the Court's divisive unpredictability, there was still plenty to worry about.

On Monday, June 5, 1950, sixty-one days after the oral arguments and on the final day of the Court's October 1949 term, the waiting came to an end. The justices had succeeded in reaching unanimity in all three of the civil rights cases.

In the matter of Elmer Henderson's shabby treatment in the dining car of the Southern Railway, the opinion was written and read by Justice Harold Burton,[13] and in his very first sentence he dashed any hopes for a sweeping ruling about the constitutionality of segregation on interstate railroads: "The question here is whether the rules and practices of the Southern Railway Company [regarding

11. Ibid., 204–207.

12. "Review of the Supreme Court's Work," *United States Law Week* 18 (June 30, 1950): 3345. When the figures were compiled for the October 1949 term, the number of dissents decreased to 98, in 126 opinions. The most dissents in the October 1949 term were filed by Black (32), Frankfurter (30), and Jackson (24). Ibid., 3346.

13. *Henderson v. United States et al.,* 339 U.S. 816 (1950). The vote was 8–0. Justice Clark recused himself because when he was attorney general, the Justice Department issued a brief in support of Henderson. Clark's successor, Howard McGrath, made an oral argument before the Court.

dining car arrangements] . . . violate §3 (1) of the Interstate Commerce Act." That section of the 1887 act, it will be recalled, made it illegal for an interstate railroad "to subject any particular person to any undue or unreasonable prejudice or disadvantage in any respect whatever."[14] But the question that Justice Burton enunciated was, obviously, not the *only* question that Henderson's lawyers hoped the Court would address. And no matter how decisively the Court declared that "we hold that those rules and practices [of the railroad] do violate the Act,"[15] there was bound to be some disappointment about the limited scope of the ruling.

Burton's opinion confronted directly the railroad's contention that its dining car seating arrangement was based on unprejudiced estimates concerning the infrequency of black passengers who actually used dining facilities. The Court affirmed the rule (previously enunciated[16]) that no particular person's rights might be ignored on the basis of such a statistical analysis—Lloyd Gaines, for example, could not be deprived of his right to a legal education simply because so few black Missourians wanted such training. Nor did the railroad's argument that white people might also be inconvenienced by the company's modified rules (if all the white seats were taken, they could not be seated at the black table even if there was space) justify the discrimination.[17] The High Court was not about to enter into regions not necessary to resolve the case, as might have been predicted by Justice Frankfurter's sharp questioning back in April (quoted above), but Justice Burton made this judicial restraint explicit: "Since §3 (1) of the Interstate Commerce Act invalidates the rules and practices before us, we do not reach the constitutional or other issues suggested. The judgment of the District Court is reversed."[18]

14. 54 Stat. 902, 49 U.S.C. §3 (1).

15. 339 U.S. at 818.

16. The Court cited an Oklahoma case, *McCabe v. Atchison, Topeka. & Santa Fe. Railroad Co.*, 235 U.S. 151 (1914), as well as *Missouri ex rel. Gaines v. Canada*, 305 U.S. 337 (1938).

17. 339 U.S., at 825–26.

18. Ibid., at 826.

The opinions in both of the NAACP cases, *Sweatt* and *McLaurin*, were written and read by Chief Justice Vinson, and both were issued without dissent. It was clear from the start that the Court regarded the two as sister cases, dealing with very similar issues. Vinson, who several times in his *Sweatt* opinion referred to "these cases," linked the two explicitly in the first words of that opinion: "This case and *McLaurin v. Oklahoma State Regents* . . . present different aspects of this general question: to what extent does the Equal Protection Clause of the Fourteenth Amendment limit the power of a state to distinguish between students of different races in professional and graduate education in a state university?"[19]

Then, in his next sentence, Vinson effectively brushed aside all of the research and expert testimony that the NAACP's attorneys had marshaled with such care and which purported to demonstrate the harmful effects of segregation on those who were segregated. "Broader issues have been urged for our consideration," Vinson acknowledged, "but we adhere to the principle of deciding constitutional questions only in the context of the particular case before the Court. We have frequently reiterated that this Court will decide constitutional questions only when necessary to the disposition of the case at hand, and that such decisions will be drawn as narrowly as possible."[20] Therefore, "because of this traditional reluctance to extend constitutional interpretations" beyond what was needed to decide a case, "much of the excellent research and detailed argument presented in these cases is unnecessary to their disposition." The chief justice returned to the matter of *Plessy v. Ferguson* at the close of his *Sweatt* opinion. The Court, he asserted, could not agree with Texas's contention that *Plessy* required that the segregationist decision of the lower court be affirmed. "Nor need we reach petitioner's contention that *Plessy v. Ferguson* should be reexamined in the light of contemporary knowledge respecting . . . the effects of racial segregation."[21] In short, there was no occasion to look at

19. *Sweatt v. Painter,* 339 U.S., at 631.
20. Ibid.
21. Ibid., at 636.

Plessy again. *Sweatt v. Painter* could be decided simply on the question of whether or not the arrangements that Texas proposed for the legal education of Heman Sweatt satisfied the requirement of the Fourteenth Amendment that every person was entitled to equal protection of the laws.

Therefore, the central thrust of the opinion was a thorough comparison of the law school at the University of Texas and the newly established law school that the state had established for black students. The university's longstanding law school had a faculty of sixteen full-time professors and three part-timers. Some of these professors were recognized authorities in their fields. The school had an enrollment of 850, a library of 65,000 volumes, a law review, a moot court, and money for scholarships. The black law school had a faculty of four part-time professors, who also taught at the University of Texas. It had an enrollment of twenty-three, and a library of 16,500 volumes. The conclusion was obvious: "We cannot find substantial equality in the educational opportunities offered white and Negro law students by the State." Thus far, the comparison between the white and the black schools was grounded on fairly concrete and visible facts. But then, in a passage of enormous significance, Vinson's opinion went further: "What is more important, the University of Texas Law School possesses to a far greater degree those qualities which are incapable of objective measurement but which make for greatness in a law school. Such qualities, to name but a few, include reputation of the faculty, experience of the administration, position and influence of the alumni, standing in the community, traditions and prestige." Vinson drove home the point: "It is difficult to believe that one who had a free choice between these law schools would consider the question close."[22]

The nonobjective factors that Vinson's opinion mentioned were soon being called "intangibles," and they had their origin in a memo that Justice Tom Clark had sent to the other justices a few days after the oral argument. In his memo, Clark enumerated seven such intangible factors, and it is evident that Vinson incorporated

22. Ibid., at 632–33.

the elements that Clark had listed.[23] In view of the inequities, both concrete and intangible, the U.S. Supreme Court ruled that Heman Sweatt was entitled to "claim his full constitutional right: legal education equivalent to that offered by the State to students of other races." Because that education could not be provided to him at the separated law school that had been created by the state, "the Equal Protection Clause of the Fourteenth Amendment requires that petitioner be admitted to the University of Texas Law School."[24]

The chief justice moved immediately to the case of George McLaurin, who was asking only to be treated like any other student. The Court's opinion in *McLaurin v. Oklahoma State Board of Regents* appears to be somewhat strained, as if the justices were struggling, almost bending over backwards, in order to avoid addressing the constitutionality of *Plessy v. Ferguson.* As in the previous opinions, Vinson began with an attempt to define (and drastically narrow) the question that the Court was called upon to adjudicate: "In this case we are faced with the question whether a state may, after admitting a student to graduate instruction in its state university, afford him different treatment from other students solely because of his race." And then, as if to make certain that nobody could think that the Court was going to review *Plessy,* Vinson added: "We decide only this issue."[25]

More than half of the opinion was a careful review of the history of George McLaurin's struggle to gain admission to the University of Oklahoma and then the conditions imposed on him while on the campus. He "uses the same classroom, library, and cafeteria as students of other races; there is no indication that the seats to which he is assigned in these rooms have any disadvantage of location. He may wait in line in the cafeteria and there stand and talk with his

---

23. For Justice Clark's four-page memo of April 7, 1950, see Tarlton Law Library, University of Texas, https://tarltonapps.law. utexas.edu/clark/pdf/sweatt /a20310.pdf (accessed May 16, 2019).

24. 339 U.S., at 635–36.

25. *McLaurin v. Oklahoma State Regents for Higher Education, et al.,* 339 U.S. 637, at 638.

fellow students, but while he eats he must remain apart." The Court understood that there would be many who felt that "the separations imposed by the State in this case are in form merely nominal." The justices also recognized that the university imposed these conditions on McLaurin "in order to comply, as nearly as could be, with the statutory requirements of Oklahoma."[26]

Under these circumstances of relative equality the Court had to wrestle with an awkward dilemma. Suppose that the justices wished to strike a blow against segregation, or, at the very least, not appear to be endorsing it. The University of Oklahoma had come about as close as possible to realizing the *Plessy* formula of separate-but-equal. Could the justices find against the university's practices without, in effect, reversing *Plessy* and saying that segregation, even under these relatively mild restrictions, was unconstitutional? But if they were to decide, as had the lower court, that the restrictions on McLaurin did not undermine his right to an equal education, would they not be endorsing a pattern of official racial separation that would probably be emulated throughout southern higher education? This was precisely why black leaders were divided about bringing McLaurin's case forward to the High Court. Some thought that a victory would be the way to getting closer to the end of separate-but-equal and, at long last, uprooting *Plessy*. Others feared that a rejection of McLaurin's claims would be an endorsement of *Plessy* that would set back race relations for years to come.

The Court's solution to this dilemma was to rule in favor of George McLaurin's contentions but to find in his favor not because *Plessy* was wrong and had been wrong for half a century, but because his treatment violated the equal protection of the laws mandated by the Fourteenth Amendment. The treatment imposed by the University of Oklahoma "sets McLaurin apart from the other students. The result is that [he] is handicapped in his pursuit of effective graduate instruction. Such restrictions impair and inhibit his ability to study, to engage in discussions and exchange views with other students, and, in general, to learn his profession. . . . We

26. Ibid., at 640–41.

conclude that the conditions under which [McLaurin] is required to receive his education deprive him of his personal and present right to the equal protection of the laws."[27] Perhaps to endow the opinion with a wider social purpose, Vinson went on to add an additional statement that connected McLaurin's treatment with the future of African Americans in general. "Those who will come under his guidance and influence must be directly affected by the education he receives. Their own education and development will necessarily suffer to the extent that his training is unequal to that of his classmates. State imposed restrictions which produce such inequalities cannot be sustained."[28] It was a curious supplement to the decision, especially since the man the justices were talking about was in his sixties, retired from teaching, and not likely to affect in the classroom the next generation of black students.

On the other hand, the Court felt the need to address a particular contention made by those in favor of maintaining the separation of the races. The segregationists sometimes argued that the government was naive to think it could somehow enact human brotherhood simply by revoking laws that required keeping the races apart. It was very likely, they asserted, that even if the university's restrictions were gone, whites would shun McLaurin, deny him and his fellow black students social acceptance, and have nothing whatever to do with them. The chief justice met this possibility with unusual eloquence:

It may be argued that [McLaurin] will be in no better position when these restrictions are removed, for he may still be set apart by his fellow students. This we think is irrelevant. There is a vast difference—a Constitutional difference— between restrictions imposed by the state which prohibit the intellectual commingling of students and the refusal of individuals to commingle where the state presents no such bar. . . . The removal of the state restrictions will not

27. Ibid., at 641–42.
28. Ibid., at 641.

necessarily abate individual and group predilections, prejudices and choices. But at the very least, the state will not be
depriving [McLaurin] of the opportunity to secure acceptance by his fellow students on his own merits.[29]

It had been a "clean sweep" as Jack Greenberg put it.[30] After June 5,
1950, black passengers on southern railways could not be relegated
to second-class citizenship. After June 5, Heman Sweatt was free
to enroll at the University of Texas School of Law, which he did
on September 19 (along with five other African Americans).[31] And
now George McLaurin and the other black students at the University of Oklahoma were to be treated in the same way as any of the
other students on campus. The afternoon of June 5 seemed like a
good time for a victory party at the New York office of the NAACP.
"There was lots of Scotch and bourbon, clouds of cigarette smoke,
lots of laughter and noise and bragging, jokes about race and racial
banter, and the almost obligatory poker game. . . . Everyone stayed
late, visitors came by, the press was on the phone. The euphoria
went on and on."[32]

For the next week, warm words of congratulation from civil
rights activists and the liberal media flooded in. "What I read seems
almost too good to be true," wrote Roscoe Dunjee the next day. "Is
this not a thrilling victory?"[33] Especially gratifying must have been
the note from Donald Murray, whose pioneering effort to enter the
law school at the University of Maryland in the mid-1930s contrib-
uted so much to the effort to desegregate professional and graduate

29. Ibid.
30. Greenberg, *Crusaders in the Courts*, 77.
31. Lavergne, *Before* Brown, 284. By a strange coincidence the dean at the University of Texas School of Law was none other than Page Keeton, who, when he was
dean at Oklahoma, testified for the NAACP that the bogus law school created by
the state could not be considered remotely equal to the University of Oklahoma's
School of Law, and who then enrolled Ada Lois Fisher as a student. Lavergne
writes (ibid.): "Dean Keeton may have been the most qualified administrator in
America to oversee the desegregation of the University of Texas Law School."
32. Greenberg, *Crusaders in the Courts*, 78.
33. RD to TM, June 10, 1950, NAACPPM, Reel 16, Frame 752.

education. He told Marshall that "all of us here in Baltimore feel very proud of your work."[34] The "First Lady" of civil rights, seventy-five-year-old Mary McLeod Bethune, called it "the most outstanding victory we have achieved" in the history of the NAACP.[35] The managing editor of one of the country's leading black newspapers, the *Pittsburgh Courier*, telegraphed Marshall to say "Congratulations to Negro America's indispensable man. I glory with you today in our victory!"[36] The editorial in *The New Republic*, entitled "Jim Crow in Handcuffs," was typical of the enthusiasm: "June 5, 1950, should be celebrated from now on as a banner day in the history of American democracy. On that day, segregation, the greatest social injustice in America was condemned by the Supreme Court."[37]

As was to be expected, not everyone was thrilled. The governor of Georgia, the vocal segregationist Herman Talmadge, announced that "as long as I am governor, Negroes will not be admitted to white schools. The line is drawn; the threats that have been held over the head of the South for four years are now pointed like a dagger ready to be plunged into the very heart of southern tradition."[38] No doubt he spoke for thousands of die-hard white southerners, and spurred on by Talmadge and others, the KKK talked about resistance and hoped for a revival in membership. Price Daniels, the Texas attorney general who had argued the *Sweatt* case back in April, listened on the phone in Austin as the verdict of June 5 was read to him. He, as well as other southern defenders of segregation, expressed the opinion that all was not lost. Daniels issued a statement on June 6, stating that because the Supreme Court did not expressly reverse *Plessy v. Ferguson* as the NAACP desired, separate-but-equal was still the law of the land. All the Court was saying was that the law school that the state had created for blacks was not equal to the one at the University of Texas. Presumably, if it were made equal, it would pass the Court's muster and segregation could

34. Donald Murray to TM, ibid., Frame 759.
35. NAACP Press Release, June 8, 1950, ibid., Frame 705.
36. Bill Nunn to TM (telegram), June 6, 1950, ibid., Frame 744.
37. "Jim Crow in Handcuffs," *New Republic*, 112 (June 19, 1950): 5.
38. Cited in Lavergne, *Before* Brown, 261.

be maintained. Officials in other southern states insisted that *their* black schools and segregationist policies *would* pass the equality test and *would* survive inspection in the judicial system.[39]

In general, the view among whites in Oklahoma seemed to be of grudging acceptance. The *Daily Oklahoman*'s front-page headline, "Negroes Win Battle to Choose Own Seats in Classrooms at OU,"[40] seemed intentionally to trivialize the issues that were contested in the *McLaurin* case. In its editorials, the paper maintained a discreet silence on the Supreme Court's decision of June 5. The editorial in the *Norman Transcript*, the hometown newspaper of the university, revealed that many of the locals were not happy about the Supreme Court's action:

> Inch by inch and foot by foot the U.S. Supreme Court is eliminating segregation throughout the South, including Oklahoma. For better or for worse the day is coming when Negroes will have the legal right to mingle with other folks at any time and in any public place, and Oklahoma people had just as well become reconciled to it. It would be better if that situation could be brought about by education and application of the Gold Rule, instead of by legal order. But the federal courts are upholding Negro groups which have forced the issue. The Supreme Court has not as yet passed on the constitutionality of segregation itself, which is based on the doctrine of equal but separate facilities. But it edges closer to that position in almost every decision relation to segregation. . . . No sooner was the ink dry on the latest decisions than Negro leaders started talking about breaking down segregation in high schools and grade schools, in other words, break down segregation in every form. If the court continues its past practice of going just a little further each time it hears a case involving segregation, it will not be long until all segregation will be ruled out.

39. Ibid., 259.
40. *DO*, June 6, 1950, 1.

Negroes Win Battle To Choose Own Seats In Classrooms at OU

The *Daily Oklahoman* breaks the news, June 6, 1950. Courtesy *The Oklahoman*.

The *Transcript* advised its readers to accept the Court's rulings "without resentment or friction," and to do so "regardless of whether we believe quick breakdown of segregation practices by legal order is less desirable than gradual elimination of them."[41]

Some of Thurgood Marshall's friends feared that he might be disappointed and unduly discouraged by the Supreme Court's failure to overturn *Plessy*, especially since many legal analysts mentioned that shortcoming in their commentaries immediately following the decisions of June 5. Pauli Murray, an activist, lawyer, and the first African American woman ordained as an Episcopal priest, hastened to send words of comfort and assurance to her friend. "I know you would have preferred a clear-cut over-ruling of *Plessy v. Ferguson*," she wrote two days after the verdicts, "but if I read the newspaper quotations correctly it would appear that the three decisions taken together have 'whittled away' further the basis of *Plessy* and that it is only a matter of time before it will be completely discredited. More power to you!"[42] Others wrote in the same consoling spirit, praising the decisions as victories and urging Marshall to keep up the fight until ultimate victory was achieved.

Although they meant well, they seemed to have misjudged Marshall's reaction. He showed no sign of discouragement and he consistently praised the decisions in *Sweatt* and *McLaurin* as substantial victories. "Of course it would have been good for the court to have

41. *NT*, June 7, 1950, 4.
42. Pauli Murray to TM, June 7, 1950, NAACPPM, Reel 16, Frame 748.

overruled Plessy v. Ferguson," he replied to Pauli Murray, "but a careful reading of the opinions will show that for all intents and purposes, Plessy v. Ferguson has been gutted. . . . [W]hatever way you look at it, the end is in sight and in view of the fact that the opinion was unanimous, there is little doubt as to what will happen on future cases to be brought."[43] To Charles Bunn, a law professor at the University of Wisconsin, Marshall wrote that "despite what has been said by the commentators and others as to what the decisions did not do, I am convinced that this is a real victory. . . . [A]lthough the Chief Justice did not overrule *Plessy v. Ferguson* he at least did one of the finest jobs of gutting the decision that I know of."[44] Marshall sounded the same note to another friend: "So far as I am concerned, the three cases were terrific victories despite what commentators and others might say." He went on to condemn the defeatism among allies to the cause: "In addition to the commentators and some of the southerners, I am sure there will be some of our folk who will belittle these opinions simply because they expect one case to do everything and are too lazy to follow the normal legal procedure which requires step-by-step action."[45] Marshall's views were echoed by numerous prominent journalists and legal writers.[46]

43. TM to Pauli Murray, June 9, 1950, ibid., Frame 749.
44. TM to Charles Bunn, June 12, 1950, ibid., Frame 763. Bunn had testified on behalf of the NAACP in Cleveland County, denying that the law school created for Fisher could be considered equal to the school at the University of Oklahoma.
45. TM to Ernest E. Johnson, June 13, 1950, ibid., Frame 766.
46. For a few examples of contemporary commentary in harmony with Thurgood Marshall's contentions, see the *New Republic*'s "Jim Crow in Handcuffs"; "Segregation," *The United States Law Week* 18 (June 13, 1950): 3342; John P. Roche, "Education, Segregation, and the Supreme Court—a Political Analysis," *University of Pennsylvania Law Review* 99 (May 1951): 949–59; Roche, "The Future of 'Separate but Equal,'" *Phylon* 12 (1951): 219–26; "The Courts and Racial Integration in Education, *Journal of Negro Education* 21 (Summer 1952): 421–30; Charles H. Thompson, "How Imminent is the Outlawing of Segregation," *Journal of Negro Education* 20 (Autumn 1951): 495–98; James M. Nabrit Jr., "Resort to the Courts as a Means of Eliminating Legalized Segregation," *Journal of Negro Education* 20 (Summer 1951): 460–74; E. H. Hobbs, "Negro Education and the Equal Protections of the Laws," *Journal of Politics* 14 (August 1952): 488–511; Katherine E. Driscoll in *Boston University Law Review* 30 (November 1950): 565–69; E. Milton Farley, III, in *Notre Dame Lawyer* 26 (Fall 1950): 134–37; and anonymous commentary in *Virginia Law Review* 36 (October 1950): 797–800.

In accord with that optimism, the NAACP sent out a barrage of press releases, all of them exulting in the victories of George McLaurin and Heman Sweatt, and all of them insisting that despite the Court's silence on *Plessy*, there was every cause for celebration. The publicity campaign began hours after the Court had spoken. In a release hastily written by Roy Wilkins ("without having carefully analyzed the complete text of the opinions"), the rulings were hailed as "a great step forward."[47] Next day, Executive Secretary Walter White issued a rapturous statement. "Yesterday the United States Supreme Court in two monumental decisions [*Sweatt* and *McLaurin*], struck the most devastating blow in American history against education segregation and discrimination." White's statement was telegraphed to a hundred faithful supporters, asking each of them to contribute $100 to help pay the $40,000 it had cost to litigate the two cases.[48]

Two days later, the New York office sent out no fewer than three separate releases celebrating the new developments. The first, largely Marshall's work, began, "The complete destruction of all enforced segregation is now in sight." The second release that day trumpeted the praise that the NAACP was receiving on account of its success: "Congratulatory messages from all parts of the country poured into the NAACP national office this week as news of the three unanimous Supreme Court decisions against segregation, handed down on June 5, swept the nation."[49] A third release, written by publicists Roy Wilkins and Henry Lee Moon, went to dozens of friendly editors and journalists across the United States and explained in detail what each of the opinions actually said.[50] When an editorial in the NAACP's principal organ, *The Crisis*, in its July issue, misinterpreted the decisions, suggesting that segregated institutions might still be maintained if "they can be proved equal," Marshall wrote the editor a testy correction. Your editorial, "to my mind, is going to be used by the 'separate but equal' boys as showing that within the NAACP there is serious dispute as to the true

47. For Wilkins's release, see NAACPPM, Reel 16, Frame 691.
48. For Walter White's telegraphed statement, see ibid., Frame 694.
49. Press releases, "End of Jim Crow Seen by Marshall," ibid., Frame 701; and "Hail NAACP Legal Staff for Supreme Court Wins," ibid., Frame 705.
50. Press release, "Note to Editors," ibid., Frames 697–700

meanings of these decisions."[51] The interpretation that *The Crisis* put on the decisions, Marshall complained, made it seem as though the Court's pronouncements did not go beyond *Gaines*, preserving the hopes of the segregationists that separation would be possible if the facilities could somehow be made "equal."

Marshall insisted, in virtually every response to his friends, that his optimistic assessment was based upon the most careful review and analysis of the Supreme Court's opinions. On the basis of his study of the chief justice's words in *Sweatt* and *McLaurin*, Marshall drew a pair of very encouraging conclusions. First, for all practical purposes the decisions outlawed segregation, at least in graduate and professional education. If (as in the *Sweatt* case), the Court was going to take into consideration such things as a school's traditions and prestige, the reputation of its faculty, the experience of its administration, and the number and influence of its alumni, it must be perfectly clear that no hastily created school for blacks could possibly be considered the equal of the long-established public institutions that whites had enjoyed for decades. And if (as in the *McLaurin* case) the Court found that even those relatively mild restrictions that George McLaurin had to endure, and the psychological and social disabilities imposed on him by those restrictions, were incompatible with the Fourteenth Amendment's stipulation of equal protection of the laws, it must be perfectly clear that no administratively enforced separation of the races would pass muster. True, the Supreme Court did not explicitly overrule *Plessy v. Ferguson*, but, as Marshall put it, the Court did a fine job of "gutting" it.

The second conclusion that Marshall and his colleagues drew as they reviewed the opinions in *Henderson, Sweatt,* and *McLaurin* was even simpler. "All three of the decisions," he told Charles Bunn, "are replete with road markings telling us where to go next."[52] What Marshall thought he saw in those decisions was a directive for the next round of civil rights litigation: stress the intangibles.

---

51. TM to James Ivy, July 13, 1950, ibid., Frame 716.
52. TM to Charles Bunn, June 12, 1950, ibid., Frame 763.

Epilogue

Where to "go next" seemed obvious to almost everyone, from the emboldened civil rights advocates to the terrified southern whites. The logical next step was to take the principles enunciated in June 1950 and use them to attack segregated elementary and secondary education. The time for demanding "equality" for segregated black institutions had passed; the time had come to launch a full onslaught on segregation itself, insisting that it was plainly incompatible with the equal protection of the laws. Marshall wasted no time. He called for a conference to take place in New York City on June 26–27, three short weeks after the decisions of June 5. The gathering was to consider strategy for moving forward and especially to make certain that southern members of the NAACP were ready to support so precipitous a move, even if it risked provoking a vicious backlash from white southerners. It was widely understood that the emotional stakes were a good deal higher and feelings would much more intense when the cases involved elementary school children rather than graduate students. Nevertheless, besides the lawyers, NAACP officers from twenty-two states and the District of Columbia came to Marshall's conference. A few of the lawyers had reservations about the new plan, but nearly all the others at the gathering were enthusiastic.[1]

The story of the 1954 landmark case of *Brown v. Board of Education of Topeka*[2] has been told so often and so thoroughly that

1. Carter, *Matter of Law*, 96–97.
2. 347 U.S. 483 (1954).

it is not necessary to repeat it here.[3] It should be perfectly clear that the argument in *Brown* drew heavily upon the verdict given in *McLaurin*. In *McLaurin*, after all, the Court had ruled that separating George McLaurin from the white students who were his peers hampered his education to such an extent that it violated the U.S. Constitution. It seemed obvious to Marshall that the *McLaurin* ruling applied also to children in public elementary and secondary schools. For him, the decision rendered in *McLaurin* adequately disposed of the arguments being offered by the defenders of segregation.[4] In that contention, Marshall was echoing a remark in the opinion in the District Court of Kansas (August 3, 1951): "If segregation within a school as in the McLaurin case" is incompatible with the Fourteenth Amendment, wrote Judge Walter Huxman, "it is difficult to see why segregation in separate schools would not result in the same" ruling.[5] So confident was Marshall that *McLaurin* effectively decided the issue that in the oral re-argument of *Brown* in December 1953, he contended that "the only way that this court can decide this case in opposition to our position . . . is to find that for some reason, Negroes are inferior to all other human beings."[6]

Among the Supreme Court justices hearing the *Brown* case, only Stanley Reed had a lingering sympathy for segregation.[7] The sole hesitation among some of the other eight was one of judicial restraint—did the Court have the authority (or the right) to overturn the segregation laws of the legislatures of so many sovereign

3. The major account remains Kluger, *Simple Justice*. See also James T. Patterson, *Brown v. Board of Education: A Civil Rights Milestone and Its Troubled Legacy* (New York: Oxford University Press, 2002); and Robert J. Cottrol, Raymond T. Diamond, and Leland B. Ware, *Brown v. Board of Education: Caste, Culture and the Constitution* (Lawrence: University Press of Kansas, 2003).

4. Cottrol, Diamond, and Ware, *Brown v. Board*, 148.

5. 98 F. Supp. 797. Nevertheless, the Kansas District Court rejected the petition in *Brown* because *Plessy* and *Gong Lum* "had never been overruled and . . . they still presently are authority for the maintenance of a segregated school system in the lower grades."

6. Quoted in Cottrol, Diamond, and Ware, *Brown v. Board*, 148.

7. Patterson, *Brown v. Board*, 65.

states? The death of Chief Justice Vinson, on September 7, 1953, and his replacement by California governor Earl Warren greatly influenced the outcome. Warren quickly proved himself a master diplomat, charming, deferential to his more learned colleagues, willing to listen and compromise. He stressed the importance of unanimity on this issue of segregation, lest the South use any dissent as a basis for resistance, even persuading Reed to concur with the final decision. On May 17, 1954, the chief justice, speaking for a unanimous Court, uttered the words that Marshall, his colleagues, and hundreds of thousands of ordinary African American citizens had been hoping to hear. They were the very words that Marshall had tried, in vain, to coax out of the Court almost four years earlier in *McLaurin*. Now at last out they came:

> We come then to the question presented: Does segregation of children in public schools solely on the basis of race, even though the physical facilities and other "tangible" factors may be equal, deprive the children of the minority group of equal educational opportunities? We believe that it does. . . . We conclude that in the field of public education the doctrine of "separate but equal" has no place. Separate educational facilities are inherently unequal. Therefore, we hold that the plaintiffs and others similarly situated for whom the actions have been brought are, by reason of the segregation complained of, deprived of the equal protection of the laws guaranteed by the Fourteenth Amendment.[8]

As Marshall had predicted, the decision rested on the social and psychological effects of segregation rather than on the usual, tangible factors. Chief Justice Warren noted that the lower courts in the particular cases leading to *Brown* had determined that "the Negro and white schools involved have been equalized, or are being equalized, with respect to buildings, curricula, qualifications and salaries of teachers, and other 'tangible' factors. Our decision,

8. 347 U.S. at 493.

therefore, cannot turn on merely a comparison of these 'tangible' factors in the Negro and white schools involved in each of the cases. We must look instead to the effect of segregation itself on public education." Citing the Court's opinion in *McLaurin*, Warren stressed the "intangible considerations," asserting that, "such considerations apply with added force to children in grade and high schools. To separate them from others of similar age and qualifications solely because of their race generates a feeling of inferiority as to their status in the community that may affect their hearts and minds in a way unlikely ever to be undone."[9]

Those who thought that the decisions in *Sweatt, McLaurin,* and *Brown* marked the hoped-for end of an effort that had occupied the NAACP at least since the mid-1920s were in for a shocking disappointment. The victories in the Supreme Court may have made illegal the state enforcement of segregation in public education. But they also triggered an explosion of fury, desperate countermeasures, and outright violence among southern whites. This "massive resistance" and extreme defiance led, in turn, to a strenuous reaction among African Americans and millions of their advocates. The Court's pronouncements marked a beginning rather than an end. And the post-1954 efforts to obtain justice for African Americans, leading to the civil rights movement, employed weapons different from those with which the NAACP was comfortable. New and angrier black voices rejected so heavy a reliance on litigation. They advocated, instead, direct action to meet the often unrestrained actions of those determined to keep segregation. The new era would be one of bus boycotts and giant protest marches, of voter registration drives and freedom rides and sit-ins at lunch counters. While some of the new leaders would urge passive resistance and moral suasion, others threatened to counter violence with violence. Many black youths gravitated away from the NAACP and toward groups that were more activist, more radical, and less constrained by the decorum and slow pace of the courtroom. Thus it was clear that while important gains had been made through the courage of such

9. Ibid., at 494.

people as Donald Murray, Lloyd Gaines, Ada Lois Fisher, Heman Sweatt, and George McLaurin, it was also clear that the fight was far from over.

On June 6, 1950, the very next day after the Supreme Court had ruled on behalf of George McLaurin, Ada Lois Sipuel Fisher quietly left her lonely chair in the back row of her classroom and moved to the front. "I have not sat in the back ever since," she was later to write. "*McLaurin* made that possible."[10]

As far as the University of Oklahoma was concerned, the victory that McLaurin had won brought some important and immediate results. Those degrading "Colored Only" signs that had not already been removed by the students themselves disappeared within a day or two. Suddenly black students found that they could sit wherever they pleased in their classrooms, in the cafeteria, and at the library. There would no longer be any question about their rights to university housing. The offensive separating wall in the stadium came down before the start of the football season. So much for the removal of state-mandated segregation.

A perusal of the *Sooner Yearbook*s for the period after the *McLaurin* decision, however, reveals that the mingling of black and white students was a very slow process. The first photograph showing students of both races sitting or standing together was, appropriately enough, of Ada Lois Fisher on the steps of Monnet Hall in the midst of her law school class.[11] By the mid-1950s, black students slowly began to appear in group pictures of the YMCA, the University Choir, the International Club, the Accounting Club, the Social Work Club, Alpha Phi Omega (the scouting fraternity), and the University Band.[12] There were a few other indications of the gradual acceptance of black students into formerly all-white situations.

10. *MBW,* 152.
11. *Sooner Yearbook* (1951), 150. In the yearbooks for 1949–51, there were at least eight thumbnail pictures of black students (including one of Penninah McLaurin), photographed separately.
12. *Sooner Yearbook* (1951), 262, 293, 296; ibid. (1952), 281, 294; ibid. (1953), 194; ibid. (1954), 154, 236.

Johnnie Davis, a black woman, was pictured as a member of the Student Senate in the 1951 yearbook.[13] Photographs of African Americans began to appear in the part of the yearbook devoted to the School of Medicine and the School of Nursing in Oklahoma City, and in the 1952 *Sooner*, black student D. W. Lee can be seen as a member of the School of Medicine's Student Council.[14] Two years later several black women were among the senior nurses and others were part of the entering class.[15]

Alongside the occasional token photo of blacks and whites in a few of the same campus organizations, there were a few more significant signs of racial progress in the 1950s. On June 5, 1950 (the same day as the Supreme Court announced its decision in *McLaurin*), the University of Oklahoma graduated its first three African American students. They were Mauderie Hancock Wilson, one of the two women who joined McLaurin on campus in the spring 1949 semester; Malcolm Whitby, the talented musician who was not allowed to play in the marching band; and Ela Mae Reynolds, the woman who sought permission to attend Lionel Hampton's concert and dance in October 1949. All three received master's degrees in Education.[16] In 1956, Prentice Gautt became the first African American to join the university's football team, and even the most bigoted racist could see that he was a young man of exceptional prowess on the field and of decency, modesty, and grace off it. One can only speculate as to how many Sooner fans who had their doubts about this desegregation business would modify their views because of this sensational running back.[17]

On January 15, 1953, the school hired its first African American teacher. She was Marie Cecelia McKnight Mink, and she began her career as a teaching assistant in the School of Nursing. The next year, she was made an instructor and, eventually, she became the

13. Ibid. (1951), 262.
14. Ibid. (1952), 180.
15. Ibid. (1954), 183, 186.
16. "State University Will Award Its First Degrees to Negroes," *DO*, May 30, 1950, 34.
17. Max Nichols, "Gautt, Prentice," *EOHC* 1:576.

first black full-time assistant professor at the University of Oklahoma.[18] On the Norman campus, the first black faculty member was Melvin Tolson Jr., the son of the famous poet. He was hired to teach French by the Modern Languages Department in 1959. For the next thirty years, Tolson excelled as a fine teacher and a steady, reliable, and respected colleague. He paved the way for other black professors, although at an agonizingly slow pace. Lennie Marie Tolliver, a graduate of the University of Chicago and a social worker with both academic and field experience, began teaching and supervising field work at the university in 1964. Three years later, in August 1967, George Henderson arrived from Michigan to establish the university's Human Relations Department. In addition to Henderson's distinguished career as a teacher, as an author of more than two dozen books, and as an able administrator and eventual dean, he, along with his wife, Barbara, quickly became the nominal parents for generations of young black students, many of them desperately needing (and receiving) words of encouragement and genuine concern.

It will seem that these gestures in the direction of including blacks in the life of the university were rather meager. Hiring four black faculty members in seventeen years does not seem like much to brag about. For every campus organization that had a black face in its yearbook photograph, there were probably twenty-five that remained entirely white for more than a decade after *McLaurin*. The Greek system of fraternities and sororities went for decades without ever pledging a black brother or sister. And one looks in vain for any photograph in those old yearbooks that show blacks and whites together at a social event such as a dance or a picnic or a party. There are also more than a few of those old photos that indicate the persistence of racial stereotyping of the standard sort. In 1952, fifteen student nurses thought it would be amusing to perform a song in blackface. The next year, the Thetas created a skit featuring three members playing African savages with blackened bodies who threatened to "boil in oil" their victims; the same year the Gamma Phi's

18. Everett and Everett, *Medical Education in Oklahoma*, 216, 225.

put on a "minstrel show" with eight black-faced women singing their ditties. For the 1954 yearbook, five Alpha Delta Pi's put on black-face to entertain their rushees, and for a rush party at the Alpha Chi Omega house, some boys did the same and posed as "bus-boys."[19]

In 2010, Professor Henderson published a memoir of his first years in Norman, and the book provides a snapshot of where race relations stood nearly twenty years after *McLaurin*. Henderson's first impression of Norman came when he discovered that nobody in town was willing to sell him a house, a sure indication of the town's quiet but widespread racism. He also learned that despite many well-meaning white students and faculty, the black students on campus felt almost completely isolated from the political and social life of the university. He quickly saw the place to which he had come as one of "white privilege, black separatism, and campus-wide indifference to bigotry." Nobody opposed the admission of blacks to the university any longer, but once on campus they were, at worst, shunned, or, at best, ignored. Henderson suggests that the years around 1967 to 1971 constituted a kind of turning point for blacks at the University of Oklahoma. Much of the change was caused by the formation, with the assistance of Henderson and Tolson, of the Afro-American Student Union in November 1967. That group offered not only fellowship and mutual support for black students, but publicly challenged and resisted formal and informal policies of exclusion and prejudice.[20] Another important sign of change came in spring 1970, when the largely white campus elected Bill Moffitt the first black president of the student body. Moffitt came into office a few days before the shattering disturbances caused by President Nixon's Cambodian incursion and the murder of four Kent State students who were protesting the Vietnam War. Moffitt, it was universally acknowledged, handled that crisis with such exquisite diplomacy, principle, and sound judgment that no one

19. *Sooner Yearbook* (1952), 187; ibid. (1953), 52, 336; ibid. (1954), 201.

20. For Henderson's view of the racial situation in Norman and at the University of Oklahoma in the late 1960s, and for his account of the early work of the Afro-American Student Union, see his *Race and the University: A Memoir* (Norman: University of Oklahoma Press, 2011).

The first African American graduates of the University of Oklahoma: Mauderie Hancock Wilson, Malcolm Whitby, and Ela Mae Reynolds, 1950. Courtesy *The Oklahoman*.

could any longer think that blacks were incapable of leadership of the highest quality.[21]

In short, just as the difficulties did not end nationally with the ruling in *Brown*, neither did they end at the University of Oklahoma with the ruling in *McLaurin* or with the small token gestures of acceptance that followed. Perhaps, as Henderson argues, a corner was turned in the late 1960s and early 1970s. But old ignorance and insensitivity are slow to die. As the writing of this book began, a group of fraternity boys on a party bus broke out into a repugnant racist song for the entertainment of their dates (one of whom filmed the outrage); and as the writing of this book was drawing to an end, two young women thought it would be fun to apply blackface and to broadcast their act on social media. If there is any ground for hope, it is in the fact that both of these incidents were met with widespread disgust and overwhelming protests across the campus.

And what of the man whose actions seven decades ago resulted in changes, however reluctant and slow, in Oklahoma and across the South? George McLaurin had always liked privacy and quiet. That moment of courage and self-assertion that he exhibited in the autumn of 1948 was probably, as the family believed, due as much to the lifelong militancy and the urging of his wife as to any inclination of his own.[22] The dignity and good humor that he demonstrated all the way through to June 1950 was doubtless his own, a part of his nature and personality, but it is likely that he did not relish the attention nor miss the notoriety once the High Court had decided his case.

Those days when his struggle to enter the University of Oklahoma was in the newspapers and his name was known, those days constituted the high point of his public life. When they were over, McLaurin retreated to near anonymity and solitude. He was seldom

21. On Moffitt and the events of May 1970, see ibid., 166–74; and William McKeen, "Field Day: Student Dissent at the University of Oklahoma, May 5–12, 1970" (PhD diss., University of Oklahoma, 1986).

22. *DO*, August 21, 1966, 10; "Mrs. McLaurin Ends Life Long Educational Fight," 1.

George and Penninah McLaurin at home. Courtesy *The Oklahoman.*

mentioned in the press. He abruptly cut short his pursuit of a doctorate and, unlike his wife, who pursued a degree in Home Economics and graduated in 1954, he never went back to the university, even to take a class. He avoided the telephone and was cautious about his rare public statements. When a reporter came to the house to interview him on the day of his victory in the Supreme Court, she was greeted by Mrs. McLaurin while George remained in his room. He finally emerged—"tall and spare, 55 years old" and wearing "a bright blue suit, crisp white shirt, red and gray tie, carefully shined brown shoes."[23] He held in his hand a written statement. When Penninah went to another room to copy it, the reporter said to him, "We don't want prepared statements . . . we want to hear what

23. It may be presumed that the reporter asked McLaurin his age and that he gave it as fifty-five. He was actually almost sixty-four. Madelaine Wilson, "June 5, 1950! McLaurin Calls It Great Day," *DO,* June 6, 1950, 1–2.

you say from the heart, not the head." McLaurin's reply was revealing: "'But I must be careful what I say,' he says, hands fidgeting. 'Because of my race I must be careful not to make a grammatical error. . . . I might say something wrong and then folks would say "look at him—and him trying to get a Ph.D degree." We colored people have to be careful to dot our i's and cross our t's.'"[24]

McLaurin took no part in the civil rights movement of the 1950s and 1960s. Unlike Donald Murray and Ada Lois Sipuel Fisher, who, after their legal battles, enlisted themselves on behalf of the movement, McLaurin remained aloof from work with the NAACP. In part this might have been due to his age. But just as important in keeping him away from the NAACP was the fact that both Roscoe Dunjee and Thurgood Marshall had taken a distinct dislike to him. A full year before the verdict, Dunjee proposed that the organization dump McLaurin and "institute another case in the name of another petitioner." One reason Dunjee gave was that McLaurin was demanding money for continuing his part in the litigation. "I am thinking about this because McLaurin is still riding us for pay," he wrote to Marshall, "and if we had another case . . . we could get rid of his payoff."[25] The day after the Supreme Court decided in McLaurin's favor, Dunjee expressed his joy at the outcome but added, "I'm really surprised at the decision because McLaurin was such a disappointment during the trial here in Oklahoma City."[26] Marshall replied with brutal candor: "I agree with you that the decision was a good one when we realize the difficulties with McLaurin. . . . However, we won it so all of us are happy." Then referring to McLaurin's demands, financial and perhaps other, Marshall wrote, "I assume that you no longer will have to bow low to McLaurin. In my book he has been wholly unsatisfactory but I do not under any circumstances intend to make

24. Another reporter, Saul Feldman, wrote in the *Miami* (Oklahoma) *News Record* (June 25, 1950, 12) that McLaurin "speaks in hushed tones and weighs each word before giving an opinion."

25. RD to TM, June 13, 1949, NAACPPM, Reel 13, Frames 966–97. See also Amos T. Hall to TM, October 20, 1949, ibid., Frame 978, which indicates that the local chapter of the NAACP was paying McLaurin's tuition.

26. RD to TM, June 6, 1950, ibid., Reel 16, Frame 752.

this known to anyone because we cannot afford to detract from the victory itself."[27] No doubt Marshall was disappointed not only by McLaurin's weak testimony two years earlier, but because of his mediocre record as a student. He had failed his PhD examinations, and his handlers had had to scramble to keep him in school so they could continue their case. The only "A" McLaurin received from any of his teachers came from a professor who bestowed that grade on every single student in the class; otherwise, with the exception of a "C," McLaurin was a solid "B" student throughout his graduate career.[28] Marshall had invited both Ada Lois Fisher (at her own request) and Heman Sweatt to Washington to listen to the arguments in their cases. He maintained cordial relations with Fisher long afterwards, greeting her warmly whenever their paths crossed. Marshall also wrote a personal letter to Sweatt, congratulating him on his victory: "You are entitled to the fullest credit for a job well done and if it had not been for your courage and refusal to be swayed by others, this victory would not have been possible."[29] No such invitation, no such note came to McLaurin. In 1948, Marshall had telephoned Fisher to convey the good news of her victory.[30] George McLaurin learned his news when his wife informed him. She had been told by a reporter.

That reporter from the *Daily Oklahoman* left a description of the modest house at 524 N. Stonewall, where the McLaurins spent the next sixteen years of their lives together. "It's a small white home in the midst of small homes. Crowded-out pieces of furniture are on the tiny porch. Weeds grow around a packing case in the front yard. Inside, the doors and windows are closed to the June air. Venetian blinds are folded against the sunshine. An open Bible is on the arm of the plastic-covered divan. A radio bringing a noisy soap opera into the living room."[31] George and Penninah lived there simply enough until Penninah's death on August 20, 1966.[32]

27. TM to RD, June 8, 1950, ibid., Frame 751.

28. *Grade Books*, 1949, 1950, Provost's Office, Evans Hall, University of Oklahoma.

29. Cited in Lavergne, *Before* Brown, 259, as TM to Sweatt, June 8, 1950, NAACP Papers.

30. *MBW*, 122.

31. Wilson, "June 5, 1950!" 1.

32. *New York Times*, August 23, 1966, 39; *DO*, August 21, 1966, 10.

Three short weeks after McLaurin's interview with that reporter, he suffered a humiliation far greater than would have been occasioned by a grammatical error. The man who said that "we colored people have to be careful to dot our i's and cross our t's" was arrested in Holdenville, Oklahoma, on June 26. He had once been principal of the high school there and had acquired a one-story brick apartment house in town that contained thirty units—part of the McLaurins' substantial real estate holdings. Apparently, the county sanitarian had warned McLaurin "three or four times" that he had to install "proper toilet facilities" for his tenants and he had failed to do it. He was held in jail for two hours and released after paying a $20 fine and posting a $100 bond. He was warned that he would lose the $100 if he did not rectify the situation within five days. Of course the story made the *Daily Oklahoman*.[33]

After the death of Penninah, after fifty-four years of marriage, George left Oklahoma and moved to Los Angeles, where he lived with his son Joffre. He died on Wednesday, September 4, 1968. A week later, the tensions of twenty years earlier apparently forgotten, the NAACP requested that he be disinterred and his body returned to Oklahoma. It is probable that they took this initiative because of the influence of his younger son, Dunbar McLaurin, who made the announcement. George McLaurin was buried next to his wife in Oklahoma City's Trice Hill Cemetery on the afternoon of September 12. He had died a few days short of eighty-one, although his grave marker doggedly insists that he was only seventy-four. Three years later, the McLaurins' daughter, Phyllis, died after a long illness and was buried alongside her parents.[34]

The state council of Oklahoma's NAACP branches held a memorial service in Oklahoma City on September 14, and the University of Oklahoma's Afro-American Student Union held a similar service in Room 161 of the Student Union. In a recent move, the University's Office of Diversity and Inclusion established the "George McLaurin and Sylvia A. Lewis Leadership Institute," whose

33. *DO*, June 27, 1950, 33.
34. Ibid., May 5, 1971. Joffre McLaurin died in 1996, but like his brother Dunbar, he was not buried in the family plot in Oklahoma City.

purpose is "to recruit, retain, and ensure the successful graduation of high achieving students from underserved communities."[35]

Clearly, George McLaurin had his flaws and weaknesses, including some serious ones. In that way, of course, he was an everyday human being very much like the rest of us. What those who have honored him since his death have chosen to remember in him, instead of his flaws, were a set of virtues. These virtues were doubly memorable, doubly worthy of celebration, precisely because they sprang, not from a man of an extraordinary strength of character or a heroic nature, but from a quite ordinary man who was able to manifest them when the moment arose. At the heart of his beliefs was the importance of education. Together with his wife, he instilled that article of faith in his children. He also believed that it was through education that downtrodden black Americans had the best chance to rise, and for more than thirty years he gave young black men and women instruction. At that crucial moment in 1948, he somehow found the strength and the will to step forward—whether at his wife's urging or on his own volition is unimportant. And throughout the long ordeal that followed, he remained firm and did not flinch or retire from the field until the victory was won. And he comported himself in public with composure and serenity, and with such an absence of bitterness and resentment, that even those fierce enemies who hated the idea of desegregation did not hate *him*. He did, by his example, make things a little easier for those who were to follow. The inscription on the family gravemarker does not tell a lie: "STEP SOFTLY. A DREAM FOR THEIR PEOPLE LIES BURIED HERE."

35. Sylvia Lewis was the first African American appointed to the University of Oklahoma Board of Regents. She joined the board in 1986.

Works Cited

Unpublished Materials

Archives and Manuscripts

Grade Books, 1949, 1950. Provost's Office, Evans Hall, University of Oklahoma, Norman.

Maryland State Archives. Archives of Maryland Online. http://aomol.msa.mary land.gov/.

McLaurin Family Collection. Schomburg Center for Research in Black Culture. New York Public Library, Harlem Library, New York, New York.

National Association for the Advancement of Colored People (NAACP) Papers. Part 3: The Campaign for Educational Equality, Legal Department and Central Office Records, 1913–1950. Series B: 1940–1950. Microfilm.

Minutes of the State Regents for Higher Education. Oklahoma City.

Minutes of the University of Oklahoma Board of Regents. Evans Hall, University of Oklahoma, Norman.

Western History Collections (WHC), Monnet Hall, University of Oklahoma, Norman.
  Cross, George Lynn, Presidential MSS
  Dale, Edward Everett, MSS
  Hengst, Herbert R., MSS
  Vertical Files (University Archives)
    Desegregation
    McLaurin, George
    Naval Air Training Center (South Base)

Legal Cases

Bluford v. Canada, 153 S.W. 2d 12 (Mo. 1941)

Brown v. Board of Education of Topeka, 347 U.S. 483 (1954)

Esther McCready v. Harry C. Byrd, et al. Md., October Term 1949

Fisher v. Hurst, 333 U.S. 147 (1948)

Guinn v. United States 238 U.S. 347 (1915)

Henderson v. United States et al., 339 U.S. 816 (1950)

Hocutt v. Wilson, N.C. Super. Ct. (1933) (unreported)

McCabe v. Atchison, Topeka, & Santa Fe Railroad Co., 235 U.S. 151 (1914)

McLaurin v. Oklahoma State Regents for Higher Education, et al., 339 U.S. 637 (1950)

Missouri ex rel. Gaines v. Canada, 113 S.W. 2d 783 (1938)

Missouri ex rel. Gaines v. Canada, 305 U.S. 337 (1938)

Mitchell v. United States, 313 U.S. 80 (1941)

Pearson v. Murray, 169 Md. 478 (1936)

Plessy v. Ferguson, 163 U.S. 537 (1896)

Sipuel v. Board of Regents of the University of Oklahoma et al., 180 P.2d 135 (1947)

Sipuel v. Board of Regents of the University of Oklahoma et al., 332 U.S. 631 (1948)

Sipuel v. Board of Regents of the University of Oklahoma et al., 190 P.2d 437–38 (1948)

Sweatt v. Painter, 339 U.S. 629 (1950)

Yick Wo v. Hopkins, 118 U.S. 356 (1886)

Unpublished Papers, Theses, and Dissertations

Carter, Bruce Gilbert. "A History of Seminole County, Oklahoma." Master's thesis, University of Oklahoma, 1932.

Clark, Carter Blue. "A History of the Ku Klux Klan in Oklahoma." PhD diss., University of Oklahoma, 1976.

Edwards, Breanna. "The Bases: The Story of Norman's Naval Bases during 1942." Student paper, 2011. WHC, Vertical File: Naval Air Training Center (South Base).

Hadley, Worth J. "Roscoe Dunjee on Education: The Improvement of Black Education in Oklahoma, 1930–1955." EdD diss., University of Oklahoma, 1981.

Hatcher, Ollie Everett. "The Development of Legal Controls in Racial Segregation in the Public Schools of Oklahoma, 1865–1952." PhD diss., University of Oklahoma, 1954.

Hodo, Julie Tart. "Fortifying a Divide: The Oklahoma Press and the Fisher Struggle." Student paper, 2005. University Archives, WHC, Vertical File: "Desegregation."

Hubbell, John T. "The Desegregation of the University of Oklahoma, 1946–1950." Master's thesis, University of Oklahoma, 1961.

McKeen, William. "Field Day: Student Dissent at the University of Oklahoma, May 5–12, 1970." PhD diss., University of Oklahoma, 1986.

Reese, Linda W. "Searching for George W. McLaurin, Forgotten Civil Rights Hero." University of Oklahoma Archives, WHC, Vertical File: "McLaurin, George."

Spears, Earnestine Beatrice. "Social Forces in the Admittance of Negroes to the University of Oklahoma." Master's thesis, University of Oklahoma, 1951.

Thompson, John H. L. "The Little Caesar of Civil Rights: Roscoe Dunjee in Oklahoma City, 1915–1955." PhD diss., Purdue University, 1990.

Published Works

Government Publications

Bureau of the Census, *Population of Oklahoma and Indian Territory 1907.* Bulletin 89. Washington, D.C.: Department of Commerce and Labor, 1907.

Eighth United States Census. Washington, D.C.: Government Printing Office, 1864.

Oklahoma: County Marriage Records, 1890–1995 (Sequoyah County, 1909–1913).

Oklahoma Statutes, 70 Supplement (1949).

Oklahoma Territory, Session Laws (1897). Article 1, sections 1–11.

Proceedings of the Oklahoma Constitutional Convention. Guthrie: Leader Printing, 1907.

Social Security Death Index, 1935–2014, genealogybank.com/doc/ssdi/news (site discontinued)

To Secure These Rights, the Report of the President's Committee on Civil Rights. Washington, D.C.: Government Printing Office, 1947.

Books

Abel, Annie Heloise. *The American Indian as a Slaveholder and Secessionist*. Vol. 1 of *Slaveholding Indians*. Cleveland: Arthur H. Clark, 1915.

Ball, Howard. *Hugo L. Black: Cold Steel Warrior*. New York: Oxford University Press, 1996.

Berman, William C. *The Politics of Civil Rights in the Truman Administration*. Columbus: Ohio State University Press, 1970.

Bond, Horace Mann. *The Education of the Negro in the American Social Order*. New York: Prentice Hall, 1934.

Burke, Bob, and Angela Monson. *Roscoe Dunjee, Champion of Civil Rights*. Edmond, Okla.: UCO Press, 1998.

Carter, Robert Lee. *A Matter of Law: A Memoir of Struggle in the Cause of Equal Rights*. New York: New Press, 2005.

Cottrol, Robert J., Raymond T. Diamond, and Leland B. Ware. *Brown v. Board of Education: Caste, Culture and the Constitution*. Lawrence: University Press of Kansas, 2003.

Crockett, Norman L. *The Black Towns*. Lawrence: Regents Press of Kansas, 1979.

Cross, George Lynn. *Blacks in White Colleges: Oklahoma's Landmark Cases*. Norman: University of Oklahoma Press, 1975.

Dorman, Robert. *Alfalfa Bill: A Life in Politics*. Norman: University of Oklahoma Press, 2018.

Dudziak, Mary. *Cold War Civil Rights: Race and the Image of American Democracy*. Princeton: Princeton University Press, 2000.

Ellsworth, Scott. *Death in a Promised Land: The Tulsa Race Riot of 1921*. Baton Rouge: Louisiana State University Press, 1982.

Everett, Mark R., and Alice Allen Everett. *Medical Education in Oklahoma: The University of Oklahoma School of Medicine and Medical Center, 1932–1964*. Norman: University of Oklahoma Press, 1980.

Fisher, Ada Lois Sipuel. *A Matter of Black and White: The Autobiography of Ada Lois Sipuel Fisher*. Norman: University of Oklahoma Press, 1996.

Foreman, Grant. *A History of Oklahoma*. Norman: University of Oklahoma Press, 1942.

———. *Indian Removal: The Emigration of the Five Civilized Tribes of Indians*. Norman: University of Oklahoma Press, 1932, 1972.

Franklin, Jimmie Lewis. *Journey toward Hope: A History of Blacks in Oklahoma*. Norman: University of Oklahoma Press, 1982.

Franklin, John Hope, and Scott Ellsworth, eds. *The Tulsa Race Riot: A Scientific, Historical and Legal Analysis*. Oklahoma City: Tulsa Race Riot Commission, 2000).

Gasman, Marybeth, and Roger L. Geiger, eds. *Higher Education for African-Americans before the Civil Rights Era, 1900–1964*. New Brunswick, N.J.: Transaction Publishers, 2012.

Goble, Danney. *Progressive Oklahoma: The Making of a New Kind of State*. Norman: University of Oklahoma Press, 1980.

Greenberg, Jack. *Crusaders in the Courts: How a Dedicated Band of Lawyers Fought for the Civil Rights Revolution*. New York: Basic Books, 1994.

Gronlund, Mimi Clark. *Supreme Court Justice Tom C. Clark: A Life of Service*. Austin: University of Texas Press, 2010.

Hamby, Alonzo. *Beyond the New Deal: Harry S. Truman and American Liberalism*. New York: Columbia University Press, 1973.

Henderson, George. *Race and the University: A Memoir*. Norman: University of Oklahoma Press, 2011.

Johnson, Hannibal B. *Acres of Aspiration: The All-Black Towns in Oklahoma*. Austin, Tex.: Eakin Press, 2002.

Kellogg, Charles Flint. *NAACP: A History of the National Association for the Advancement of Colored People*. Baltimore: Johns Hopkins University Press, 1967.

Klarman, Michael J. *From Jim Crow to Civil Rights: The Supreme Court and the Struggle for Racial Equality*. New York: Oxford University Press, 2004.

Kluger, Richard. *Simple Justice: The History of* Brown v. Board of Education *and Black America's Struggle for Equality*. New York: Alfred A. Knopf, 1976.

Lavergne, Gary M. *Before* Brown: *Heman Marion Sweatt, Thurgood Marshall, and the Long Road to Justice*. Austin: University of Texas Press, 2010.

Levy, David W. *The University of Oklahoma: A History*. Vol. 2, *1917–1950*. Norman: University of Oklahoma Press, 2015.

Loewen, James. *Sundown Towns: A Hidden Dimension of American Racism*. New York: New Press, 2005.

Luxenberg, Steve. *Separate: The Story of* Plessy v. Ferguson, *and America's Journey from Slavery to Segregation*. New York: W. W. Norton, 2019.

McCuistion, Fred. *Graduate Instruction for Negroes in the United States*. Nashville: George Peabody College for Teachers, 1939.

McMurry, Linda O. *Recorder of the Black Experience: A Biography of Monroe Nathan Work*. Baton Rouge: Louisiana State University Press, 1985.

Mendelson, Wallace. *Justices Black and Frankfurter: Conflict in the Court*. Chicago: University of Chicago Press, 1961.

Motley, Constance Baker. *Equal Justice under the Law: An Autobiography*. New York: Farrar, Straus, and Giroux, 1998.

Mulroy, Kevin. *The Seminole Freedmen: A History*. Norman: University of Oklahoma Press, 2016.

Myrdal, Gunnar. *An American Dilemma: The Negro Problem and Modern Democracy*. New York: Harper & Brothers, 1944.

Painter, Nell Irvin. *The Exodusters: Black Migration to Kansas after Reconstruction*. New York: Alfred A. Knopf, 1977.

Palmer, Jan. *The Vinson Court Era: The Supreme Court's Conference Votes*. New York: AMS Press, 1990.

Patterson, James T. Brown v. Board of Education: *A Civil Rights Milestone and Its Troubled Legacy*. New York: Oxford University Press, 2002.

Patterson, Zella J. Black. *Langston University: A History*. Norman: University of Oklahoma Press, 1982.

Porter, Kenneth W. *The Black Seminoles: A History of a Freedom-Seeking People*. Gainesville: University of Florida Press, 2013.

Rampp, Lary C., and Donald L. Rampp. *The Civil War in the Indian Territory*. Austin, Tex.: Presidial Press, 1975.

Sullivan, Patricia. *Lift Every Voice: The NAACP and the Making of the Civil Rights Movement*. New York: The New Press, 2010.

Thoburn, Joseph B., and Muriel H. Wright. *Oklahoma: A History of the State and Its People*. 4 vols. New York: Lewis Historical Publishing, 1929.

Tolson, Arthur L. *The Black Oklahomans: A History, 1541–1972*. New Orleans: Edwards Printing, 1974.

Tushnet, Mark V. *Making Civil Rights Law: Thurgood Marshall and the Supreme Court, 1936–1961*. New York: Oxford University Press, 1994.

———. *The NAACP's Legal Strategy against Segregated Education, 1925–1950*. Chapel Hill: University of North Carolina Press, 1987.

Urofsky, Melvin I. *Division and Discord: The Supreme Court under Stone and Vinson, 1941–1953*. Columbia: University of South Carolina Press, 1997.

Ware, Gilbert. *William Hastie: Grace under Pressure*. New York: Oxford University Press, 1984.

Wattley, Cheryl Elizabeth Brown. *A Step toward Brown v. Board of Education: Ada Lois Sipuel Fisher and Her Fight to End Segregation*. Norman: University of Oklahoma Press, 2014.

Womack, John. *Norman: An Early History, 1820–1900*. Norman: Privately printed, 1976.

Woodward, C. Vann. *The Strange Career of Jim Crow*. New York: Oxford University Press, 1955.

Articles

"Abolish the Technicalities." *NT*, February 7, 1949, 4.

"All the Way." *DO*, November 21, 1947, 2.

"The Anita Hill Chair: A New Chapter in the Long Racial History of the University of Oklahoma College of Law." *Journal of Blacks in Higher Education* 11 (Spring 1996): 20.

Atkins, Hannah D. "Hall, Amos T. (1896–1971)." *EOHC* 1:639.

Balyeat, F. A. "Segregation in Public Schools of Oklahoma Territory." *ChO* 39 (Summer 1961): 191–97.

"Banker Dunbar S. McLaurin Suicide Victim in N.Y. Home." *Jet*, July 26, 1973.

"Bill's Author Has Criticism for Cross." *DO*, June 18, 1949, 5.

Bittle, William. "The Desegregated All-White Institution . . . The University of Oklahoma." *Journal of Educational Sociology* 32 (February 1959): 275–82.

Bluford, Lucile H. "The Lloyd Gaines Story." *Journal of Educational Sociology* 32 (February 1959): 242–46.

"Board Recommends End to Segregation in Graduate Schools." *DO,* January 30, 1949, 1.

Callis, H. A. "The Need and Training of Negro Physicians." *Journal of Negro Education* 4 (Winter 1935): 32–41.

Celarier, Michelle. "A Study of Public Opinion on Desegregation in Oklahoma Higher Education." *ChO* 47 (Autumn 1969): 268–81.

"Class Moves to New Room So Negro Can Sit to One Side." *DO,* October 15, 1948, 1.

Clayton, Edward T. "The Strange Disappearance of Lloyd Gaines." *Ebony* 6 (May 1951): 26–34.

"The Courts and Racial Integration in Education." *Journal of Negro Education* 21 (Summer 1952): 421–30.

Curtis, Gene. "First Black Student at OU Still Faced Obstacles." *Tulsa World,* February 18, 2007.

Dale, Edward Everett. "David Ross Boyd: Pioneer Educator." *ChO* 42 (1964): 2–35.

Darcy, R. "Constructing Segregation: Race Politics in the Territorial Legislature, 1890–1907." *ChO* 86 (Fall 2008): 260–89.

———. "Did African Americans Vote between 1910 and 1943?" *ChO* 93 (Spring 2015): 72–98.

———. "The Oklahoma Territorial Legislature, 1890–1905." *ChO* 83 (Summer 2005): 144–77.

Davis, J. B. "Slavery in the Cherokee Nation." *ChO* 11 (1933): 1056–72.

Doolittle, Sara. "Contingencies of Place and Time: The Significance of *Wilson v. Marion* and Oklahoma Territory in the History of School Segregation." *History of Education Quarterly* 58 (August 2018): 393–419.

Doran, Michael F. "Negro Slaves of the Five Civilized Tribes." *Annals of the Association of American Geographers* 68 (September 1978): 335–50.

———. "Population Statistics of Nineteenth Century Indian Territory." *ChO* 53 (1975–76): 492–513.

Dycus, Ed. "Ada Sipuel Fisher Denied Admission for Third Time." *OD,* June 17, 1949, 1.

———. "Segregation Procedure Announced by Cross." *OD,* June 17, 1949, 1.

Edwards, Paul K. "The Need for and Education of Negro Business Men." *Journal of Negro Education* 4 (Winter 1935): 71–75.

"Enrollment in Negro Colleges and Universities." *School and Society* 50 (July 29, 1939): 141.

"Equal Rights in Education." *New York Times,* January 15, 1948, 22.

"Federal Judges to Hear Negro's Plea August 23." *DO,* August 6, 1948, 1.

"56-Year-Old Segregation Rule Broken at Okla. University." *Black Dispatch,* October 16, 1948, 1–2, 5.

Fishman, Joel. "This Banker Had a Heart." *Daily Argus* (Mt. Vernon, N.Y.), July 14, 1973.

Gasman, Marybeth, and Roger L. Geiger, eds. *Higher Education for African-Americans before the Civil Rights Era, 1900–1964.* New Brunswick, N.J.: Transaction Publishers, 2012.

"GI Business Wizard." *Ebony* 4 (December 1948): 43.

Goble, Danney. "The Southern Influence on Oklahoma." In *"An Oklahoma I Had Never Seen Before": Alternative Views of Oklahoma History,* edited by Davis D. Joyce, 280–301. Norman: University of Oklahoma Press, 1994.

Grinde, Donald A., Jr., and Quintard Taylor, "Red vs. Black: Conflict and Accommodation in the Post Civil War Indian Territory." *American Indian Quarterly* 8 (Summer 1984): 211–29.

Hobbs, E. H. "Negro Education and the Equal Protections of the Laws." *Journal of Politics* 14 (August 1952): 488–511.

Hockett, Jeffrey D. "Justices Frankfurter and Black: Social Theory and Constitutional Interpretation." *Political Science Quarterly* 107 (Autumn 1992): 479–99.

"Holdenville Fine Given McLaurin." *DO,* June 27, 1950, 33.

Houston, Charles H. "The Need for Negro Lawyers." *Journal of Negro Education* 4 (Winter 1935): 49–52.

Hubbell, John T. "Some Reactions to the Desegregation of the University of Oklahoma, 1946–1950." *Phylon* 34 (1960): 187–96.

Huston, James L. "Civil War Era." *EOHC* 1:290–93.

Hutchinson, Dennis J. "The Black-Jackson Feud." *Supreme Court Review* (1988): 203–43.

Jeltz, Wyatt F. "Relations of Negroes and Choctaw and Chickasaw Indians." *Journal of Negro History* 33 (January 1948): 24–37.

Jessup, Michael M. "Consorting with Blood and Violence: The Decline of the Oklahoma Ku Klux Klan." *ChO* 78 (Fall 2000): 296–315.

"Jim Crow in Handcuffs." *New Republic* 112 (June 19, 1950): 5.

Johnson, Herbert A. "Editor's Preface." In *Division and Discord: The Supreme Court under Stone and Vinson, 1941–1953,* by Melvin I. Urofsky, ix–xii. Columbia: University of South Carolina Press, 1997.

Levy, David W. "The Week the President Went Fishing." *SM* 18 (Winter 1998): 26–30.

Logan, Ron. "Whitby Is First Negro Vet at OU." *OD,* June 22, 1949, 1.

"Logan Protest on Segregation Plan Produces Hot Words from Boatman." *DO,* June 19, 1949, 34.

Lomazoff, Eric, and Bailie Gregory. "Thurgood Marshall's 'Broom Closet': The Structure of Segregation in *McLaurin v. Oklahoma State Regents.*" *ChO* 97 (Spring 2019): 26–43.

"More Separate Classes Ready." *NT,* June 26, 1949, 1.

"Mrs. McLaurin Ends Life Long Educational Fight in State." *Black Dispatch,* August 26, 1966, 1.

"Music Professor Named to Teach Negroes at O.U." *NT,* June 24, 1949, 1.

Nabrit, James M., Jr. "Resort to the Courts as a Means of Eliminating Legalized Segregation." *Journal of Negro Education* 20 (Summer 1951): 460–74.

"Negro Admitted to O.U." *SM* 21 (October 1948): 9, 22.

"Negro Checks on Enrolment." *DO,* February 3, 1949, 4.

"Negro Seating Rushed." *DO,* November 23, 1948, 1.

"Negro to Have Own Anteroom for OU Work." *DO,* October 14, 1948, 1–2.

"Negro to Make Another Try." *El Reno* (Okla.) *Daily Tribune*, September 10, 1948.

Nichols, Max. "Gautt, Prentice." *EOHC* 1:576.

Nolen, Eunice. "The Real Reason?" *DO*, January 25, 1948, 6.

"No New State Move Is Likely in Negro Case." *DO*, August 25, 1948, 1.

"Oklahoma Honors McLaurin Family." *The Sphinx* 57 (December 1971): 37.

"OU Asks Ruling on Entry Case." *DO*, October 16, 1948, 25.

"OU Still Says No to Negro." *DO*, September 17, 1948, 1.

"OU to Ask Extra Funds for Negro Instruction." *NT*, June 19, 1949, 1.

Parr, Ray. "Six More Negroes Knock on OU's Door to Test Segregation." *DO*, January 29, 1948, 1.

Pogue, John. "Cress Hired to Teach OU Negroes." *OD*, June 22, 1949, 1.

"Railings Are Up at OU; Negroes Are Due Monday." *DO*, June 19, 1949, 38.

Reese, Linda W. "McLaurin, George W." In *African American National Biography*, vol. 5, edited by Henry Louis Gates, Jr., and Evelyn Brooks Higginbotham, 531–33. New York: Oxford University Press, 2008.

"'Reserved for Colored': Memories of Legalized Bigotry at the University of Oklahoma (1948)." *Journal of Blacks in Higher Education* 31 (Spring 2001): 75.

"Review of the Supreme Court's Work." *United States Law Week* 18 (June 30, 1950): 3345.

Rich, Spencer. "William O. Douglas Dies at 81." *Washington Post*, January 20, 1980, A1.

Roche, John P. "The Future of 'Separate but Equal.'" *Phylon* 12 (1951): 219–26.

———. "Education, Segregation and the Supreme Court—A Political Analysis." *University of Pennsylvania Law Review* 99 (May 1951): 949–59.

Schreiber, R. L. "Five Named to Instruct Negro Classes." *OD*, June 23, 1949, 1.

"Segregation." *The United States Law Week* 18 (June 13, 1950): 3342.

"Separate Instruction Will Require $100,000." *OD*, June 21, 1949, 1.

Spivey, Donald. "Crisis on a Black Campus: Langston University and Its Struggle for Survival." *ChO* 59 (Winter 1981–82): 430–47.

"State NAACP Conference Plans Bold Attack upon Education Inequalities in Sooner State." *Black Dispatch*, November 8, 1945, 1.

"State Negroes Plan Education Equality Fight." *DO*, November 4, 1945, 1.

"State University Will Award Its First Degrees to Negroes." *DO*, May 30, 1950, 34.

Stephenson, Larry. "The Sipuel Case." *SM* 20 (January 1948): 5, 26.

Stokes, Dillard. "Supreme Court Hears Negro's Schooling Plea." *Washington Post*, January 9, 1948, 1.

Stout, David. "Quiet Hero of Civil Rights History: A Supreme Triumph, Then into the Shadows." *New York Times*, July 11, 2009, A19.

Sullivant, Otis. "Legal Change to Let Negroes in OU, A&M Proposed by Deans." *DO*, March 23, 1948, 1.

Thompson, Charles H. "How Imminent is the Outlawing of Segregation." *Journal of Negro Education* 20 (Autumn 1951): 495–98.

———. "Separate but Not Equal: The *Sweatt* Case." *Southwest Review* 33 (Spring 1948): 105–12.

"University of Oklahoma's First Negro Student Dies." *Sacramento Bee*, September 7, 1968, 3.

Urofsky, Melvin I. "Conflict among the Brethren: Felix Frankfurter, William O. Douglas, and the Clash of Personalities and Philosophies on the United States Supreme Court." *Duke Law Journal* (February 1988): 71–113.

Wilson, Madelaine. "June 5, 1950! McLaurin Calls It Great Day." *DO*, June 6, 1950, 1–2.

Wood, Lewis. "Bar Segregation, High Court Asked." *New York Times*, April 4, 1950, 41.

Acknowledgments

I have incurred many debts in writing this book, and it is a pleasure to acknowledge them. I must begin by expressing my deep gratitude to the scholars whose work in African American, Oklahoman, and legal history has been indispensable to me. It is not feasible to thank each of them here, but I hope that my footnotes and bibliography will reveal how much I owe them.

I want to thank Linda W. Reese for her pioneering explorations into George McLaurin's life. Betty Jean Shapiro and Andre Head helped me navigate some of the genealogical and biographical mysteries relating to McLaurin. Darlita Bullard and Tabitha Terrell-Brooks of Jackson State University, and Rebecca Schute of the University of Kansas supplied information about McLaurin's academic career. Lauren Stark at the Schomburg Center for Research in Black Culture in New York City graciously facilitated my access to the McLaurin Family Collection. At the University of Oklahoma's Bizzell Memorial Library, Karen Rupp Serano, Laurie Scrivener, and Jeffrey Wilhite provided consistent and helpful assistance.

For a quarter of a century, I have benefited from the expertise and enjoyed the cordial hospitality of the staff at the Western History Collections at the University of Oklahoma. The welcome I first received from Don DeWitt and John Lovett has continued unbroken by Lina Ortega, David Wrobel, and Todd Fuller. I owe them and others on the staff a great deal. It would be hard to adequately measure my debt to Jacquelyn Reese, the Librarian at Western History; her knowledge of the Collections is unsurpassed, her patience with my numerous requests and her cheerful readiness to render aid have been remarkable. She is entirely responsible for the illustrations that appear in this book.

A version of chapter 4 originally appeared in the March 2020 number of *The Journal of Supreme Court History*. I have imposed on some old friends by asking them to read preliminary drafts of this book, and they have kindly loaned me their critical eyes and sharp minds to make the final product much better than it would have otherwise been. I have profited from the constructive suggestions of Sara Doolittle, Drew Kershen, Robert Shalhope, and Melvin Urofsky, and I deeply appreciate their willingness to take the time and make the effort on my behalf. Three especially well-qualified readers selected by the University of Oklahoma Press also made valuable suggestions for improvement, and I thank Guy Lavergne, Cheryl Elizabeth Brown Wattley, and Merline Pitri for their helpful observations and suggestions. I need hardly mention that any errors or other flaws that escaped their scrutiny can be attributed to only one person. I also wish to thank, for various matters in connection with writing this book, Dianna Crissman, Bruce Fisher, Kyle Harper, James Hart, George Henderson, Nancy Mergler, Ronald Schleifer, and Christa Seedorf.

This is the sixth book I have written or co-edited for the University of Oklahoma Press, and I continue to be impressed by the professionalism and the good will of the experts with whom I have worked. For their words of encouragement concerning this project, I am especially grateful to Byron Price and Adam Kane. Kent Calder and Steven Baker have combined their cool competence and efficiency with a friendly informality that have made working with them a pleasure; they have wisely guided the project through some unexpected difficulties. And my friend Alice Stanton has done her usual splendid job of copyediting the manuscript with high intelligence and sound judgment and sympathetic understanding. Every page of this book has been improved by her skill.

As always, my principal debt is to my wife, Lynne, for her encouragement, her saintly patience, and her willingness to excuse me from chores that I should have done, but which she selflessly undertook so that I might have the freedom to study and write. These (and the many other) gifts that she has bestowed on me and our children cannot be adequately expressed in words.

December 10, 2019
Norman, Oklahoma

Index

CPSIA information can be obtained
at www.ICGtesting.com
Printed in the USA
LVHW010041081020
668215LV00004B/243